NICHO

GUIDE TO THE

London, Gra

Oxford & Lee

Nicholson

An imprint of HarperCollins*Publishers*

Also available:

Nicholson Guide to the Waterways

2. Severn, Avon & Birmingham

3. Birmingham & the Heart of England

4. Four Counties & the Welsh Canals

5. North West & the Pennines

6. Nottingham, York & the North East

7. Thames, Wey, Kennet & Avon

Nicholson Inland Waterways Map of Great Britain

Published by Nicholson
An imprint of HarperCollins*Publishers*
77–85 Fulham Palace Road
Hammersmith, London W6 8JB

www.**fire**and**water**.com
www.bartholomewmaps.com

First published by Nicholson and Ordnance Survey 1997
Reprinted 1998
New edition published by Nicholson 2000

Researched and written by David Perrott and Jonathan Mosse.
Design by Bob Vickers.

The publishers gratefully acknowledge the assistance given by British Waterways and its staff in the preparation of this guide.

Grateful thanks is also due to members of the Inland Waterways Association and CAMRA representatives and branch members.

Photographs reproduced by kind permission of the following picture libraries:
British Waterways Photo Library pages 107; Bill Meadows Picture Library pages 105, 140, 14;
Derek Pratt Photography pages 17, 25, 29, 42, 55, 87, 91, 111, 117, 156.

Printed in Italy.

ISBN 0 7028 4161 7
ME10287
97/2/35

The publishers welcome comments from readers. Please address your letters to:
Nicholson Guides to the Waterways, HarperCollins Cartographic, HarperCollins Publishers,
Westerhill Road, Bishopbriggs, Glasgow, G64 2QT.

The canals and river navigations of Britain were built as a system of new trade routes, at a time when roads were virtually non-existent. After their desperately short boom period in the late 18th and early 19th centuries, they gracefully declined in the face of competition from the railways. A few canals disappeared completely, but thankfully most just decayed gently, carrying the odd working boat, and becoming havens for wildlife and the retreat of the waterways devotee.

It was two such enthusiasts, L.T.C. Rolt and Robert Aickman who, in 1946, formed the Inland Waterways Association, bringing together like-minded people from all walks of life to campaign for the preservation and restoration of the inland waterways. Their far-sightedness has at last seen its reward for, all over the country, an amazing transformation is taking place. British Waterways, the IWA, local councils, canal societies and volunteers have brought back to life great lengths of canal, and much of the dereliction which was once commonplace has been replaced with a network of 'linear parks'.

The canals provide something for everyone to enjoy: engineering feats such as aqueducts, tunnels and flights of locks; the brightly decorated narrow boats; a wealth of birds, animals and plants; the mellow unpretentious architecture of canalside buildings; friendly waterside pubs and the sheer beauty and quiet isolation that is a feature of so much of our inland waterways.

It is easy to enjoy this remarkable facet of our history, either on foot, often by bicycle, or on a boat. This book, with its splendid Ordnance Survey® mapping, is one of a series covering the waterways network, and gives you all the information you need.

CONTENTS

IRISH SEA
BRISTOL CHANNEL
R Lune
Carnforth
Lancaster
Glasson
Lancaster Canal
Blackpool
Preston
R Ribble
Leeds & Liverpool Canal
Skipton
Shipley
Burnley
Blackburn
Calder Hebble
Halifax
Huddersfield
Rochdale Canal
Rochdale
Huddersfield Narrow Canal
Rufford
Leeds & Liverpool Canal
Aintree
Liverpool
Leigh
Manchester
Ashton Canal
Peak Forest Canal
Manchester Ship Canal
Bridgewater Canal
Marple
Whaley Bridge
Ellesmere Port
River Weaver
Anderton
Macclesfield
Macclesfield Canal
Winsford
Middlewich
Chester
Middlewich Branch
Trent & Mersey Canal
Leek
Caldon Canal
Froghall
Nantwich
R Dee
Stoke-on-Trent
Llangollen
Llangollen Canal
Whitchurch
Market Drayton
Stone
Shropshire Union Canal
Montgomery Canal
Welshpool
Newtown
R Severn
Staffordshire & Worcestershire Canal
Trent &
Co
Tamworth
Birm & Fazeley Canal
BCN
Birmingham
Grand
Bewdley
Kidderminster
Stourport-on-Severn
Droitwich Canal
Worcester & Birmingham Canal
Stratford-on-Avon Canal
Worcester
River Avon
Evesham
River Severn
Tewkesbury
Gloucester
Gloucester & Sharpness Canal
Sharpness
Lechlade
Brecon
Monmouthshire & Brecon Canal
Abergavenny
R Usk
Pontypool
Cardiff
Bristol
R Avon
Bath
Kennet & Avon
Devizes

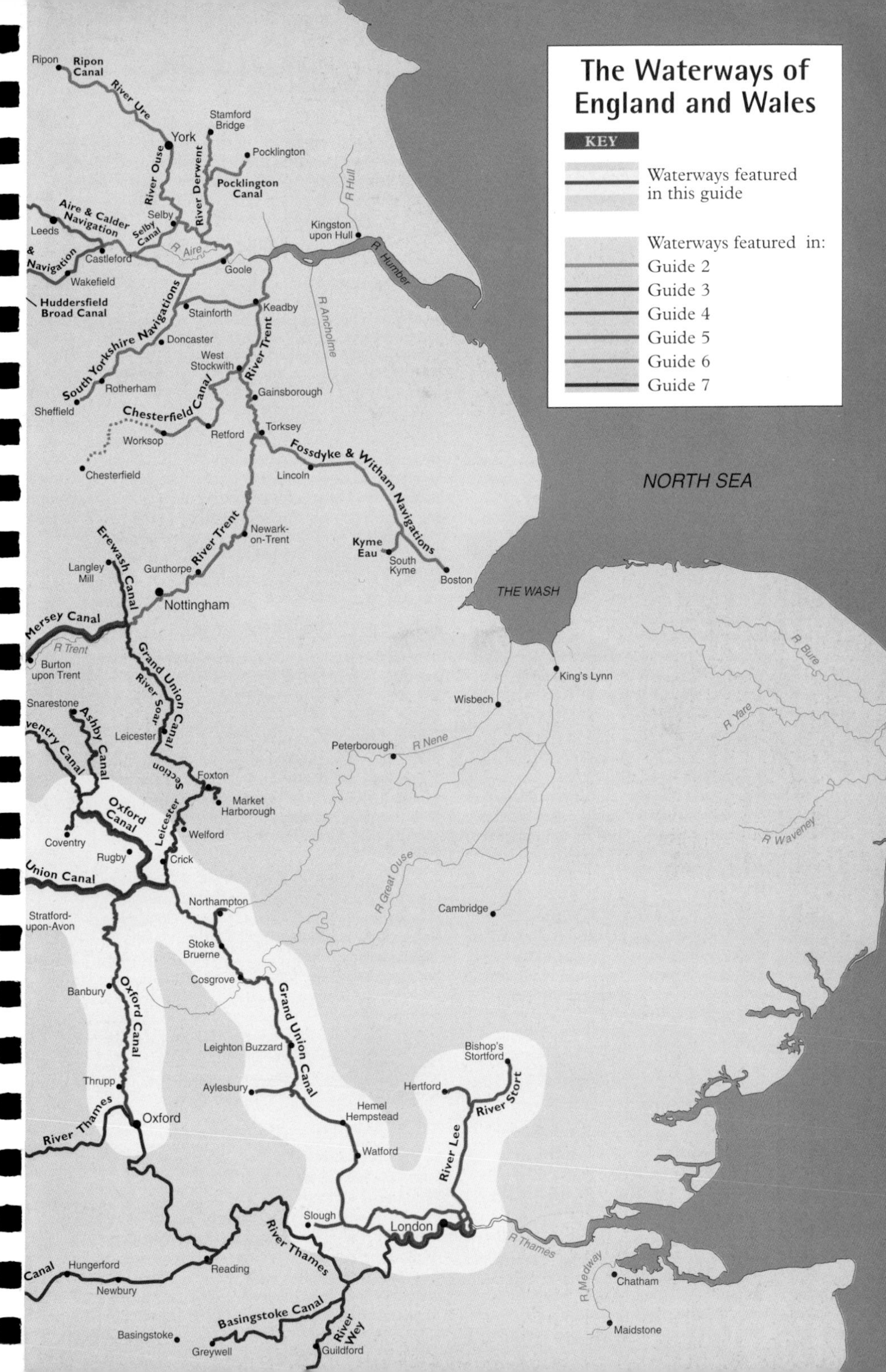

The Waterways of England and Wales
KEY
Waterways featured in this guide
Waterways featured in:
Guide 2
Guide 3
Guide 4
Guide 5
Guide 6
Guide 7
NORTH SEA
THE WASH
Ripon
Ripon Canal
River Ure
York
River Ouse
Stamford Bridge
Pocklington
River Derwent
Pocklington Canal
Aire & Calder Navigation
Leeds
Selby
Selby Canal
R Aire
Castleford
& Navigation
Wakefield
Goole
Huddersfield Broad Canal
R Hull
Kingston upon Hull
R Humber
Stainforth
Keadby
R Ancholme
South Yorkshire Navigations
Doncaster
River Trent
West Stockwith
Rotherham
Sheffield
Gainsborough
Chesterfield Canal
Worksop
Retford
Torksey
Chesterfield
Fossdyke & Witham Navigations
Lincoln
Newark-on-Trent
Kyme Eau
South Kyme
Boston
Erewash Canal
Langley Mill
Gunthorpe
Nottingham
Mersey Canal
R Trent
Burton upon Trent
Grand Union Canal
River Soar
King's Lynn
R Bure
Wisbech
Snarestone
Ashby Canal
ventry Canal
Leicester
R Yare
Peterborough
R Nene
Leicester Section
Foxton
Market Harborough
Oxford Canal
Coventry
Welford
R Waveney
Rugby
Crick
Union Canal
R Great Ouse
Northampton
Stratford-upon-Avon
Cambridge
Stoke Bruerne
Cosgrove
Banbury
Grand Union Canal
Oxford Canal
Leighton Buzzard
Bishop's Stortford
Thrupp
Aylesbury
Hertford
River Stort
Hemel Hempstead
River Thames
Oxford
Watford
River Lee
Slough
London
R Thames
River Thames
Canal
Hungerford
Reading
R Medway
Chatham
Newbury
Basingstoke Canal
River Wey
Basingstoke
Greywell
Guildford
Maidstone

GENERAL INFORMATION FOR CANAL USERS

The slogan Waterways For All was coined to take account of the wide diversity of people using the inland waterways for recreation.

Today boaters, walkers, fishermen, cyclists and gongoozlers (on-lookers) throng our canals and rivers, to share in the enjoyment of our quite amazing waterway heritage. British Waterways (BW), along with other navigation authorities, is empowered to develop, maintain and control this resource in order to maximise its potential: namely our enjoyment. It is to this end that a series of guides, codes, and regulations have come into existence over the years, evolving to match a burgeoning – and occasionally conflicting – demand. Set out below are the key points as they relate to everyone wishing to enjoy the waterways.

LICENSING – BOATS

The majority of the navigations covered in this book are controlled by BW and are managed on a day-to-day basis by local waterway offices. Waterway Managers are detailed in the introduction to each waterway. All craft using BW waterways must be licenced and charges are based on the length of the craft. This licence covers all navigable waterways under BW's control and in a few cases includes reciprocal agreements with other waterway authorities (as indicated in the text). As this edition goes to print, BW and the Environment Agency are preparing to go to consultation on an optional joint licence to cover both authorities' waterways. Permits for permanent mooring on the canals are also issued by BW. For further information contact BW Customer Services (see inside front cover). You can download licence fees and charges and an application form from the BW website (see inside front cover).

Since 1 January 1997, BW and the Environment Agency have introduced the Boat Safety Scheme, setting technical requirements for good and safe boat-building practice. A Boat Safety Certificate or, for new boats, a Declaration of Conformity, is necessary to obtain a craft licence. For powered boats proof of insurance for Third Party Liability for a minimum of £1,000,000 is also required. Further details from BW Customer Services. Other navigational authorities relevant to this book are mentioned where appropriate.

LICENSING – CYCLISTS

Not all towpaths are open to cyclists. This is because many stretches are too rough or narrow, or because cyclists cause too great a risk to other users. The maps on the BW website show which stretches of towpaths are open to cyclists. This information is also available from your local waterway office, which you should contact in any case to obtain the necessary permit to cycle on the towpath and a copy of the Waterways Code. When using the towpaths for cycling, you will encounter other towpath users, such as fishermen, walkers and boaters. The Waterways Code gives advice on taking care and staying safe, considering others and helping to look after the waterways. A complete list of towpaths available for cycling is available in a National Cycle Pack, price £5.00 from BW Customer Services.

TOWPATHS

Few, if any, artificial cuts or canals in this country are without an intact towpath accessible to the walker at least. However, on river navigations towpaths have on occasion fallen into disuse or, sometimes, been lost to erosion. In today's leisure climate considerable efforts are being made to provide access to all towpaths with some available to the disabled. Notes on individual waterways in this book detail the supposed status of the path, but the indication of a towpath does not necessarily imply a public right of way or mean that a right to cycle along it exists. Maps on the BW website show all towpaths on the BW network, and whether they are open to cyclists. Motorcycling and horse riding are forbidden on all towpaths.

INDIVIDUAL WATERWAY GUIDES

No national guide can cover the minutiae of individual waterways and some Waterway Managers produce guides to specific navigations under their charge. Copies of individual guides (where they are available) can be obtained from the Waterway Office detailed in the introduction. Please note that times – such as operating times of bridges and locks – do change year by year and from winter to summer.

STOPPAGES

BW works hard to programme its major engineering works into the winter period when demand for cruising is low. It publishes a National Stoppage Programme and Winter Opening Hours leaflet which is sent out to all licence holders, boatyards and hire companies. Inevitably, emergencies occur necessitating the unexpected closure of a waterway, perhaps during the peak season. You can check for stoppages on individual waterways between specific dates on the BW website. Details are also announced on lockside noticeboards and on Canalphone (see inside front cover).

STARTING OUT

Extensive information and advice on booking a boating holiday is available on the BW website. Please book a waterway holiday from a licenced operator – only in this way can you be sure that you have proper insurance cover, service and support during your holiday. It is illegal for private boat owners to hire out their craft. If in doubt, please contact BW Customer Services. If you are hiring a canal boat for the first time, the boatyard will brief you thoroughly. Take notes, follow their instructions and *don't be afraid to ask* if there is anything you do not understand. BW have produced a short video giving basic information on using a boat safely. Copies of the video, and the Waterways Code for Boaters, are available free of charge from BW Customer Services.

GENERAL CRUISING NOTES

Most canals are saucer-shaped in section so are deepest at the middle. Few have more than 3–4ft of water and many have much less. Keep to the centre of the channel except on bends, where the deepest water is on the outside of the bend. When you meet another boat, keep to the right, slow down and aim to miss the approaching craft by a couple of yards: do not steer right over to the bank or you are likely to run aground. If you meet a loaded commercial boat keep right out of the way and be prepared to follow his instructions. Do not assume that you should pass on the right. If you meet a boat being towed from the bank, pass it on the outside. When overtaking, keep the other boat on your right side.

A large number of BW facilities in their north-east region – pump-outs, showers, electrical hook-ups and so on – are currently operated by smart cards, obtainable from BW Regional Office, Neptune Street, Leeds (0113 281 6800); local waterways offices (see introductions to individual navigations); lock keepers and some boatyards within the region. At the time of printing, a £6 card will purchase one pump-out, about 12 showers and electricity pro rata. Please note that if you are a weekend visitor, you should purchase cards *in advance*.

Speed

There is a general speed limit of 4 mph on most BW canals. This is not just an arbitrary limit: there is no need to go any faster and in many cases it is impossible to cruise even at this speed: if the wash is breaking against the bank or causing large waves, slow down.

Slow down also when passing moored craft, engineering works and anglers; when there is a lot of floating rubbish on the water (and try to drift over obvious obstructions in neutral); when approaching blind corners, narrow bridges and junctions.

Mooring

Generally speaking you may moor where you wish on BW property, as long as there is sufficient depth of water, and you are *not causing an obstruction*. Your boat should carry metal mooring stakes, and these should be driven firmly into the ground with a mallet if there are no mooring rings. Do not stretch mooring lines across the towpath. Always consider the security of your boat when there is no one aboard. On tideways and commercial waterways it is advisable to moor only at recognised sites, and allow for any rise or fall of the tide.

Bridges

On narrow canals slow down and aim to miss one side (usually the towpath side) by about 9 inches. *Keep everyone inboard when passing under bridges*, and take special care with moveable structures – the crew member operating the bridge should hold it steady as the boat passes through.

Tunnels

Make sure the tunnel is clear before you enter, and use your headlight. Follow any instructions given on notice boards by the entrance.

Fuel

Hire craft usually carry fuel sufficient for the rental period.

Water

It is advisable to top up every day.

Lavatories

Hire craft usually have pump-out toilets. Have these emptied *before* things become critical. Keep the receipt and your boatyard will usually reimburse you for this expense.

Boatyards

Hire fleets are usually turned around on a Saturday, making this a bad time to call in for services. Remember that moorings at popular destinations fill quickly during the summer months, so do not assume there will be room for your boat. Always ask.

LOCKS AND THEIR USE

A lock is a simple and ingenious device for transporting your craft from one water level to another.

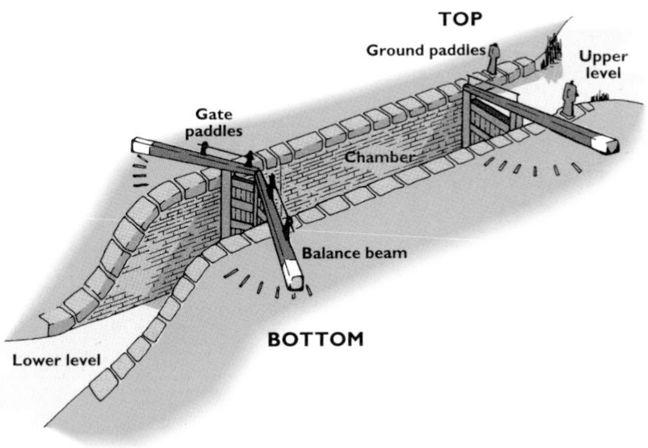

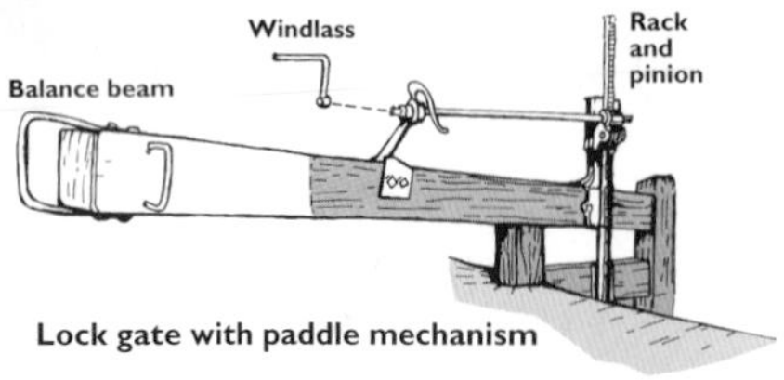

Lock gate with paddle mechanism

When both sets of gates are closed it may be filled or emptied using gate or ground paddles at the top or bottom of the lock. These are operated with a windlass.

General tips

- Make safety your prime concern. *Keep a close eye on young children.*
- Always take your time, and do not leap about.
- Never open the paddles at one end without ensuring those at the other are closed.
- Never drop the paddles – always wind them down.
- Keep to the landward side of the balance beam when opening and closing gates.
- Never leave your windlass slotted onto the paddle spindle – it will be dangerous should anything slip.
- Keep your boat away from the top and bottom gates to prevent it getting caught on the gate or the lock cill.
- Be wary of fierce *top gate* paddles, especially in wide locks. Operate them slowly, and close them if there is *any* adverse effect.
- Always follow the navigation authority's instructions, where these are given on notices or by their staff.

PLANNING A CRUISE

Many a canal holiday has been spoiled by trying to go too far too fast. Go slowly, don't be too ambitious, and enjoy the experience. Note that mileages indicated on the maps are for guidance only.

A *rough* calculation of time taken to cover the ground is the lock-miles system:

Add the number of *miles* to the number of *locks* on your proposed journey, and divide the resulting figure by three. This will give you a guide to the number of *hours* it will take. But don't forget your service stops (water, shopping, pump-out), and allow plenty of time to visit that special pub!

TIDAL WATERWAYS

The typical steel narrow boat found on the inland waterways system has the sea-going characteristics of a bathtub, which renders it totally unsuitable for all-weather cruising on tidal estuaries. However, the more adventurous will inevitably wish to add additional ring cruises to the more predictable circuits within the calm havens of inland Britain. Passage is possible in most estuaries if careful consideration is given to the key factors of weather conditions, crew experience, the condition of the boat and its equipment and, perhaps of overriding importance, the need to take expert advice. In many cases it will be prudent to employ the skilled services of a local pilot. Within the text, where inland navigations connect with a tidal waterway, details are given of sources of both advice and pilotage. This guide is to the inland waterways of Britain and therefore recognizes that tideways – and especially estuaries – require a different skill and approach. We therefore do not hesitate to draw the boater's attention to the appropriate source material.

GENERAL

Most inland navigations are managed by BW or the Environment Agency, but there are several other navigation authorities responsible for smaller stretches of canals and rivers. For details of these, contact the Association of Inland Navigation Authorities at www.cam.net.uk/home/aina or BW Customer Services. The boater, conditioned perhaps by the uniformity of our national road network, should be sensitive to the need to observe different codes and operating practices. Similarly it is important to be aware that some waterways are only available for navigation today solely because of the care and dedication of a particular restoration body, often using volunteer labour and usually taking several decades to complete the project. This is the reason that, in cruising the national waterways network, additional licence charges are sometimes incurred. The introduction to each waterway gives its background history, details of recent restoration (where relevant) and also lists the operating authority.

BW is a public corporation, responsible to the Department of the Environment, Transport and the Regions and, as subscribers to the Citizen's Charter, they are linked with an ombudsman. BW has a comprehensive complaints procedure and a free explanatory leaflet is available from Customer Services. Problems and complaints should be addressed to the local Waterway Manager in the first instance – the telephone number is listed in the introduction to individual waterways.

The Inland Waterways Association campaigns for the 'conservation, use, maintenance, restoration and development of the inland waterways', through branches all over the country. For more information contact them at PO Box 114, Rickmansworth, WD3 1ZY, telephone 01923 711114, fax 01923 897000, email iwa@waterways.org.uk or visit their website at www.waterways.org.uk/index.htm.

FREEPHONE CANALS

Emergency help is available from BW outside normal office hours on weekdays and throughout weekends via Freephone Canals (see inside front cover). You should give details of the problem and your location.

GRAND UNION CANAL

MAXIMUM DIMENSIONS

Regent's Canal
Length: 72'
Beam: 14' 6"
Headroom: 8' 6"

Brentford and Paddington to Berkhamsted Lock, including the Slough Arm
Length: 72'
Beam: 14'
Headroom: 7' 6"

Berkhamsted Lock to Camp Hill
Length: 72'
Beam: 7'
Headroom: 7' 6"
Craft up to 12' 6" beam are permitted between Berkhamsted and Camp Hill but all craft of this size must seek advice before proceeding. Permission must be obtained from BW for passage through the tunnels.

Camp Hill to Aston Junction and Salford Junction
Length: 70'
Beam: 7'
Headroom: 6' 6"

Aylesbury and Northampton Arms
Length: 72'
Beam: 7'
Headroom: 7' 6"

MANAGER
Brentford to Cowley, Paddington and Slough Arms: 0208 571 8900
Cowley to Stowe Hill and Aylesbury, Wendover and Northampton Arms: 01442 825938
Stowe Hill to Napton, Foxton and Welford: 01788 890666
Napton to Camp Hill: 01564 784634
Camp Hill to Salford Junction: 0121 506 1300

MILEAGE
Thames, BRENTFORD to:
Bull's Bridge: 6 miles
Black Jack's Lock: 16 miles
Watford: 22 miles
Berkhamsted: 33 miles
Bulbourne: 38 miles
Leighton Buzzard: 47½ miles
Fenny Stratford: 55 miles
Cosgrove: 67 miles
Stoke Bruerne: 73 miles
Gayton Junction: 89 miles
Braunston: 93½ miles
Napton Junction: 98½ miles
Leamington Spa: 109 miles
Shrewley: 115½ miles
Salford Junction: 137 miles
Locks: 166

Paddington Arm: 13½ miles
No locks

The Grand Union Canal is unique among English canals in being composed of at least eight separate canals. This system links London with Birmingham, Leicester and Nottingham. The original – and still the most important – part of the system was the Grand Junction Canal. This was constructed at the turn of the 18thC to provide a short cut between Braunston on the Oxford canal and Brentford, west of London on the Thames. Previously, all London-bound traffic from the Midlands had to follow the winding, narrow Fazeley, Coventry and Oxford canals down to Oxford, there to tranship into lighters to make the 100-mile trip down river to Brentford and London. The new Grand Junction Canal cut this distance by fully 60 miles, and with its 14ft wide locks and numerous branches to important towns rapidly became busy and profitable. The building of wide locks to take 70-ton barges was a brave attempt to persuade neighbouring canal companies – the Oxford, Coventry and the distant Trent and Mersey – to widen their navigations and establish a 70-ton barge standard throughout the waterways of the Midlands. Unfortunately, the other companies were deterred by the cost of widening, and to this day those same canals – and many others – can only pass boats 7ft wide. The mere proposal of the building of the Grand Junction Canal was enough to generate and justify plans for other canals linked to it. Before the Grand Junction itself was completed, independent canals were built linking it in a direct line to Warwick and Birmingham, and later a connection was established from the Grand Junction to Market Harborough and Leicester, and thence via the canalised River Soar to the Trent. Note: craft up to 12' 6" beam are permitted between Berkhamsted and Camp Hill but all craft of this size should seek advice from British Waterways before proceeding. There is also no passage through tunnels without permission.

Limehouse

In the Greater London area little specific information is given that does not relate directly to the canal. However whilst canalside pubs and restaurants are marked on the map details are only given of some of the less obvious (and often more rewarding) places to eat and drink. The Regent's Canal begins at Limehouse Basin (previously known as Regent's Canal Dock) in London's dockland and climbs up round central London towards Paddington. It is mostly flanked by the backs of houses and factories which usually enclose the canal in a remarkably private and peaceful world of its own. The towpath can now be followed from Limehouse Basin along the whole length of the Regent's Canal to West London, and there are frequent access points. Visitor moorings are provided in Kingsland (*pump-out*), Battlebridge (*toilet, showers*) and Cumberland Basins () (all by prior arrangement) and at St Pancras, Camden, east of Islington Tunnel, Little Venice, Bulls Bridge, Cowley Lock, Limehouse and Brentford Gauging Lock. The IWA, in conjunction with Original London Walks,

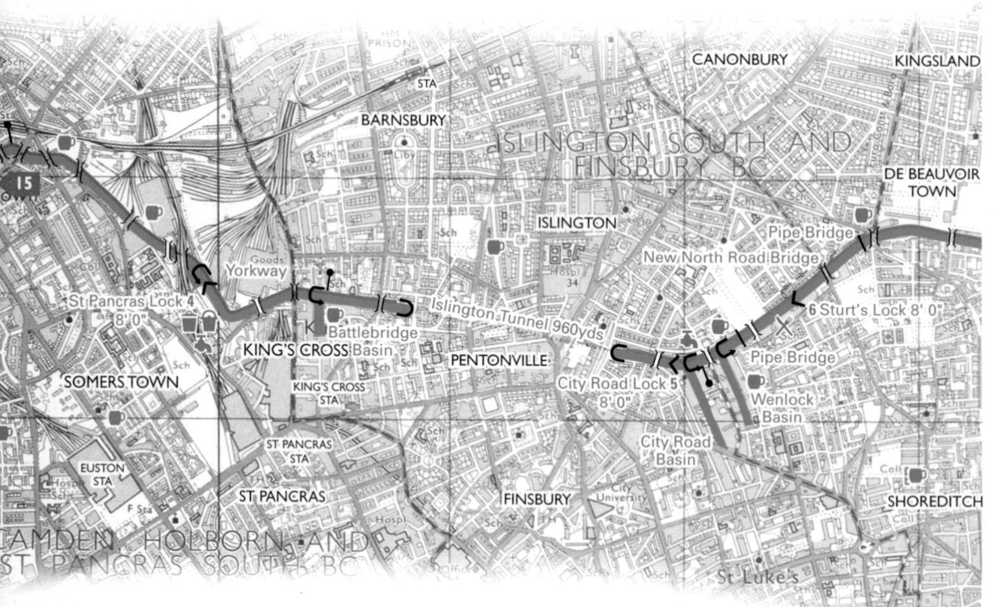

organise guided towpath walks, details available on 0207 624 3978 (charge). The entrance to the Regent's Canal and to the River Lee Navigation from the Thames is through Limehouse Lock. The Hertford Union Canal (often known as Duckett's), is a useful short cut between the Regent's Canal and the Lee Navigation, running along the attractive Victoria Park. The canal continues to climb, passing two large basins before plunging under Islington through a 1/2 mile tunnel (forbidden to unpowered craft), then round the back of St Pancras and Camden Town passing Battlebridge Basin, site of the London Canal Museum.

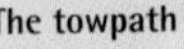

The towpath
Throughout the entire Grand Union Canal system, including all the arms, the towpath is in good condition, offering an unrivalled and versatile long distance route to walker and cyclist alike. Along certain marked sections there is a no cycling régime in operation.

● **London Canal Museum** 12–13 New Wharf Road, N1 (0207 713 0836). By Battlebridge Basin. Housed in an ice warehouse built for Carlo Catti, the famous ice-cream maker, the museum tells the story of London's canals, and features the history of the trade in natural ice. Visitors can see the huge well where the ice was once stored. Book and gift shop. *Open Tue–Sun & B. Hol Mons 10.00–16.30. Closed Xmas.* Charge.

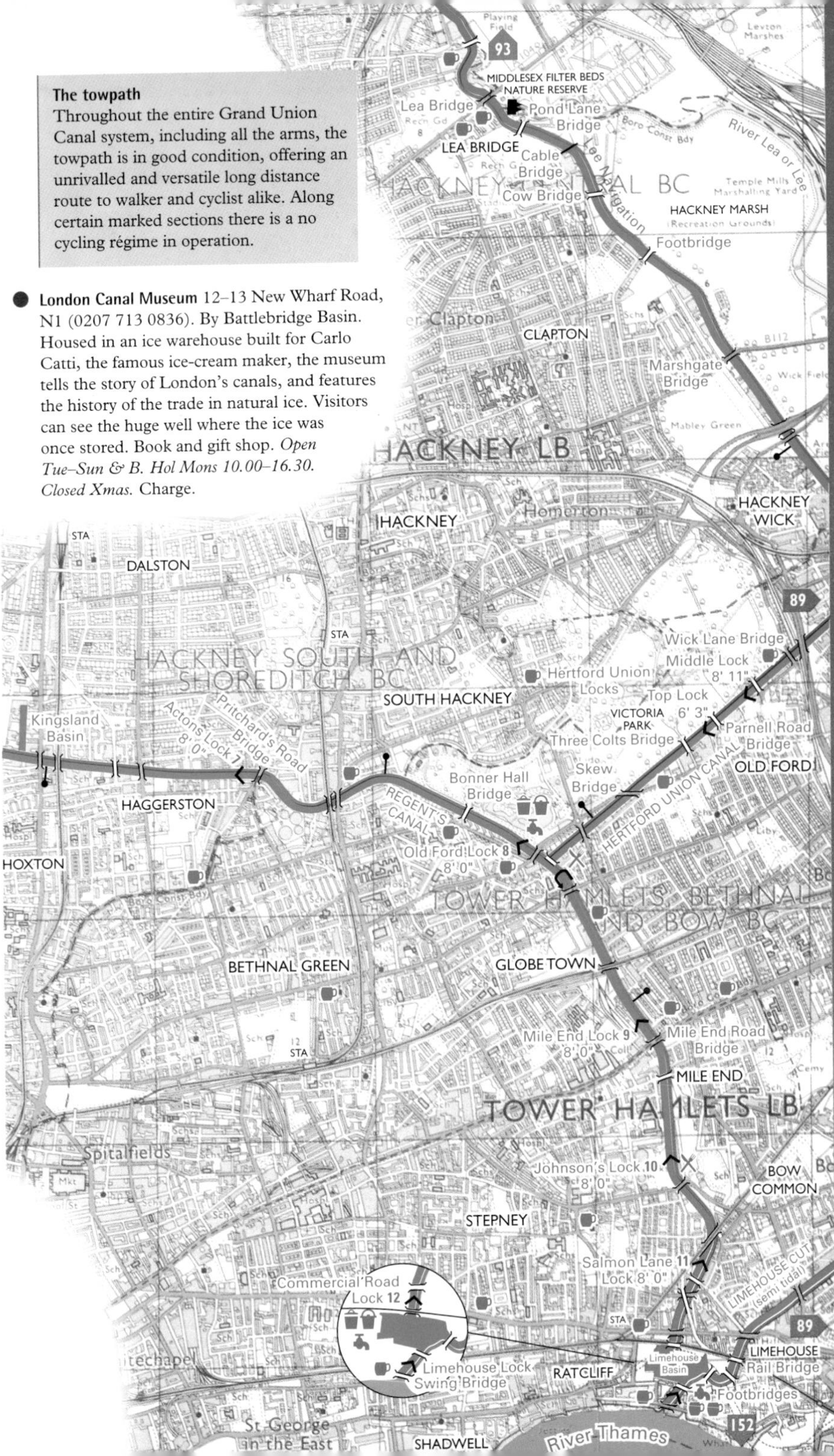

NAVIGATIONAL NOTES

1 Limehouse Lock can accommodate craft 91' x 24'4" x 8' draught. It is *open Apr-Oct, daily 08.00–18.00; Nov–Mar, daily 08.00-16.00. It is also available on a pre-booked basis (24hrs notice) within the core-hour period 05.00-22.00.* Telephone 0207 308 9930 for further information.

2 For further details on navigating the tidal Thames, read the section on the London Thames, commencing on page 141.

3 Craft entering the canal from the Thames without the necessary BW licence may complete the formalities at Limehouse.

4 As with most inner city canals, there is a risk of vandalism. Locks on the Regent's Canal are padlocked – a BW handcuff lock key is required.

5 Useful advice on navigating the tideway is contained in the IWA London Region's Tideway Notes available from Limehouse, Brentford, Teddington and Bow Locks.

● **Limehouse Basin** Limehouse. The terminus of the Regent's Canal and of the Lee Navigation where they meet the Thames. Once known as the Regent's Canal Dock, this basin has now been developed as a marina. Running underneath is a newly constructed road tunnel offering easy access to the Canary Wharf development.
Ragged School Museum 46-50 Copperfield Road, Mile End, E3 (0208 980 6405). Situated in three canalside warehouse buildings that once housed the largest Dr Barnardo Ragged School in London, this museum brings to life the unique history of the East End and, in particular, the history of the Copperfield Road School. *Open Wed & Thu 10.00-17.00 & first Sun in month 14.00-17.00.* Café *open same times.* Free – donations appreciated.
Victoria Park Hackney. Beside the canal. Almost 300 acres of parkland which comes as a relief after so much townscape. Designed by James Pennthorne, a protege of Nash, and laid out between 1842 and 1845.
Islington Tunnel 960yds long, the tunnel was opened in 1816. In 1826 a towing boat was introduced, which pulled itself to and fro along a chain laid on the canal bed. This system remained until the 1930s. The attractive borough of Islington lies to the north of the tunnel where there are useful shops, a street market and a laundrette.

Boatyards

Ⓑ **Limehouse Basin Marina** 1 Northey Street, E14 (0207 537 2828). Administered by the Cruising Association. Pump-out, overnight mooring, long-term mooring, BW licences and keys, windlasses, telephone, toilets, showers, laundry facilities, café & restaurant. Resident marine engineer.
Ⓑ **Pumpkin Marine** 100 The Highway, E1 (0207 480 6630). Extensive range of chandlery, electronic marine equipment and clothing.
Ⓑ **St Pancras Cruising Club** St Pancras Basin, Camley Street, NW1 (0207 278 2805). Pump-out, overnight mooring, dry dock, long-term mooring, toilet. Clubhouse open to the public *Sat afternoons & evenings; Sun lunchtimes & Wed evenings.*

REGENT'S CANAL COMPANY

In 1812 the Regent's Canal Company was formed to cut a new canal from the Grand Junction's busy Paddington Arm, around London to Limehouse, where a big dock was planned at the junction with the Thames. This was duly opened in 1820, narrowly escaping conversion at an early stage into a railway, and proved extremely successful. Ten years later a 1½-mile-long canal – the Hertford Union – was built: this remains a useful short cut from Regent's Canal to the River Lee. Together with the Grand Junction Canal (and its associated spurs to the Trent and to Birmingham), these were the canals that made up the spine of southern England's transport system until the advent of the railways. When in this century the Regent's Canal Company acquired the Grand Junction and others, the whole system was integrated as the Grand Union Canal Company in 1929. In 1932 the new company, aided by the government, launched a massive programme of modernisation: widening the 52 locks from Braunston to Knowle, piling and dredging, etc. But when the grant was all spent, the task was unfinished and broad beam boats never became common on the Grand Union Canal. The great attempt to break loose from narrow boat carrying had failed, and after this the Grand Union could only begin to decline. Now narrow boat carrying on the canal is finished and pleasure craft have taken their place.

Pubs and Restaurants

Barley Mow 44 Narrow Street, Limehouse, E14 (0207 265 8931). In the original Dockmaster's office, at the entrance to Limehouse Dock. Burton and Tetley's real ales in a waterside pub, now part of the Big Steak Pub chain. Meals served *lunchtimes and evenings* and snacks available *all day*. Children and vegetarians catered for. Riverside patio seating. *Open all day.*

Grapes 76 Narrow Street, Limehouse, E14 (0207 987 4396). Fine riverside pub (east of Limehouse Lock) serving Burton, Friary Meux, Tetley's and guest real ales. Bar food and an exciting (though expensive) fish restaurant upstairs *open L & D except Sun.* No children. *Closed all day Sat until 19.00.*

The House They Left Behind Narrow Street, Limehouse, E14 (0207 538 5102). 1/4 mile east of Limehouse Dock. Once the only building left standing in a demolished terrace, this pub offers a warm welcome and an appetising range of home-cooked food *lunchtimes and evenings (Mon–Fri and Sat lunchtimes)*. Free barbecues *Sun in summer.* Children and vegetarians catered for. Rotating guest real ales. Outside seating. Music *Mon & Thu. Open all day Fri–Sun.*

Queens Head 8 Flamborough Street, Stepney, E14. North west of Limehouse Basin. Bustling, friendly little local serving Young's real ales and *lunchtime food Mon–Fri.* Traditional pub games.

Hollands Brayforde Square, Stepney, E1 (0207 790 3057). 1/4 mile west of Limehouse Basin along Commercial Road. A Grade II listed interior with original Victorian fittings and press cuttings together with Young's real ales. *Open all day.*

Top O' The Morning Hackney E9 (0208 985 9917). Adjacent to Middle Lock on north side of Hertford Union Canal. Sandwiches and bar snacks *lunchtimes and evenings, 7 days a week* in this boater-friendly pub. Children and vegetarians catered for. Beer garden and *Sat & Sun afternoon* barbecues and music. *Open all day.*

Coborn Arms 8 Coborn Road, Bow, E3 (0208 980 3793). ¼ mile east of Mile End Road Bridge. Serving a variety of Young's ales and food *lunchtimes and evenings*. This friendly, comfortable local offers outside seating and pub games. *Open all day.* Disabled access.

Falcon & Firkin 360 Victoria Park Road, Hackney E9 (0208 986 0102). Further east from Actons Lock or across Victoria Park, north of Upper Lock. One of Firkin's main brew pubs serving a range of their own real ales, real cider and food *lunchtimes and evenings.* Children's room, large outside seating area and disabled access. *Open all day.*

Approach Tavern 47 Approach Road, Bethnal Green, E2 (0208 980 2321). 300 yds south west of Bonner Hall Bridge. Adnams, Fuller's, Marston's, Wadworth and guest real ales served in a roomy city local with an upstairs art galley. Food available *lunchtimes and evenings.* Outside seating, pub games and a real fire. *Open all day.*

Marksman 254 Hackney Road, Hackney, E2 (0207 739 7393). 500 yds south west of Pritchard's Road Bridge. Single bar pub, dispensing Courage and guest real ales, to a largely local clientele. Framed posters on the walls reflect both local and military themes. *Open all day.*

Wenlock Arms 26 Wenlock Road, Hoxton, N1 (0207 608 3406). Immediately east of Wenlock Basin. Tastefully renovated pub dispensing Adnams, Nethergate, and Tetleys real ales. Also real ciders. Open fires and traditional pub games. Regular *Sun lunchtime* jazz sessions. *Open all day.*

Marquess Tavern 32 Canonbury Street, Canonbury, N1 (0207 354 2975). ½ mile north west of New North Road Bridge. Young's real ales and superb, home-cooked food *(lunchtimes and evenings)* served in a splendid old Victorian pub. A real fire in winter and pavement seating in summer. Open all day.

Spread Eagle 141 Albert Street, Camden Town, NW1 (0207 264 1410). South of Camden Lock. Visitors are welcome in this thriving pub serving Young's real ales and lunchtime food. Traditional pub games in spacious, wood-lined bar areas. Outside seating. *Open all day.*

Perseverance 11 Shroton street, Marylebone, NW1 (0207 723 7469). ¼ mile south east of Lisson Grove Bridge. Originally a 19th-C coaching house this friendly pub, with attentive staff, now dispenses Bass and Fuller's real ales. Food is available *lunchtimes and evenings* together with outside seating and pub games. Disabled access.

Little Venice

At Camden High Road, the top locks are reached and the long level begins (27 miles of canal without a lock). Near the top lock is a castellated youth club; boatmen should beware of the many young persons rowing and canoeing nearby. Soon the industrial surroundings melt away and, rounding a right-angled bend, the canal suddenly enters London Zoo and Regent's Park – which look splendid from the water. (Do not attempt to tie up and walk into the zoo without paying.) The canal continues through a long wooded cutting, then leaves Regent's Park and skirts the former Marylebone goods yard – now a housing estate – beyond which is the short Maida Hill Tunnel. One emerges into one of the finest stretches of urban canal in the country. Tree-lined and flanked by fine Regency houses, the Regent's Canal ends gloriously at Little Venice. To the left, under the Westway bridge, is the vast Paddington Basin. To the right is the Paddington Arm of the former Grand Junction Canal. The two stop places seen at Little Venice were used for gauging boats for tolls. There are good moorings, toilets and a BW operated pump-out by the Canal Office. Groceries are available nearby. The Paddington Arm continues west, passing a large housing estate and the backs of houses in Harrow Road, before running along the side of the well-known Kensal Green Cemetery. There is a useful Sainsbury's with moorings, and easy access immediately west of Kensal Green Bridge. The huge concrete structure sweeping out over the canal is a further section of the elevated Westway Road. The main Western region tracks run just below the canal, to the south, while at Old Oak Common there are extensive carriage sidings, including new stabling for the Eurostar trains. Beyond them can be seen the towers of Wormwood Scrubs.

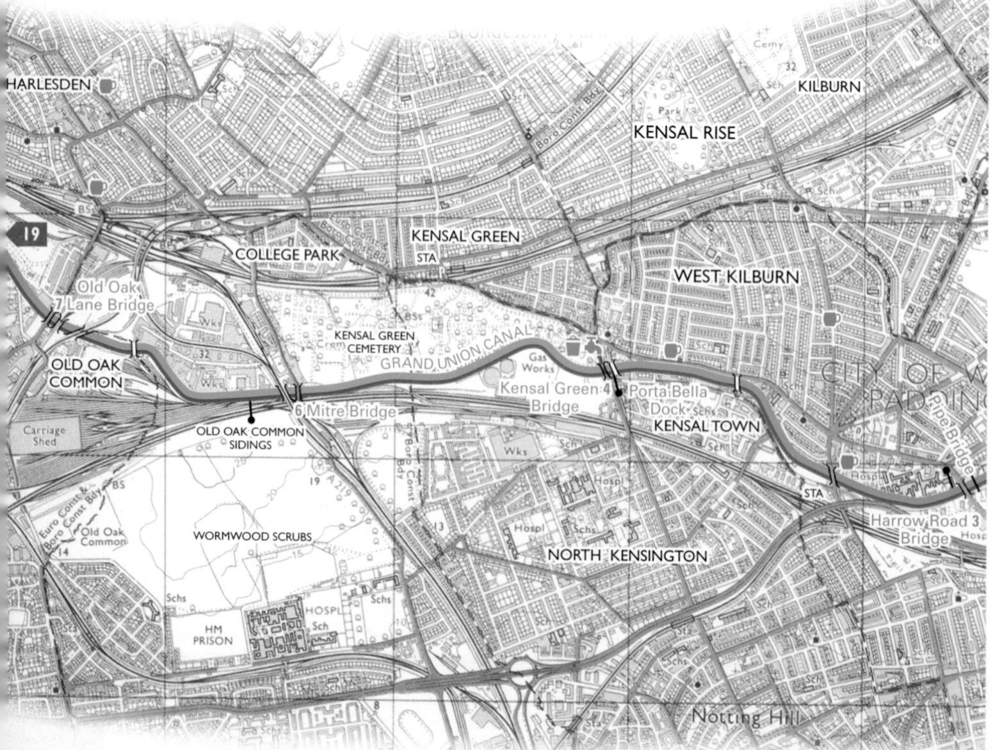

BOAT TRIPS

London Waterbus Co. Camden Lock (0207 482 2660/0207 482 2550). A *50 minute* trip from Little Venice through Regent's Park to the zoo (stopping for admission) and then continuing on to Camden Lock. *Hourly service both ways in summer, reduced service on winter weekends.* Regular day trips to Limehouse Basin, Brentford and Harefield with commentary *May-Sep.* Group Bookings.

Jason's Trip Opposite Blomfield Road moorings. (0207 286 3428). *1½ hour* trip in a narrow boat through Regent's Park and Zoo to Camden Locks. Commentary on return trip, advisable to book. Also *Lace Plate* restaurant boat available for private hire. Seats 35.

Canal Cruises 250 Camden High Street, NW1 (0207 485 6210/4433). *Nb Jenny Wren* makes a *1½ hour* trip through Regent's Park, the Zoo and Maida Hill Tunnel to Little Venice and back. Live commentary. Advisable to book. Also *My Fair Lady* cruising restaurant makes an *evening dinner cruise Tue–Sat, and lunchtime cruise on Sun.* Must book.

Lady Rose of Regents Little Venice, east of BW canal office. Cruising restaurant. For further details and bookings telephone 0207 286 3428.

Camden Lock A fascinating craft and canal centre, with a busy weekend market, around what was once a timber wharf. Stalls crowd every nook and cranny of the wharf and spill out into several squares south of the canal. The market is a good place to purchase fresh fruit and vegetables; the opportunities to buy designer clothing at knock down prices are legion and the selection of take-away food is truly cosmopolitan. Compendium Books, on Camden High Street, must be unique in the range of material stocked, offering an unrivalled service to readers over several decades.

Regent's Park Originally part of Henry VIII's great hunting forest in the 16thC. In 1811 the Prince Regent planned to connect the park and a new palace via the newly built Regent Street to Carlton House. Although never completed, the design by John Nash is very impressive: the park is surrounded by handsome Regency terraces and gateways. The sanctuary and the north east corner of the park are excellent points for watching migrant birds, including willow warblers, chiffchaff, white throats, redstarts and redpolls.

London Zoo Regent's Park (0207 722 3333). The canal passes along the edge of the zoo, one of the largest in the world. Lord Snowdon's aviary can be seen from the canal. The zoo was originally laid out by Decimus Burton in 1827, but since then many famous architects have designed special animal houses. *Closed Christmas.*

Cumberland Basin A small canal basin by the zoo which used to form the junction of the Regent's Canal Main Line with an arm that led off round the park to Cumberland Market near Euston Station. Much of the arm was filled in during the last war and the zoo car park now sits on top of it. Cumberland Basin is now full of moored boats; there is also a floating restaurant.

Lord's Cricket Ground St John's Wood Road NW7 (0207 289 1611). The ground of the MCC, which is also the governing body for British cricket.

Canalside walk From Lisson Grove (at the east end of Maida Hill Tunnel) to Regent's Park Zoo, 2 miles of the canal towpath make one of London's most attractive waterside walks. The bridges are nicely painted and wooden seats installed at intervals. With the ducks, the overhanging trees, the passing boats and London Zoo on either side, this is a remarkable stretch of urban canal. A *no cycling* regime operates along most of this section.

Little Venice A very canal-conscious area centred on the junction of the Regent's and Grand Junction canals, famous for its elegant houses, colourful boats and excellent canalside views. There is a floating café and the floating **Cascade Art Gallery** (0207 289 7050). The island and pool were named after Robert Browning. The area is sometimes referred to as Paddington Stop. There are shops and a laundrette nearby.

St Mary Magdalene Alongside the canal west of Little Venice. Built by Street, 1868–78, the church with its tall Gothic spire is now curiously isolated among modern flats. The richly decorated crypt is very striking.

Porta Bella Dock Ladbroke Grove W10. A private dock, market and office complex.

Kensal Green Cemetery North bank of canal. Opened in 1833, the huge cemetery flanks the canal. The monuments are now all romantically overgrown, and scattered among trees. Water gates set in the wall indicate that at one time coffins for burial could be brought up by barge. Leigh Hunt, Thackeray, Macready, Trollope, Wilkie Collins and Blondin are among the famous buried here.

Wormwood Scrubs South of canal. Expanse of open space with the famous prison on the southern boundary.

Boatyards

London Narrow Boat Assn Battlebridge Moorings, Wharfdale Road, N1 (0207 837 9256). Temporary moorings by prior arrangement only. Laundry, baths available for moorers.

GREAT CENTRAL RAILWAY

On passing the site of the old Great Central Railway's goods yard, beside its Marylebone terminus, it is worth reflecting on this illustrious company's original aims: a railway link from the industrial north via the capital, and a *channel tunnel* into Europe; constructed to a loading gauge compatible with continental railways. And this was in *1899*.

Further west, whilst navigating under the concrete spans of the Westway, with its nonstop roar of heavy goods traffic, it is hard to conceive that a plan to resurrect this line – its original loading gauge even today capable of conveying, piggy back, fully laden articulated lorries, continental-style – was recently rejected, by Parliament, for debate.

Little Venice

Pubs and Restaurants

Clifton St John's Wood, NW8 (0207 624 5233). West of Blow up Bridge. Adnams, Abbot, Marston's, Tetley's and guest real ales in an upmarket establishment, once a Victorian residence. Interesting menu served *(lunchtimes and evenings – no food after 18.00 Sun evenings)* in conservatory dining area. Open fire, children's area, beer garden and pub games. *Open all day.*

Bridge House 13 Westbourne Terrace Road, Little Venice, W2 (0207 286 7925). Bass and Worthington real ales, together with food *lunchtimes and evenings*, served in this bustling, canalside pub. Theatre upstairs. *Open all day.*

Warwick Castle 6 Warwick Place, Little Venice, W9 (0207 286 6868). Very much the same as the Bridge House, but with no theatre and some interesting glass in the bar windows.

Warrington Hotel 93 Warrington Crescent, Maida Vale, W9 (0207 286 2929). ¼ mile north of Little Venice. Mellow decadence is a term that might well apply to the bar which dispenses Brakspear, Fuller's, Young's and guest real ales. Food available *lunchtimes and evenings*. There is also an upstairs Thai Restaurant *open in the evening*. Bar *open all day.*

Archery Tavern 4 Bathurst Street, Paddington W2 (0207 402 4916). Immediately south of Paddington Station. Adorned with sombre wood panelling this pub serves Hall & Woodhouse, Wells and an interesting selection of guest real ales. Bar meals available *lunchtimes and evenings.* Pub games. *Open all day.*

Victoria 10a Strathearn Place, Paddington, W2 (0207 724 1191). South east of Paddington Station. Victorian through and through with all original features, a model of an old royal yacht and Fuller's real ales. *Food available lunchtimes and evenings (except Sun, all day).* Upstairs piano bar *open Fri & Sat evenings.* Pub *open all day.*

Truscott Arms 55 Shirland Road, Maida Vale, W9 (0207 236 0310). ¼ mile north of the Carlton Bridge Tavern. A large pub, sporting rather more hand pumps than ales for sale, dispensing Bass, Courage and Abbot real ales. Food available *lunchtimes and evenings.* Pub games. *Open all day.*

Also popular with boaters are the **Paddington Stop**, canalside at Little Venice and **Crocker's Folly**, above Maida Hill Tunnel.

Carlton Bridge Tavern 45 Woodfield Road W9 (0207 286 1886). A welcoming canalside pub serving John Smith's and Theakston real ales and *lunchtime food.* Vegetarians catered for, children welcome until *20.00.* Moorings and garden. *Open all day.*

Coliseum 2 Manor Park Road, Harlesden, NW10 (0208 961 6570). Once a cinema now transformed (albeit with Gary Cooper mural and film posters) into a comfortable pub serving Courage, Theakston, Younger and guest real ales. Food available *lunchtimes and evenings.* Outside seating area and disabled access. *Open all day.*

Alperton

Acton Lane Power Station straddles the canal; not far away are the twin townships of Harlesden and Willesden. The canal crosses the North Circular road on a large aqueduct: a strange contrast between the tranquillity of the canal and the roaring traffic below. The Paddington Arm continues west through Alperton and Greenford. Between bridges 11 and 12 there is a useful Sainsbury's right by the canal, with and moorings. The surroundings are mostly flat, but Horsenden Hill and Perivale Wood provide a long stretch of beautiful hilly parkland and Greenford Golf Course adjoins the canal. Soon afterwards the canal turns south into suburban Middlesex.

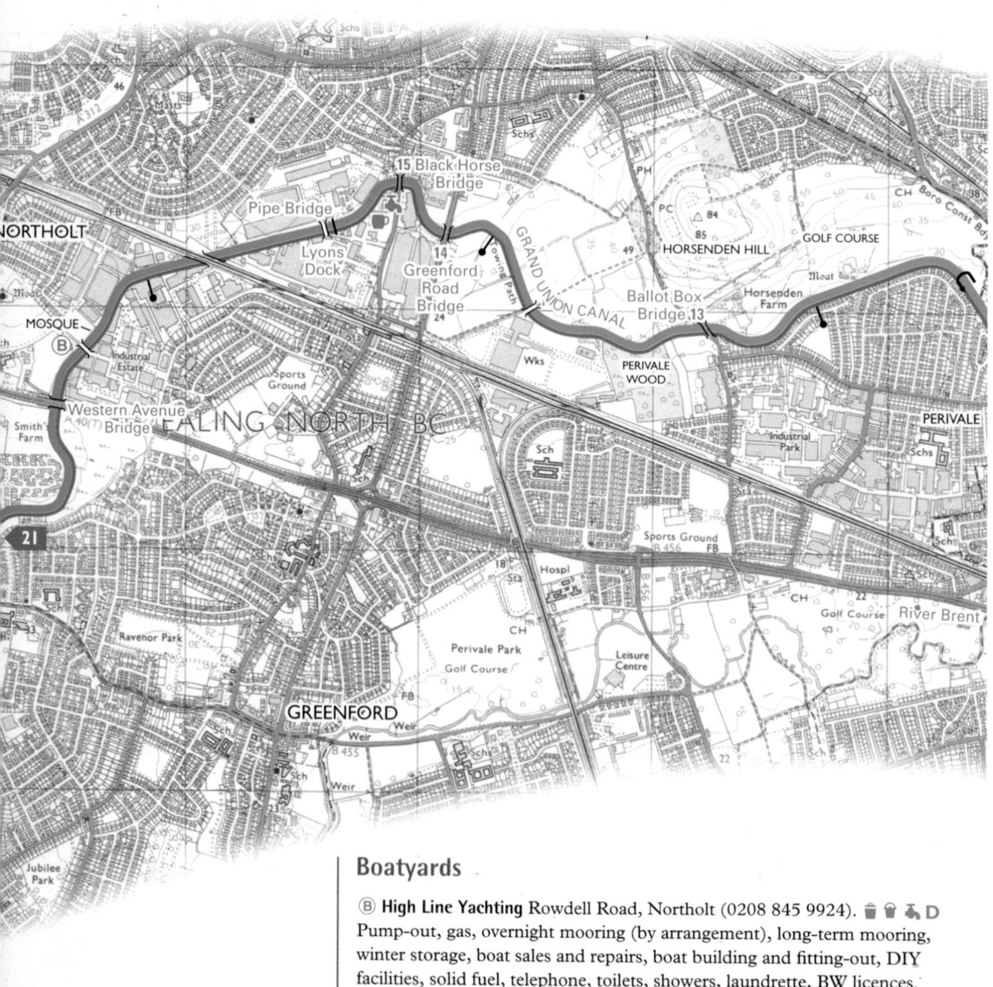

Boatyards

Ⓑ **High Line Yachting** Rowdell Road, Northolt (0208 845 9924). D
Pump-out, gas, overnight mooring (by arrangement), long-term mooring, winter storage, boat sales and repairs, boat building and fitting-out, DIY facilities, solid fuel, telephone, toilets, showers, laundrette, BW licences. Contact head office on 01753 651496 for details of opening times.

Pubs and Restaurants

Castle 140 Victoria Road, Acton W3 (0208 992 2027). South of Actons bridge, near North Acton tube station. Time warp back to the BBC radio era with a large lounge hung with nostalgic pictures and a bar dispensing Fuller's real ales. Food available *lunchtimes and evenings.* Outside seating and traditional pub games. *Open all day.*

Grand Junction Arms Acton Lane NW10 (0208 965 5670). A large pub with good moorings and a children's playground. *Open all day* serving Young's real ale and good value bar food *lunchtimes and evenings and all day Sat.* Vegetarians catered for. Terraced garden and traditional pub games. Children welcome *until 21.00.* Disabled access.

Pleasure Boat 346 Ealing Road, Alperton (0208 902 4516). A wooden skiff over the entrance porch echoes this pub's name. Tetley's real ale and food available *lunchtimes and evenings, Mon–Fri.* Children welcome *until 20.00.* Garden with play area. *Fri* music. *Open all day from 12.00.*

Black Horse 425 Oldfield Lane, Greenford (0208 578 1384). Near Black Horse Bridge 15. Bustling traditional pub, *open all day,* serving Fuller's real ale. Food available *lunchtimes Mon–Fri.* Vegetarians catered for. Children's play area, large garden and overnight mooring for patrons. Traditional pub games.

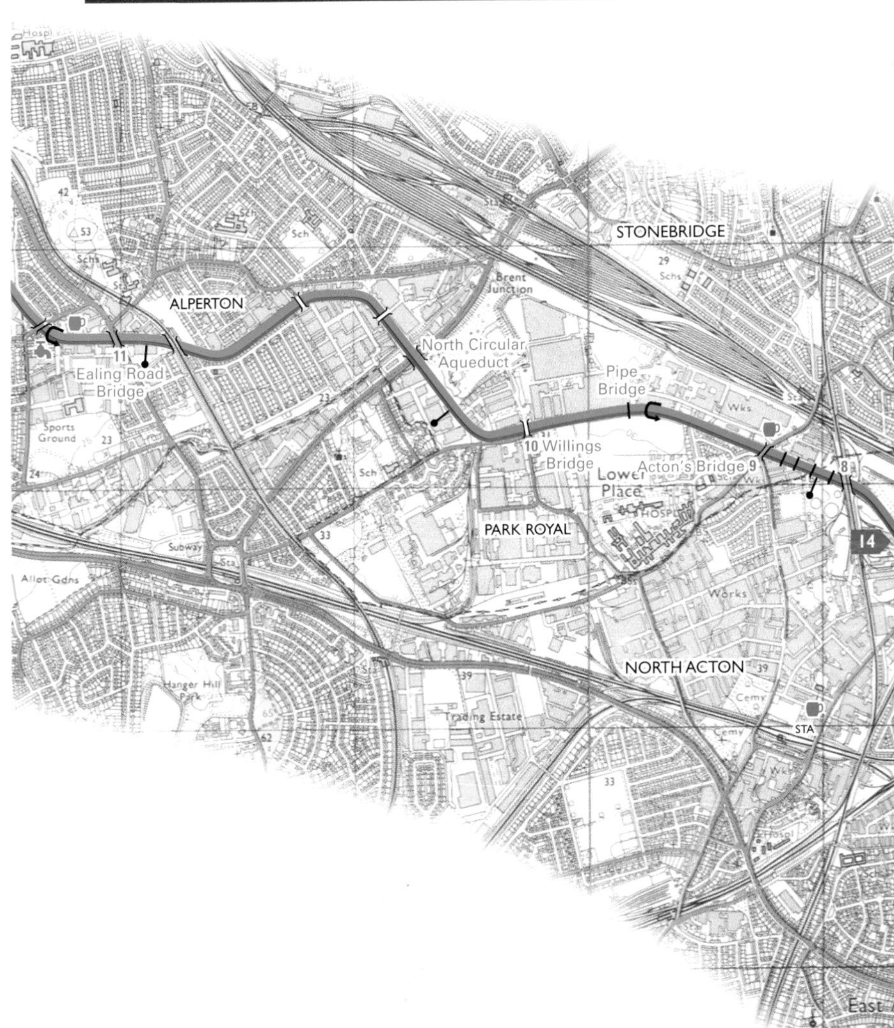

Bull's Bridge

Continuing south through the industrial estate, the Paddington Arm soon reaches the junction with the main line of the Grand Union at Bull's Bridge. This was once a large BW yard (and formerly the Grand Union Canal Carrying Fleet depot) where maintenance boats were built and repaired. It has now been developed by Tesco and offers *24 hr shopping (Mon-Fri)*, temporary moorings and [water tap symbol]. Turning left, the waterway leads east towards Brentford and the Thames past a colourful collection of houseboats; whilst, turning right, the canal goes to Birmingham and beyond. First the navigation enters the indivisible conurbation of Hayes, Harlington, West Drayton and Yiewsley: a good area for shops and pubs before starting to bend towards the north. At bridge 192 the canal passes the site of Colham Wharf. An incised stone from the wharf has been preserved and built into the new building – now visible from road rather than from the canal.

● **Hayes & Harlington**
Middx. All services. Much-industrialised area and distribution base; home of such famous brand names as Nestles, Heinz, EMI and many of the large supermarket chains. There are laundrettes in Hayes (between bridge 200 and the railway station) and at Bull's Bridge (east of bridge 201).

● **Southall**
Middx. All services. Extensive modern shopping centre.
Martinware Pottery Collection Southall Public Library, Osterley Park Road. (0208 574 3412). Representative collection of Martinware, including birds, face mugs and grotesqueries. Of exceptional interest to admirers of Art Nouveau. *Open Tue & Thu 09.30-19.45, Wed & Sat 09.30-17.00. Closed Fri, Sun & Mon.*

Boatyards

Ⓑ **Willowtree Marina** West Quay Drive, Yeading (0208 841 6585). [symbols] Pump-out, gas, narrow boat hire, day hire craft, overnight moorings, long-term mooring, DIY facilities, chandlery, winter storage, slipway, boat sales, solid fuel, books, maps, gifts, telephone, laundrette, showers, toilets. Quayside Bistro & Wine Bar (see page 21).

Ⓑ **Highline Yachting** Packet Boat Lane, Cowley Peachey, Uxbridge (01895 442290). [symbols] D Pump-out, gas, overnight mooring (by arrangement), long-term mooring, covered wet dock, boat building, boat sales and repairs, DIY facilities, boat fitting-out, solid fuel. *Open Tue–Sat 09.00–18.00.*

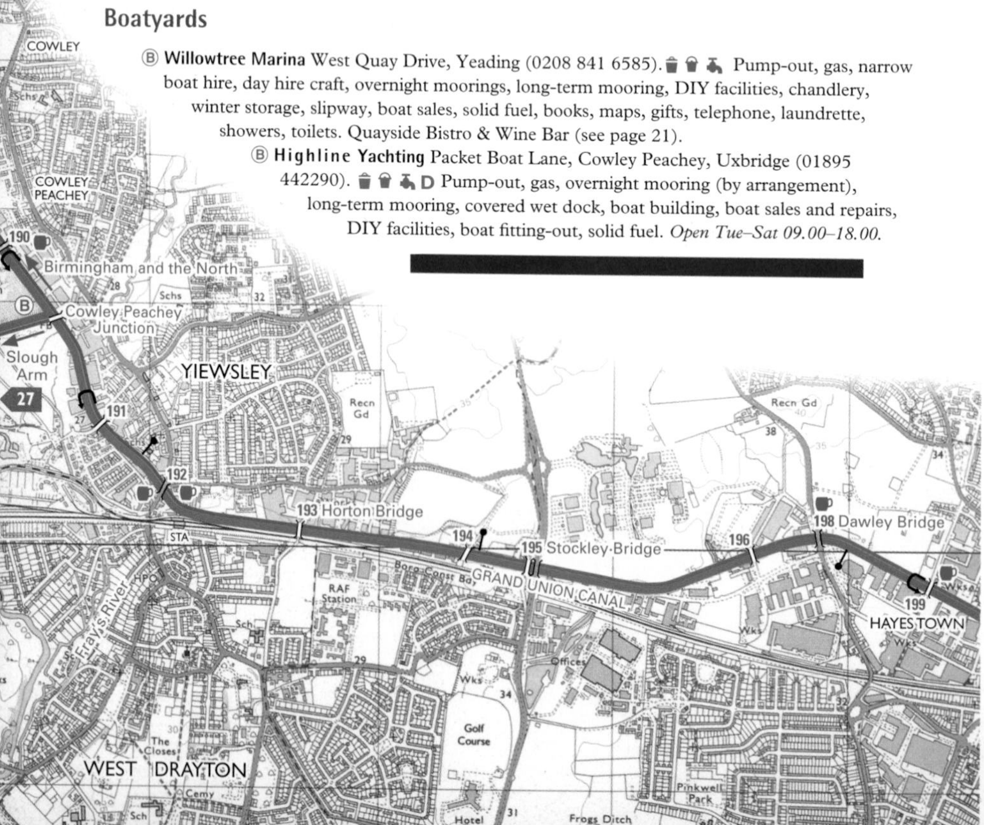

Pubs and Restaurants

Civil Engineer 550 Ruislip Road, Southall (0208 842 1340). Beside bridge 18. Inexpensive bar meals *lunchtimes and evenings, 7 days a week.* Children and vegetarians catered for. Garden. Music and karaoke *Thu–Mon. Open all day.*

Quayside Bistro & Wine Bar Willowtree Marina, West Quay Drive, Yeading (0208 841 2500). English and continental cuisine in a bistro overlooking the marina basin. Food available *L & D Mon–Sat together with Sunday lunches.* Also afternoon tea *at weekends.*

Hambrough Tavern The Broadway, Southall (0208 574 9008). Canal-side at bridge 20. Fairly plush new pub (replacing an earlier waterside tavern) serving a constantly changing range of four real ales. Outside seating, no children in the bars. Traditional pub games. *Open all day.*

Blue Anchor Printing House Lane, Hayes (0208 569 3396). Canalside, at bridge 199. Smart one-bar pub serving rotating guest real ales. Food available *lunchtimes and evenings Mon–Sat (all day Sat).* Children and vegetarians catered for. Garden. Mooring. *Open all day.*

Woolpack North of bridge 198. Ruddles and Webster's real ales and a diet of strip-tease artistes *daily from lunchtime onwards.* Burger bar outside. Unsuitable for children. *Open all day.*

De Burgh Arms Station Approach, West Drayton (01895 442018). Near bridge 192. Smart and comfortable pub, serving Tetley's, Eldridge Pope, Burton and guest real ales. Food available *lunchtimes and evenings.* Outside seating area and disabled access. No smoking area. *Open all day.*

Turning Point Packet Boat Lane, Cowley Peachey (01895 440550). Beside Highline Yachting. A well-kept family restaurant and bar serving Bass real ale. Bar food and à la Carte restaurant menu (offering traditional English cooking) available *L & D (no food Sun evening), together with Sunday lunchtime roasts.* Vegetarians catered for. Children welcome in the restaurant. Attractive waterside patio garden. *Open all day.* Dine and disco *Sat until 01.00.*

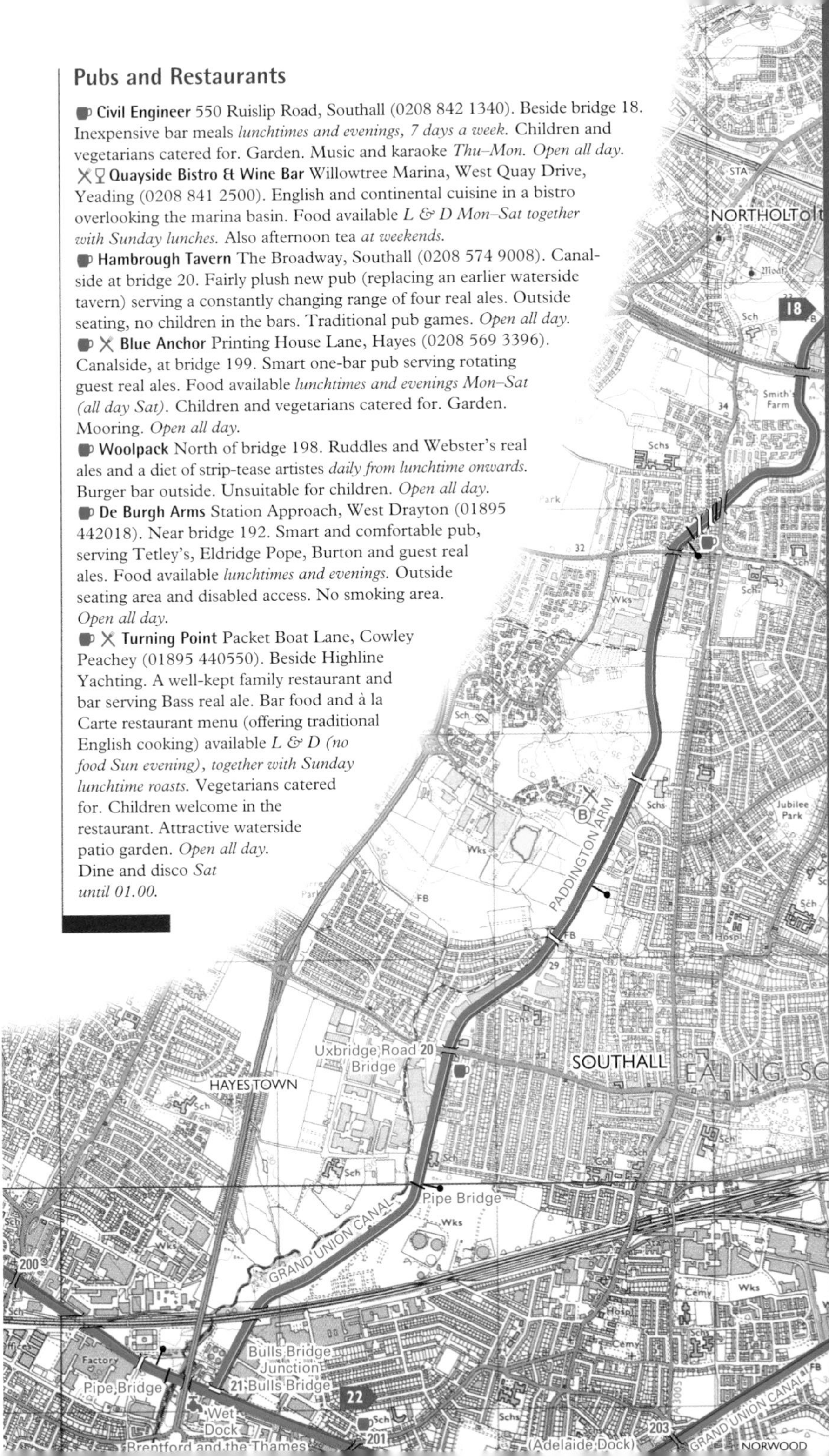

Brentford

This section follows the main line of the Grand Union east from Norwood down to the junction with the Thames at Brentford. At Norwood there is a BW maintenance yard and the beginning of the 12-lock drop to the river, including the Hanwell flight of six locks. It is in parts an interesting and attractive stretch: Osterley and Syon parks are nearby. The River Brent joins the canal at the bottom of Hanwell Locks; there is a rare intersection of canal, road and railway at the top of these locks and several of the bridges are of the brick arched type more commonly seen on the rural canals. Near the big M4 embankment is a very attractive cast iron roving bridge, dated 1820. Immediately below this bridge, is a very poorly signed and unprotected weir, *hazardous* when there is fresh water in the river. Towards Brentford, the towing path disappears under the roof of a large BW warehouse – an odd experience for walkers and cyclists. Kew Gardens are just across the Thames.

Boatyards

BW Norwood Yard at Norwood top lock. (0208 571 8900).

Ⓑ **Adelaide Marine** Adelaide Dock, Endsleigh Road, Endsleigh Industrial Estate, Norwood Green, Southall (0208 571 5678). D E Pump-out, gas, narrow boat hire, winter storage, slipway, crane and straddler (20 tons), boat fitting-out, boat repairs, engine sales, wet dock, DIY facilities, chandlery, toilet. *24 hr* emergency call-out.

Ⓑ **Brent Wharf Services** Brent Wharf, 198 High Street, Brentford (0208 568 7041). Gas, crane (15 ton), chandlery, boat building, boat fitting-out, boat storage, engine sales and repairs, telephone, toilets, café, gifts, solid fuel, laundrette.

Ⓑ **Brentford Marine Services** Ridgeways Wharf, Brent Way, Brentford (0208 568 0287). Slipway, boat sales and repairs, engine sales and repairs (including outboards), boat building and fitting-out, wet dock, hoist (5 tons). Emergency call-out.

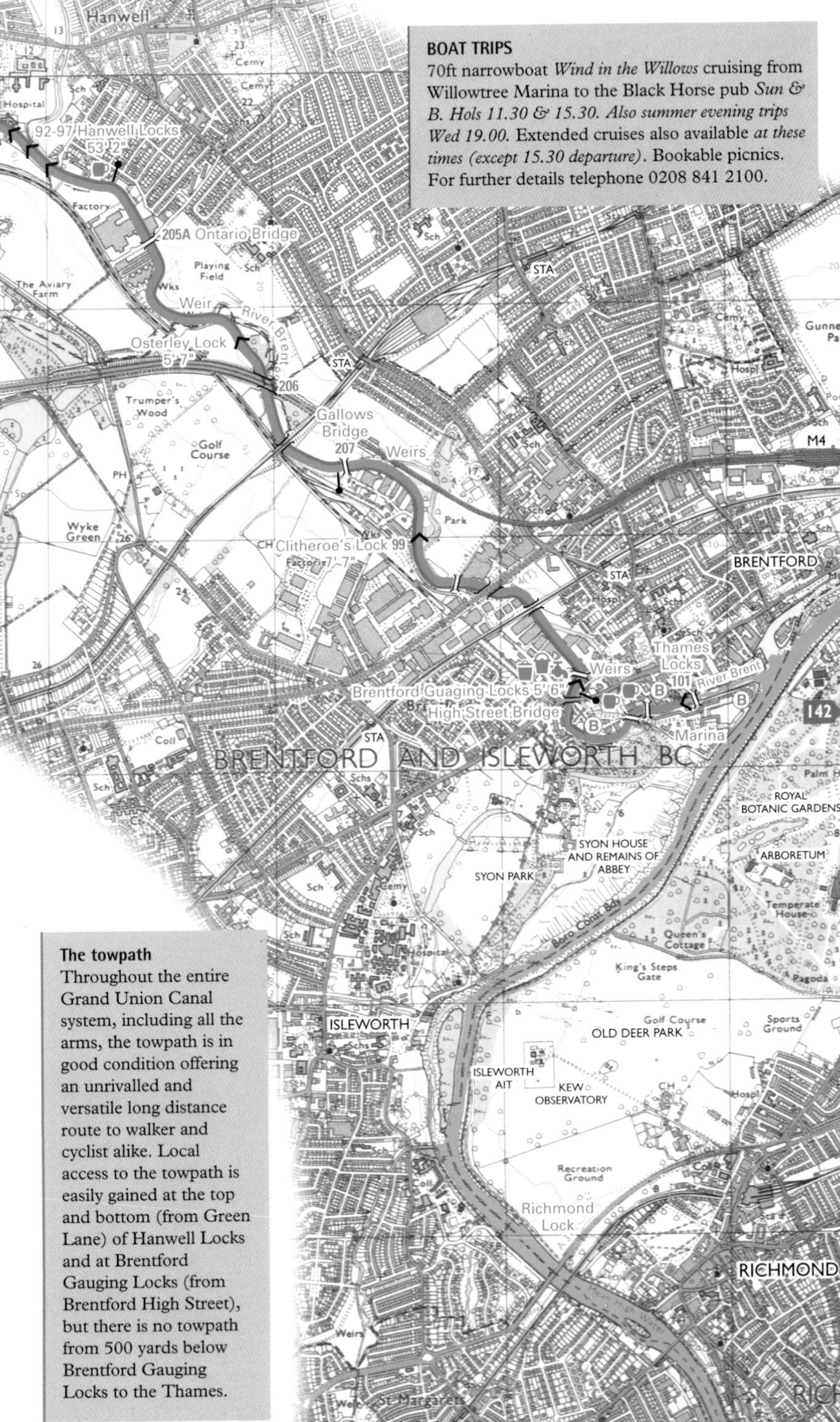

See Book 7

BOAT TRIPS

70ft narrowboat *Wind in the Willows* cruising from Willowtree Marina to the Black Horse pub *Sun & B. Hols 11.30 & 15.30. Also summer evening trips Wed 19.00.* Extended cruises also available *at these times (except 15.30 departure)*. Bookable picnics. For further details telephone 0208 841 2100.

The towpath

Throughout the entire Grand Union Canal system, including all the arms, the towpath is in good condition offering an unrivalled and versatile long distance route to walker and cyclist alike. Local access to the towpath is easily gained at the top and bottom (from Green Lane) of Hanwell Locks and at Brentford Gauging Locks (from Brentford High Street), but there is no towpath from 500 yards below Brentford Gauging Locks to the Thames.

NAVIGATIONAL NOTES

1 Norwood and Hanwell Locks are kept padlocked and can be operated with a BW key.
2 The Thames at Brentford is tidal; Teddington Locks (the upper limit of the Thames tideway) are 5 miles upstream. Application to navigate the non-tidal Thames should be made in advance to the Environment Agency, Thames Region, King's Meadow House, King's Meadow Road, Reading, Berks, RG1 8DQ (01734 535000). Craft entering the canal from the Thames without the necessary BW licence may complete the formalities at Brentford. No licence is required on the tidal river. Craft entering the the non-tidal Thames without the necessary licence can complete the formalities for a visitor licence at Teddington Lock.
3 Thames Lock is controlled by a lock keeper and, together with Brentford Gauging Locks, is of course subject to the tide. It is manned *for a period before and following high water (2hrs each side if this falls within normal working hours: Apr–Oct 08.00–18.00 & Nov–Mar 08.00–16.30)* and you should contact the lock keeper – giving at least *24hrs notice* – to pre-book passage *outside the normal working hours*. Passage may only be booked within the core hours of 05.00–22.00. The lock keeper can be contacted on 0208 560 1120 and VHF channel 74.
4 Brentford Gauging Locks are boater operated using a BW sanitary station key. Pairs and single boats are requested to use the single lock on the toll office side to minimise the use of water. Please keep dogs inside your boat at all times whilst using the two tidal locks. Boaters should note that the section of the waterway between Brentford Gauging Locks and Thames Lock is **tidal** and therefore if the tide is still rising the headroom under the bridges is still *decreasing*. Brentford High Street Bridge is unnavigable at the top of *spring* tides due to less than 4ft headroom.
5 For further details on navigating the tidal Thames read the section on the London Thames, commencing on page 144.

● **Osterley Park House** Jersey Road, Isleworth (0208 560 3918). Set in a large park – a superb remodelled mansion with elegant interior decorations by Robert Adam, 1760–80. Gobelins and Beauvais tapestries and fine carpets. Elizabethan stables in large park. *Open Apr–Oct, Wed–Sun 13.00–17.00 & B. Hol Mon 11.00–17.00. Closed G. Fri. Last admission 16.30.* Charge. Access is unfortunately on the south side of the M4, 1 1/2 miles from the canal. But Osterley Park tube station is close to the entrance, which is just north of the A4.

Boston Manor House Boston Manor Road, Brentford, 1/2 mile north of bridge 208. (0208 560 6597). Tudor and Jacobean house with excellent examples of period ceilings. *Open to visitors – telephone for details.* Nearest tube station is Boston Manor (1/4 mile north of the house).

Syon House Brentford (0208 560 0883). Entrance 300yds west of Brentford Gauging Locks on A315. Seat of the Duke of Northumberland. Noted for its fine Adam interior and period furniture, also its paintings. Its historical associations go back to the 15thC. *Open to visitors – telephone for details.*

Syon Park Gardening Centre Park Road, Brentford (0208 580 0134). Very wide selection of plants and gardening equipment for sale.

Syon Park Gardens Brentford (0208 560 0883). 55 acres of Capability Brown gardens. In the grounds are the Gardening Centre, Live Butterfly House, reptile house and children's indoor adventure playground. Charge.. Gardens *closed Xmas Day & Boxing Day.*

Musical Museum St George's Church, 368 High Street, Brentford (0208 560 8108). A fascinating collection of around 200 automatic, old and odd musical instruments. Many of the instruments are played during the *one-hour* conducted tour. *Telephone for details of opening times..* Charge. No small children.

Kew Bridge Steam Museum Green Dragon Lane, Brentford (0208 568 4757). Huge Victorian building housing six gigantic beam engines, restored to working order by volunteers. Under steam at *weekends.* Also a collection of old traction engines and a working forge. Tearoom *(weekends only). Open 11.00–17.00 Mon–Sun inc B. Hols.* Charge (under 5s free).

Kew Gardens Kew (0208 940 1171/8332 5655). On the south bank of the Thames, opposite Brentford. (Access from the south side of the Gardens or from the Thames towpath.) One of the world's great botanic gardens, with thousands of rare outdoor and hothouse plants. Kew Palace, also worth a visit, was built in 1631 in the Dutch style. Gardens *open daily 09.30-18.30 (weekends & B. Hols 19.30).* Glasshouses, gallery and museum *close 17.30.* Charge.

Pubs and Restaurants

Grand Junction Arms Acton Lane, Southall NW10 (0208 965 5670). Canalside, by bridge 201. A cosy family pub serving a varied selection of food *lunchtimes and evenings every day*. Young's real ale. Children and vegetarians catered for. Garden and large children's play area. Live entertainment *Fri. Open all day.*

Old Oak Common Road, Southall (0208 574 5851). Families are made very welcome in this canalside pub (bridge 202) which serves a selection of real ales and traditional English, home-cooked food daily, *lunchtimes and evenings*. Large screen TV and karaoke *Fri nights. Open all day.*

Lamb Norwood (0208 574 3578). At bridge 203. Courage real ale in this canalside pub. Outside seating, moorings. *Open all day.*

Plough Tentelow Lane, Norwood Green (0208 574 1945). Fuller's oldest pub (serving their range of real ales) and a building of some considerable historic significance in the area. Food available at *lunchtimes (not Sun)*. Open fires, garden and traditional pub games. *Open all day.*

Fox Green Lane, Hanwell W7 (0208 567 3912). At bottom of Hanwell Locks, 50yds from canal. In virtually a village location this pub offers Courage and Marston's real ales and *lunchtime* food (including excellent *Sunday* roasts). Vegetarians catered for. Large garden. Children welcome. Pub games, camping and disabled access. *Open all day.*

Dolphin 13 Lower Boston Road, Hanwell, W7 (0208 840 0850). ¼ mile past the Fox. Always an interesting selection of food available (*lunchtimes and evenings*) together with a wide range of real ales (often from micro-breweries) which includes Bass and Gibbs Mew: well worth the short walk from the canal. Outside seating, a no smoking area and pub games. *Open all day.*

Bridge Wine Bar High Street, Brentford (0208 847 3941). Beside High Street Bridge. Bright and friendly establishment beside the canal offering an interesting, varied and very reasonably priced menu. Telephone for hours of opening.

Magpie and Crown 128 High Street, Brentford (0208 560 5658). Between Brentford and Thames Locks. The landlord has created a welcoming family atmosphere and offers an interesting variety of good value food *lunchtimes Mon–Fri*. Vegetarians catered for. Three rotating guest ales. Outside seating. Live music *Tue & Thu*. B & B. *Open all day.*

Brewery Tap Catherine Wheel Road, Brentford (0208 560 5200). Between the canal and the High Street. Fuller's real ale, food *lunchtimes and evenings until 20.00 (not Sun evenings)* and a range of live music *Tue & Thu–Sat* make this Victorian pub a lively (yet cosy) venue. Outside seating and traditional pub games. *Open all day.*

Beehive 113 High Street, Brentford (0208 952 2446). North of Thames Lock. Traditional town pub with a fine blue and green tiled exterior. Fuller's real ale, food available *all day Mon–Sat. Open all day.*

Watermans Arms 11 Ferry Lane, Brentford (0208 560 5665). ¼ mile east of Thames Lock, just off the High Street. Small, friendly side-street pub offering Morland and Ruddles real ales. Bar snacks available *lunchtimes only. Open all day.*

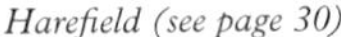

Harefield (see page 30)

Cowley Peachey Junction

At Cowley Peachey Junction, the 5-mile Slough Arm branches off to the west in an almost straight line. Built as late as 1882 (the last canal to be built in Britain except for the New Junction and Manchester Ship Canals), it sweeps easily over several aqueducts and through a long cutting. The main traffic on the waterway was bricks made from the copious clay deposits along its length and used to fuel the capital's prodigious construction appetite. In a neat and reciprocal manner boats returned with the city's waste which was used to backfill the brick pits. It can be seen that the canal was built after the rise of the railways and is, perhaps, unique in that it represented the more economic mode of transport. East of Iver the water is relatively clear, and there are often attractive weeds and reeds to be seen growing in the canal in summer. Continuing westwards under the A412, the Slough arm passes dull housing and industrial estates on its way to the terminal basin on the outskirts of the town. On the main line, Cowley Lock marks the end of the 27-mile pound and the start of the climb up the Colne valley and the Chiltern Hills. Uxbridge, just to the north, signals the limit of the outer-suburban belt that surrounds London. Uxbridge Lock has an attractive setting with its lock cottage, a turnover bridge and a tall modern flour mill standing nearby in grounds that are splendidly landscaped down to the water's edge. The *Paddington Packet* Boat used to run daily from Paddington to Cowley – one of the few passenger boats plying regularly along the Grand Junction Canal. It was pulled by four horses and had precedence over all other boats, so it covered the 15-mile lock-free run in a time that was remarkable at the beginning of the 19thC.

Iver
Bucks. PO, tel, stores, garage, station. The church has a Saxon nave with Roman bricks visible in the walls. Norman arches, medieval art and Tudor monuments. The 700-year-old tower owes its great height to the 15th-C bell chamber.

Old Slade Nature Reserve 1 mile south of Iver station. Gravel pit taken over by the Berkshire, Buckinghamshire and Oxfordshire Naturalists' Trust and now a wealth of bird and animal life.
Iver Grove Shredding Green, Iver (north of the boatyard). A fine mansion built by Sir John Vanbrugh in 1724. Not open to the public.

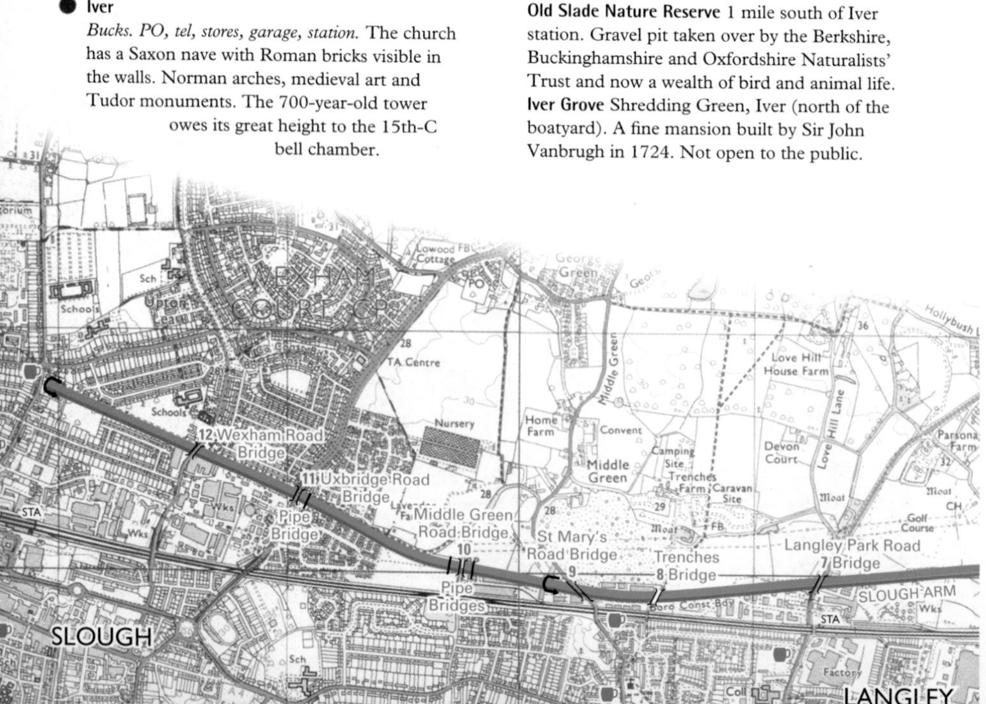

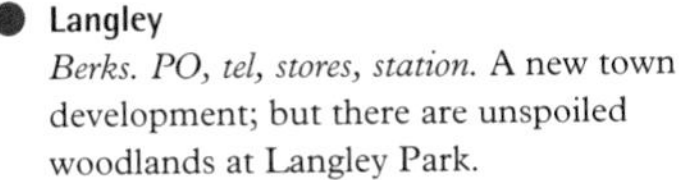

Langley

Berks. PO, tel, stores, station. A new town development; but there are unspoiled woodlands at Langley Park.

Slough

Berks. MD Tue. PO, tel, stores, garage, station, cinema. This is the largest town in Berkshire; it is a new town, undistinguished architecturally and remembered more for its wide range of light industries and its immortalization in verse by John Betjeman who wrote (in 1981):

> 'Come, friendly bombs, and fall on Slough
> It isn't fit for humans now
> There isn't grass to graze a cow.'

St Mary's Church is, however, interesting for its stained glass by Kempe and Alfred J. Wolmark: the church was completed in 1876. Herschel Park, in the town centre, is also worth a visit. South of the basin (towards the town centre) there is a parade of shops including a chemist, PO, stores and greengrocer, take-aways and the like. The town plays host to a rash of the new breed of pubs with double-barrel names.

Uxbridge

Middx. PO, tel, stores, garage, station, cinema, laundrette. The Battle of Britain was directed by the late Air Marshal Lord Dowding from the RAF Headquarters in Uxbridge. The town is perhaps noteworthy for its selection of modern and futuristic buildings in a variety of competing styles.

Pubs and Restaurants

Fox & Pheasant Thorney Lane, Iver (01753 653175). Friendly, bustling establishment between the canal and the village with some form of entertainment *every evening*. Real cider together with Burton, Courage and guest real ales. Food available *all day until 22.00, 7 days a week*. Garden, children's play area and bouncy castle. Pool, darts, dominoes, chess and hoopla.

Bull High Street, Iver (01753 651115). Basic village pub serving Burton and Flowers real ales together with inexpensive bar meals and snacks *lunchtimes and evenings (except Sun)*. Children and vegetarians catered for. Pub games including pool. *Open all day Sat.*

X Swan High Street, Iver (01753 655776). An old, traditional and heavily-beamed pub with a relaxed atmosphere dispensing Courage and guest real ales. Food is available in both the bar and restaurant *L & D, 7 days a week*. Children and vegetarians catered for. Garden and darts.. *Open all day.*

Gurkha Shredding Green, Iver (01753 654257). Undergoing refurbishment at time of writing.

Willow Tree Langley (01753 811491). Immediately south of Langley station. Courage and Webster's real ales together with bar snacks *lunchtimes and evenings*. Beer garden and games room adjoining the large, single bar. *Over 21s only.*

Chestnuts St Mary's Road, Langley (01753 544238). Mature chestnut trees crowd the front of this pub which serves Courage and Webster's real ales, along with bar meals *lunchtimes and evenings*. Children welcome. Garden and outside seating. Pool, darts, quiz *alternate Weds.*

X Red Lion St Mary's Road, Langley (01753 582235). Past the Chestnuts, opposite the church. A 16th-C inn with low-beamed ceilings serving Greene King and guest real ales. Food available *lunchtimes, evenings and all day Sun*. Children and vegetarians catered for. Garden. Disabled access.

Nags Head Slough (01753 551964). Near the basin. Spacious, friendly, modern pub serving Courage and Webster's real ales together with *lunchtime* bar meals *Mon–Fri* (snacks available *Sat lunchtimes)*. Vegetarians and children catered for. Patio seating. *Open all day.*

Printers Devil Slough (01753 520140). South of the basin. A youngish persons establishment (18–35) with sports TV and enthusiastic football and pool teams. Tetley's and Marston's real ales and *lunchtime* food. Snacks available *lunchtimes and evenings*. Disco *Thu–Sat* and pop quiz *Sun.*

Grapes Slough (01752 531720). South of the basin, past the station, in the town centre. Long established hostelry with an attractive, wood-panelled interior, dispensing Boddingtons, Flowers and guest real ales together with inexpensive food *lunchtimes, Mon–Sat*. Vegetarians catered for and children welcome in the garden. Disco *Thu & Sat. Open all day.*

X Turning Point Packet Boat Lane, Cowley Peachey (01895 440550). Beside Highline Yachting. A well-kept family restaurant and bar serving Bass real ale. Bar food and à la carte restaurant menu (offering traditional English cooking) available *L & D (no food Sun evenings), together with Sunday lunchtime roasts*. Vegetarians catered for. Children welcome in the restaurant. Attractive waterside patio garden. *Open all day.* Diner and disco *Sat until 01.00.*

Paddington Packet Boat Packet Boat Lane, Cowley Peachey (01895 442392). Down the road from bridge 190. Fuller's real ale and home-cooked food available *lunchtimes and evenings* in a fine traditional pub. Children welcome in the garden and non-smoking area only. Live music *Sat.* B & B. Disabled access. There is a laundrette to the left of the junction between Packet Boat Lane and the High Street.

X Shovel Cowley Peachey (01895 233121). At Cowley Lock. Restaurant, steak bar and bar, with attractive canal decor and full-length bookcases. Food available *lunchtimes, evenings and all day Sat & Sun*. Children and vegetarians catered for. Canalside garden. Moorings outside.

Dolphin St John's Road, Uxbridge. At bridge 186. Compact local serving Courage and Brakspear real ales and inexpensive food *lunchtimes and evenings, Mon–Fri*. Children and vegetarians catered for. Small canalside beer garden. Darts, pool and crib. Moorings.

General Elliot St John's Road, Uxbridge (01895 237385). At bridge 186. A boisterous canalside pub of great character, serving Marston's, Tetley's, Wadworth, and Adnams real ales. Bar food available *lunchtimes and evenings (not Sun evenings)*. Children and vegetarians catered for. Canalside terrace. Darts. Moorings.

Crown & Treaty Oxford Road, Uxbridge (01895 233891). Near bridge 185. A very handsome pub dating from 1576, where unsuccessful negotiations were held between King and Parliament during the Civil War. Marston's, Flowers and six guest real ales and food available *lunchtimes and evenings, five days a week*. Vegetarians catered for, patio seating. Quiz *alternate Mon, jazz alternate Sun and karaoke Tue.* No children.

X Swan and Bottle Oxford Road, Uxbridge (01895 234047). Busy pub and restaurant serving bar meals *all day, every day*, and John Smith's and Courage real ales. A steak-based restaurant menu is available *L & D Mon–Sat and all day Sun*. Children and vegetarians catered for. Moorings.

Boatyards

Ⓑ **Highline Yachting** Packet Boat Lane, Cowley Peachey, Uxbridge (01895 442290). D Pump-out, gas, overnight mooring (by arrangement), long-term mooring, covered wet dock, boat building, boat sales and repairs, DIY facilities, boat fitting-out, solid fuel. *Open Tue–Sat 09.00–18.00.*

Ⓑ **Highline Yachting** Mansion Lane, Iver (01753 651496/653151). D E Pump-out, gas, overnight mooring, long-term mooring, winter storage, slipway, chandlery, books, gifts and maps, boat building and fitting-out, boat sales and repairs, engine repairs, DIY facilities, solid fuel, toilet, showers, laundrette, telephone. Emergency call-out. *Open Tue–Sat 09.00-18.00, Sun 10.00-17.00.*

Ⓑ **Uxbridge Boat Centre** Uxbridge Wharf, Waterloo Road, Uxbridge (01895 252019). D E Gas, overnight mooring, long-term mooring, winter storage, slipway, dry dock, wet dock, crane, DIY facilities, chandlery, books, maps and gifts, boat building and fitting-out, boat and engine repairs (including outboards), engine sales, solid fuel, toilet. *Closed Mon (also Sun Dec & Jan).*

Ⓑ **Marine Engine Services** Uxbridge Wharf, Waterloo Road, Uxbridge (01895 270422). Engine sales and repairs. Lister engine specialist.

Ⓑ **Denham Yacht Station** 100 Acres, Sandersons Road, Uxbridge (01895 239811). By bridge 184. D E Pump-out, gas, overnight mooring (by arrangement), long-term mooring, winter storage, chandlery, boat sales and repairs, engine repairs (including outboards), DIY facilities, telephone, solid fuel, toilets, club house. Emergency call-out.

Cowley Lock

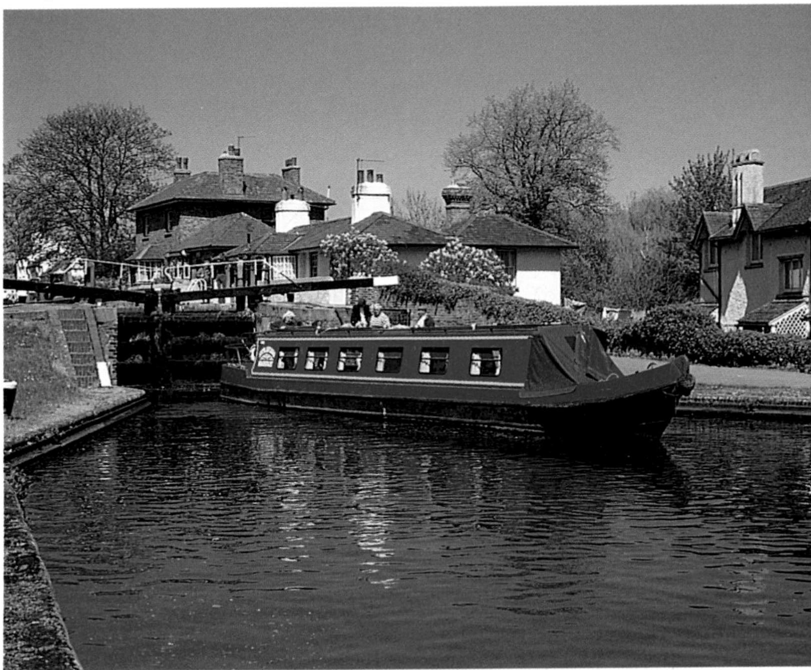

Harefield

The main line of the canal continues northwards past the village of Denham and across Harefield Moor, a stretch of common land of considerable interest to naturalists. Denham Lock, with a rise of 11ft 1in, is the deepest on the Grand Union. Leaving Widewater Lock, the canal continues up the Colne valley through a landscape of interesting contrasts which contains woods, mills, lakes and a large sewage works. Black Jack's Lock is beautifully framed by a small mill and a tiny timbered cottage, while Copper Mill Lock is just upstream of an attractive group of canalside buildings.

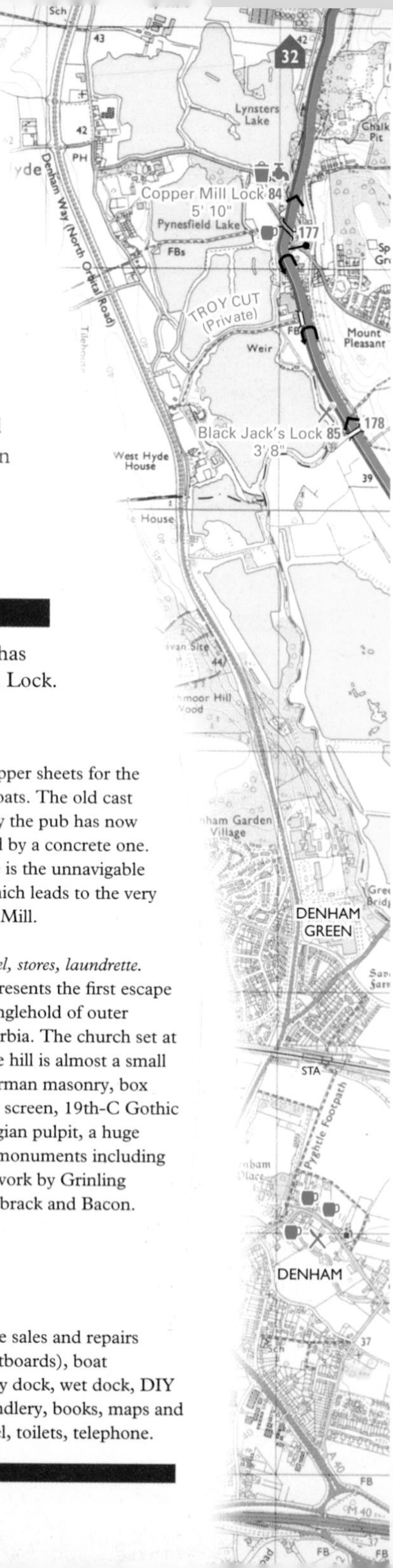

NAVIGATIONAL NOTES

There is a strong cross current, especially when there has been heavy rain, between bridge 177 and Copper Mill Lock.

● **Denham**
Bucks. PO, tel, stores, station. West of the canal and of the River Colne, Denham is split into two parts: the new part is north of the railway. In the old village is the church set among the cottages. It contains a Doom painting of 1460 and some Renaissance effigies and monuments. Denham Court, which stands in the Colne meadows, and Denham Place, the 17th-C home of the Vansittart family, are both fine examples of English architecture. The old village is quintessential Old England with immense charm, albeit in what has become a very exclusive area of the Home Counties.

Copper Mill An interesting canal settlement. The big mill was once a paper mill, but after the canal was built it turned to making copper sheets for the bottoms of boats. The old cast iron bridge by the pub has now been replaced by a concrete one. South of here is the unnavigable Troy Cut, which leads to the very ancient Troy Mill.

● **Harefield**
Middx. PO, tel, stores, laundrette. Harefield represents the first escape from the stranglehold of outer London suburbia. The church set at the foot of the hill is almost a small museum: Norman masonry, box pews, 16th-C screen, 19th-C Gothic gallery, Georgian pulpit, a huge collection of monuments including brasses, and work by Grinling Gibbons, Rysbrack and Bacon.

Boatyards

Ⓑ **Harefield Marina** Moorhall Road, Harefield (01895 822036). Beside bridge 180. **D E** Pump-out, gas, overnight mooring, long-term mooring, winter storage, slipway, crane, boat sales and repairs, engine sales and repairs (including outboards), boat fitting-out, dry dock, wet dock, DIY facilities, chandlery, books, maps and gifts, solid fuel, toilets, telephone.

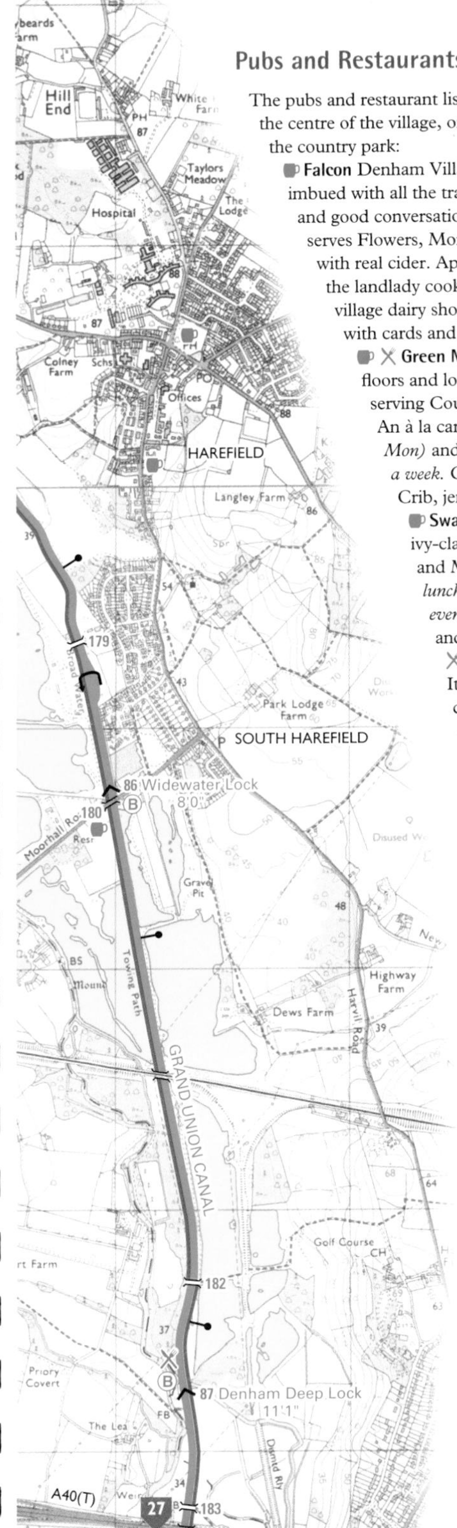

Pubs and Restaurants

The pubs and restaurant listed for Denham are all within 100yds of each other in the centre of the village, one mile north west of the lock, by footpath through the country park:

Falcon Denham Village (01895 832125). The archetypal village pub, imbued with all the traditional values: excellent ales, honest home-cooking and good conversation. This one-roomed local, approached by stone steps, serves Flowers, Morland, Marston's and Brakspear real ales, together with real cider. Appetising food is available *lunchtimes, Mon–Sat,* whilst the landlady cooks a fish and chip supper on *Fri evenings.* Once the village dairy shop, the atmosphere is both homely and welcoming, with cards and dominoes the only (welcome) intrusion. No children.

Green Man Denham Village (01895 832760). Flag stone floors and low-beamed ceilings in a pub built in 1780 and now serving Courage, Greene King, Rebellion and Webster's real ales. An à la carte menu is offered in the restaurant for *D, (except Mon)* and bar meals are available *lunchtimes and evenings, 7 days a week.* Garden and children's play area. Quiz *Thu & Sun.* Crib, jenga, dominoes and cards.

Swan Denham Village (01895 832085). Attractive, old ivy-clad building, wood-panelled inside and serving Courage and Marston's real ales. Friendly staff. Bar meals available *lunchtimes and evenings (except all day Mon & Sun evenings).* Children and vegetarians catered for. Garden and pet animals.

Da Remo Denham Village (01895 832425). Classic Italian cuisine in an old, dark beamed building with contrasting panelling in polished oak, providing a delightful setting for a special meal. *Open for L Mon–Fri & D Mon–Sat* and offering a choice of table d'hôte and à la carte menus.

Fran's Tea Garden Denham Deep Lock, Denham. Hot and cold snacks, home produce, tea and coffee all served in an idyllic location. *Open Easter-Oct 10.00-19.00; Nov-Easter 10.00-16.30. Closed Mon.* Coal.

Horse & Barge Moorhall Road, Harefield (01895 834080). By bridge 180. Family pub serving Courage and guest real ales and food available *all day.* Vegetarians catered for. Quiz *Mon* and disco *Tue & Thu–Sun.* Darts. Karaoke *Sat.*

White Horse Church Hill, Harefield (01895 822144). Take the footpath east from Black Jack's Lock. Tetley's, Greenalls, Wadworth, Shipstone's and guest real ales served in a friendly, Grade II listed pub dating from 17thC. Food available *lunchtimes and evenings.*

Black Jack's Mill Restaurant Harefield (01895 822205). Startlingly pretty situation overlooking Black Jack's Lock. *Closed at the time of writing.*

Fisheries Inn Harefield (01895 825623). Canalside at bridge 177. A fine old pub, virtually surrounded by water, now a part of the Big Steak Pub empire. Burton, Tetley's and Benskins real ales together with real cider. Food available *lunchtimes, evenings and all day Sun.* Canalside patio and children's play area. *Open all day.*

Rickmansworth

Old chalk quarries adjoin the canal as it turns north east towards Rickmansworth. Passing Stocker's Lock with an interesting group of old farm buildings close by – they date from the 16thC – the canal soon reaches Batchworth Lock on the outskirts of Rickmansworth. (There are in fact two locks here, one of them leading up into the River Chess, which is navigable for a short distance. Northbound navigators should take the right hand lock to stay on the Grand Union Canal.) Here the River Colne comes in from the east and the Chess from the north west, while the Gade continues to accompany the canal to the north east. Just before the lock is a useful Tesco, complete with moorings for patrons. Past Rickmansworth is Common Moor and north of this is Croxley and the outskirts of Watford. The canal keeps well away from this town and climbs instead into the superb Cassiobury Park, a long and lovely stretch of wooded parkland. A commemorative plaque at Iron Bridge Lock, unveiled by the Duke of Marlborough, is inscribed 1787–1987, to mark 200 years of the Grand Union Canal's existence. The A404 crosses at Rickmansworth and the A412 at Croxley.

● **Springwell and Stocker's Locks** This stretch is of interest to naturalists: there is a great variety of plants along here and disused watercress beds are nearby. Orchids have been found growing in the adjacent chalk pits.

Batchworth Lock Canal Centre beside Batchworth Locks (01923 778382). Canal Memorabilia, postcards, drinks and ice-creams and reconstruction of *nb Roger. Open Feb–Oct, Mon, Tue, Thu, Fri and Sun 11.00-17.00.*

● **Rickmansworth**

Herts. PO, tel, stores, station. Very little of the medieval town remains today: the Vicarage in Church Street has late medieval timberwork, but 18th-C and 19th-C alterations are intermingled. Despite this, there are several other buildings well worth a look: the 17thC Bury and the timber-framed but much restored Priory, both lying near the 19th-C Church of St Mary, which lends a wonderful feeling of unity because it is almost entirely the work of one man – Sir Arthur Blomfield. The town centre is north of bridge 173.

Tourist Information Centre Three Rivers House, Northway, Rickmansworth (01923 776611). *Open Mon–Fri 08.30–17.00.*

● **Croxley Green**

Herts. PO, tel, stores, garage, laundrette, station. Despite being swamped by new housing, part of the old village survives around the green, where there are several attractive houses. There is a large medieval barn south of the village.

Cassiobury Park Cassiobury Avenue, Watford (01923 226400 ext 2555). The canal flows through the park, once part of the 17th-C gardens of the Earls of Essex. The avenue of limes was planted by Moses Cook in 1672 and many of the trees are as old as 300 years. The park stretches for 190 acres and is adjoined by Whippendell Woods. Watford's carnival takes place here every *Whitsun* and there are regular *B. Hol* fairs. Tennis courts and café.

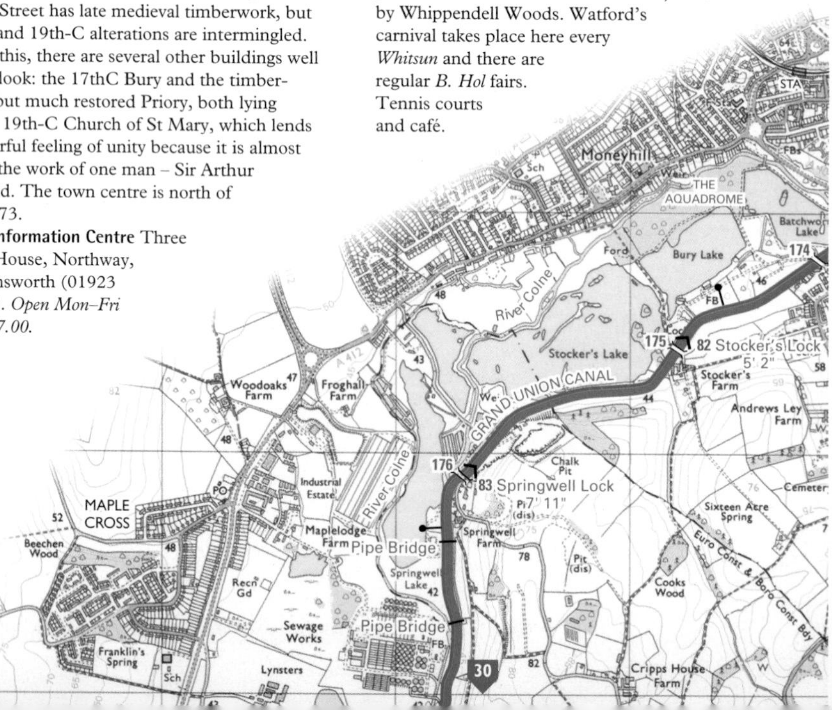

Boatyards

Ⓑ **Bridgewater Basin** Cassio Bridge, Croxley Green, Watford (01923 211448). D Gas, pump-out, long-term mooring, slipway.

BOAT TRIPS

Arcturus Cruises Cassio Wharf, Watford. Part or whole day cruises by narrow boat, for parties of up to 54 passengers. Public trips *Sun afternoon – and Tue & Thur afternoons in Aug* – from lock 77. Telephone 01438 714528 for further details.

Batchworth Lock Canal Centre (01923 778382). *25 min* trips to Stoker's Lock and back operating *Apr-Oct, Sun afternoons 14.00 onwards.*

Pubs and Restaurants

✕ **Batchworth Brasserie** Batchworth Locks, Rickmansworth (01923 778382). Enterprising venture in conjunction with the Canal Centre based in a marquee on a lawn between the locks. Enjoy hot and cold drinks and a tasty selection of snacks while helping to fund *Roger's* restoration. *Open Apr-Oct, Sat & Sun & B. Hols 10.30-17.00.*

White Bear Rickmansworth (01923 772381). Near Batchworth Lock. Boddingtons, Bass and Courage real ales in a member of the Magic Pub chain. Mirrors and a cottagey interior with moorings outside. Bar meals *lunchtimes and evenings (not Sun evenings)*. Children and vegetarians catered for. Outside seating. Darts.

Fox & Hounds High Street, Rickmansworth (01923 441119). Cosy local serving Courage and a selection of changing guest real ales. Bar meals available *Mon–Sat lunchtimes*. Open fire and traditional pub games. Garden. *Open all day.*

Kings Langley

The canal climbs in a northerly direction through Cassiobury Park to Grove Mill, a water mill where the mill stream doubles as a private canal arm. Just north of the mill is the deservedly famous ornamental stone bridge ordered by the Earl of Essex before he would allow the Grand Junction Canal Company to cut a navigation through his park. The canal winds considerably along this valley as it follows the course of the River Gade. This results in several wide stretches; do not attempt to turn in these without ascertaining the depth. The M25 north orbital road and the A41 cross the canal as it approaches the lovely village of Hunton Bridge. A little further north is Kings Langley, where there is a useful store and off-licence just west of bridge 158.

● **Hunton Bridge**
Herts. PO, tel, stores. Peaceful canalside village, with a spired church and the pleasing Langleybury Park.

● **Abbots Langley**
Herts. PO, tel, stores, station (shared with Kings Langley). The Church of St Lawrence has 12th-C arcades to the nave and a 14th-C south chapel, an octagonal Perpendicular font and a 14th-C wall painting of Saints Thomas and Lawrence.

● **Kings Langley**
Herts. PO, tel, stores, laundrette, station. Somewhere between a large village and a small country town, Kings Langley derives its name from its royal associations; there are still the remains of a palace in the town. The tomb of Edmund de Langley, brother of the Black Prince, lies in the Norman Church of All Saints. Sir John Evans, the famous archaeologist, is also buried here. With the construction of the bypass both are now able to rest in peace.

Pubs and Restaurants

Kings Head Bridge Road, Hunton Bridge (01923 262307). A village pub of great character which is in danger of brewery refurbishment. Marston's and Morland and guest real ales, and food *lunchtimes and evenings (not Sun evenings).* Children and vegetarians catered for. Extensive canalside garden with imaginative adventure playground.

Dog and Partridge Old Mill Lane, Hunton Bridge. (01923 441116). Morland and guest real ales and *lunchtime* bar snacks. Vegetarians and children catered for. Darts, dominoes, cards and pool. Quiz *winter Wed* and disco *Sat. Open all day.*

Rose and Crown High Street, Kings Langley (01923 262462). An unusual and heavily beamed pub combining live music, a range of well kept real ales and a striking interior. Once reputed to be the best jazz venue outside London (jazz *now only Tue),* the musical range now embraces indie, funk, soul and rock (*on Thu, Fri & Sat nights)* played in the intimate surroundings of a wood panelled bar lit by a stained glass lantern window. Tables stand in alcoves hung with old enamel advertising signs and photographs of music greats. Tetley's, Burton and Marston's are dispensed from two bars. *Lunchtime food, including Sunday* roasts. Garden. No children *after 20.30. Open all day Fri, Sat & Sun.*

Saracens Head High Street, Kings Langley (01923 400144). There are always four real ales to choose from in this traditional pub, given over to good beer and good company. Regular ales include Fuller's, Wadworth and Tring. Bar food *lunchtimes Mon–Sat.* Vegetarians catered for. Outside seating. No children, no special nights and no games.

La Casetta 18 High Street, Kings Langley (01923 263823). Hospitable Italian restaurant in a delightfully random timber-framed building, dating from 1509. Classic Italian cuisine prepared from fresh ingredients. *Open L Mon–Fri & D Mon–Sat. Booking essential at weekends.*

Oscar's Pizza Company High Street, Kings Langley (01923 263823). Lively Italian eating place, inexpensive and welcoming, *open lunchtimes and evenings. Closed Sun.*

Grand Union Canal

Kings Langley

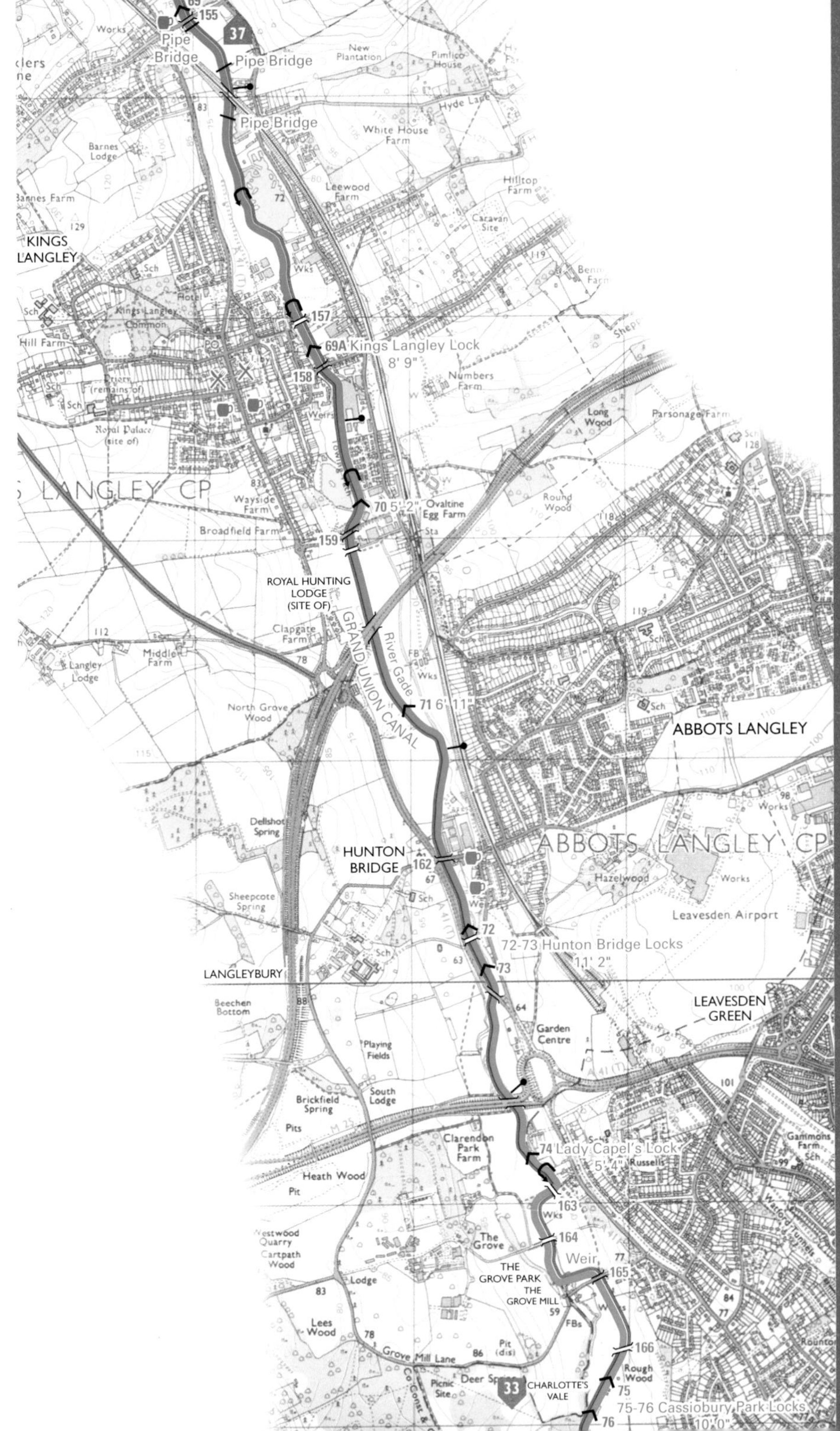

Hemel Hempstead

The canal begins to climb more steeply to the north west, passing several large paper mills in Apsley and the quaint double arch of bridge 154. The River Gade leaves the canal for Hemel Hempstead, a handsome modern town (somewhat dominated by the towering Kodak office block) standing back from the canal beyond spacious urban parkland known as Boxmoor, which includes an excellent children's playground to the north of the waterway, west of bridge 150. The canal turns further west, accompanied now by the little River Bulbourne. There is an excellent interpretation board beside lock 61.

NAVIGATIONAL NOTES

1 A BW key is required to operate Winkwell Swing Bridge.
2 Beware of mooring between locks 57 and 58, as the water level can drop overnight.

● **Apsley**
Herts. PO, stores, chemist, garage, take-aways. The shops (south of bridge 152) are much closer to the navigation than in nearby Hemel.

● **Hemel Hempstead**
Herts. MD Tue, Wed, Thu, Fri, Sat. PO, tel, stores, garage, station, cinema. A developing, well-planned new town with excellent shops, built around a charming old town with attractive streets.

Old Town Hall High Street, Hemel Hempstead (01442 228091). Thriving regional arts centre for theatre, dance, comedy and music: home to a popular jazz club. Box office *open 12.00-18.00 (20.00 on performance nights).*

Piccotts End Medieval Murals 138 Piccotts End. Remarkable 14th-C wall paintings in a hall believed to have been a pilgrims' hospice. Also an Elizabethan painted room. Not open to the public.

Tourist Information Centre Dacorum Information Centre, Marlowes, Hemel Hempstead (01442 234222). *Open Mon–Fri 09.30–17.00 & Sat 10.00–16.00.*

Boatyards

Ⓑ **Middlesex and Herts Boat Services** Winkwell Dock, Winkwell, Bourne End (01442 872985). **D E** Pump-out, gas, overnight mooring, long-term mooring, residential mooring, winter storage, slipway, boat sales and repairs, engine sales and repairs (including outboards), boat building and fitting-out, dry dock, wet dock, DIY facilities, specialist welding, chandlery, books, maps and gifts, emergency telephone, solid fuel, toilets, showers, washing machine, groceries (nearby). Emergency call-out.

Pubs and Restaurants

Ye Olde Red Lion Nash Mills Lane, Apsley. Large garden with children's play area stretching down to the towpath at lock 69. Families welcome. Inexpensive food, together with Tetley's and Marston's real ales. Pool. *Open all day.*

White Lion London Road, Apsley (01442 268948). Quiet, friendly pub with an open fire and newspapers where you can enjoy Fuller's real ale, together with inexpensive bar snacks *lunchtimes Mon-Fri.* Outside seating. *Open all day.*

Bell Inn Two Waters, London Road, Apsley (01442 252389). East of the intersection between Two Waters Way and the old A41 (south of bridge 151). Marston's, Fuller's, Tring, Morland and guest real ales in a family pub dating back more than 400 years. Traditional English home-made food is available *lunchtimes and evenings, 7 days a week,* in both the bar and restaurant.

K2 Balti House Two Waters Way, Hemel Hempstead (01442 239993). Wide range of Indian and Pakistani cuisine in a comfortable restaurant beside bridge 151. Vegetarians and children catered for. *Open 12.00-14.30 & 17.30-23.00 every day except Xmas Day & Box. Day.*

Ristorante Alfonso 10 St John's Road, Hemel Hempstead (01442 264846/251792). Family-run restaurant and small hotel serving traditional Italian fare *7 days a week. L 12.00-14.30 & D 18.00-22.30.*

Three Blackbirds 194 St John's Road, Boxmoor (01442 253523). Moor west of bridge 150 and walk across the western edge of Boxmoor. Greene King, Tetley's, Benskins and guest real ales in a friendly pub that is *open all day.* Bar meals and snacks *lunchtimes Mon-Sat.*

Boxmoor Vintners 25-27 St John's Road (01442 252171). An off-licence sporting an array of hand pumps offering the boater a chance to return to his craft with an interesting selection of draught real ales. *Open Mon-Sat 09.30-13.00 & 16.30-21.30; Sun 12.00-14.00 & 19.00-21.00.*

Post Office Arms 46 Puller Road, Boxmoor (01442 261235). Walk across Boxmoor. Fuller's real ale and *lunchtime* bar meals in this welcoming, back street local. Open fire, outside seating and pub games. *Open all day.*

Fishery Inn Fishery Road, Boxmoor (01442 61628). A large and often busy canalside pub, recently refurbished, serving Greene King and Tetley's real ales and meals *until 20.00* (in a non-smoking area). Children welcome inside if eating. Children's menu. Moorings outside. *Open all day.*

Three Horseshoes Winkwell (01442 862585). By bridge 147. A popular inn, dating from 1535, with a real fire, a most unusual stone sett and tile floor and Marston's, Morland and Tetley real ales. Meals (including a children's menu) are served *lunchtimes and evenings (except Sun evenings).* Canalside garden and moorings. *Summer* barbecues when fine. *Open all day in summer only.*

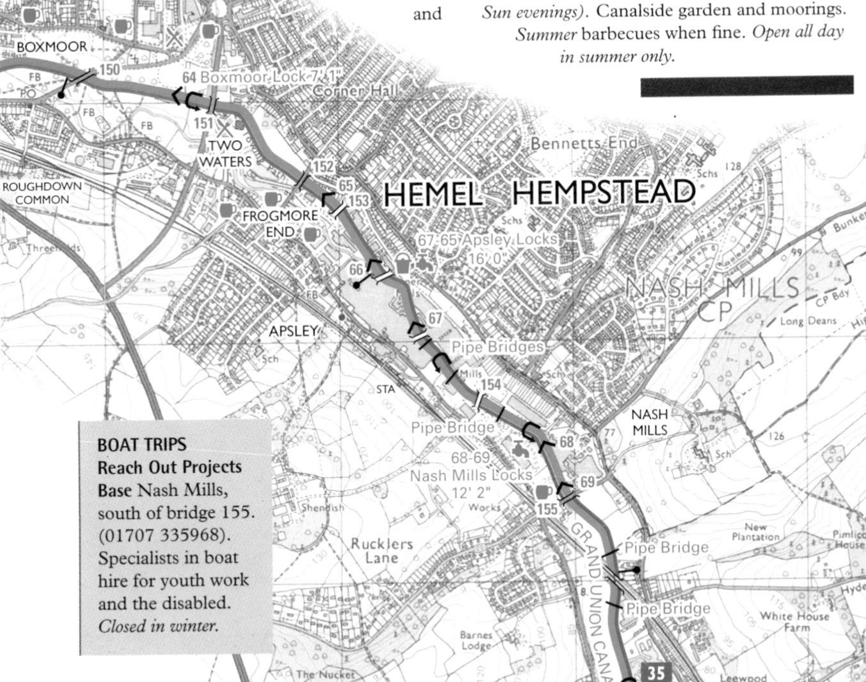

BOAT TRIPS
Reach Out Projects Base Nash Mills, south of bridge 155. (01707 335968). Specialists in boat hire for youth work and the disabled. *Closed in winter.*

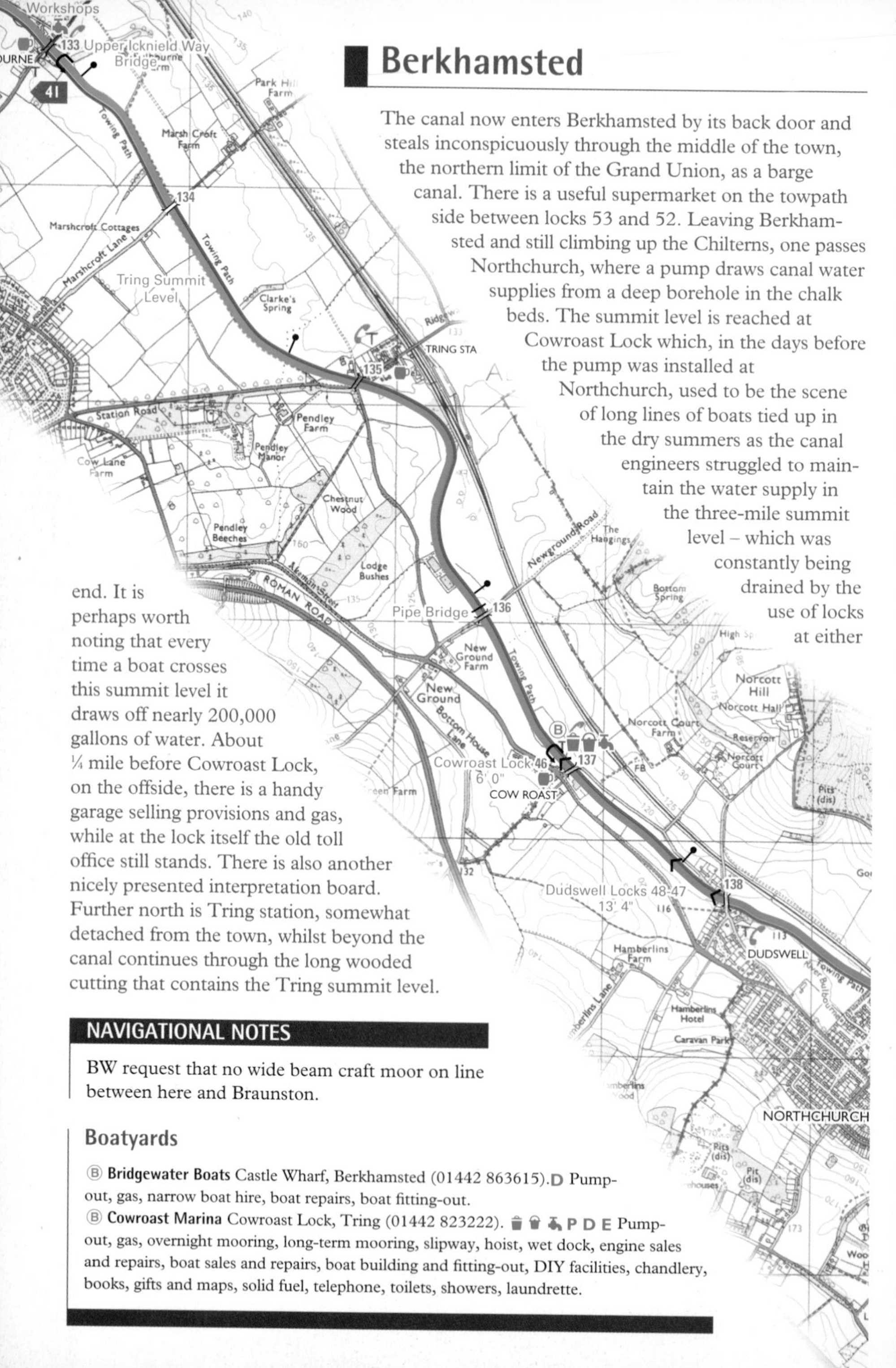

Berkhamsted

The canal now enters Berkhamsted by its back door and steals inconspicuously through the middle of the town, the northern limit of the Grand Union, as a barge canal. There is a useful supermarket on the towpath side between locks 53 and 52. Leaving Berkhamsted and still climbing up the Chilterns, one passes Northchurch, where a pump draws canal water supplies from a deep borehole in the chalk beds. The summit level is reached at Cowroast Lock which, in the days before the pump was installed at Northchurch, used to be the scene of long lines of boats tied up in the dry summers as the canal engineers struggled to maintain the water supply in the three-mile summit level – which was constantly being drained by the use of locks at either end. It is perhaps worth noting that every time a boat crosses this summit level it draws off nearly 200,000 gallons of water. About ¼ mile before Cowroast Lock, on the offside, there is a handy garage selling provisions and gas, while at the lock itself the old toll office still stands. There is also another nicely presented interpretation board. Further north is Tring station, somewhat detached from the town, whilst beyond the canal continues through the long wooded cutting that contains the Tring summit level.

NAVIGATIONAL NOTES

BW request that no wide beam craft moor on line between here and Braunston.

Boatyards

Ⓑ **Bridgewater Boats** Castle Wharf, Berkhamsted (01442 863615). D Pump-out, gas, narrow boat hire, boat repairs, boat fitting-out.

Ⓑ **Cowroast Marina** Cowroast Lock, Tring (01442 823222). P D E Pump-out, gas, overnight mooring, long-term mooring, slipway, hoist, wet dock, engine sales and repairs, boat sales and repairs, boat building and fitting-out, DIY facilities, chandlery, books, gifts and maps, solid fuel, telephone, toilets, showers, laundrette.

Berkhamsted
Herts. MD Sat. All services, laundrette. Good-looking large town with buildings of all periods which, until recently, was being shaken apart by the A41 running through the middle. The bypass has provided the community with the chance, once again, to savour the richness and diversity of its architectural heritage. The High Street is dominated by the Church of St Peter, which contains work from practically every period, including a restoration by Butterfield of 1871. There are several brasses. Only the ruins of the Norman castle remain where William I received the offer of the English crown in 1066.

Northchurch
Herts. PO, tel, stores.
Ashridge House *Herts.* 3 1/2 miles north of Berkhamsted. (01442 843491). Built in 1808 as a large romantic mansion in the Gothic taste by James Wyatt, the house gives an impression of what his famous Fonthill must have been like; the chapel is particularly splendid. The grounds were laid out by Capability Brown, and altered later by Repton. *Gardens only open, Easter–Sep weekend afternoons.*

Aldbury
Herts. PO, tel, stores. A charming village pond and stocks are sheltered below the hillside which rises to the east towards Ashridge. The monument to the third Duke of Bridgewater (an urn and a Greek Doric column) was erected on the brow of the hill beyond Stocks Road in 1832 to commemorate his pioneering work for the English canals.

Pubs and Restaurants

There is a good choice of pubs and restaurants either on, or close to, the High Street in Berkhamsted. These are a selection close to the canal.

Bull High Street, Berkhamsted (01442 870364). Pleasant 18th-C pub with canalside garden and moorings. Courage and a guest real ale together with *lunchtime food (not Sun)*. Vegetarians and children catered for. Darts, dominoes, pool and board games. *Weekend* music and the occasional quiz. *Open all day.*

Boat Gravel Path, Raven's Lane, Berkhamsted (01442 877152). By bridge 142. Fuller's real ale and excellent food available *lunchtimes (except winter Sun).* Canalside patio and disabled access. Traditional pub games. Busy *at weekends.*

Crystal Palace Station Road, Berkhamsted (01442 862998). Panelled pub near the castle remains.

Aylesbury and Flowers real ales. Canalside patio. Moorings. Darts, pool and cards. *Open all day.*

Cow Roast Cowroast Lock (01442 822287). Large, smart 17th-C inn near the marina with the emphasis on family eating. Young's, Greene King and Bass real ales. Home-made, traditional English bar food served *lunchtimes and evenings, 7 days a week.* Massive garden with children's play area and bouncy castle *in summer.* No food *Sun evenings.*

Royal Hotel Station Road, Tring (01442 827616). Hotel with a single, large bar, where Courage real ale can be enjoyed. Home-made food is available *lunchtimes and evenings (7 days a week) in the bar, together with a table d'hôte menu served in the restaurant.* Children and vegetarians catered for. Garden. Pool. B & B.

Greyhound 19 Stocks Road, Aldbury (01442 851228). Unadulterated village pub dispensing Tetley and four guest real ales together with food *lunchtimes and evenings.* Real cider in summer. Open fires in a massive fireplace and pub games. Garden and disabled access. B & B. *Open all day.*

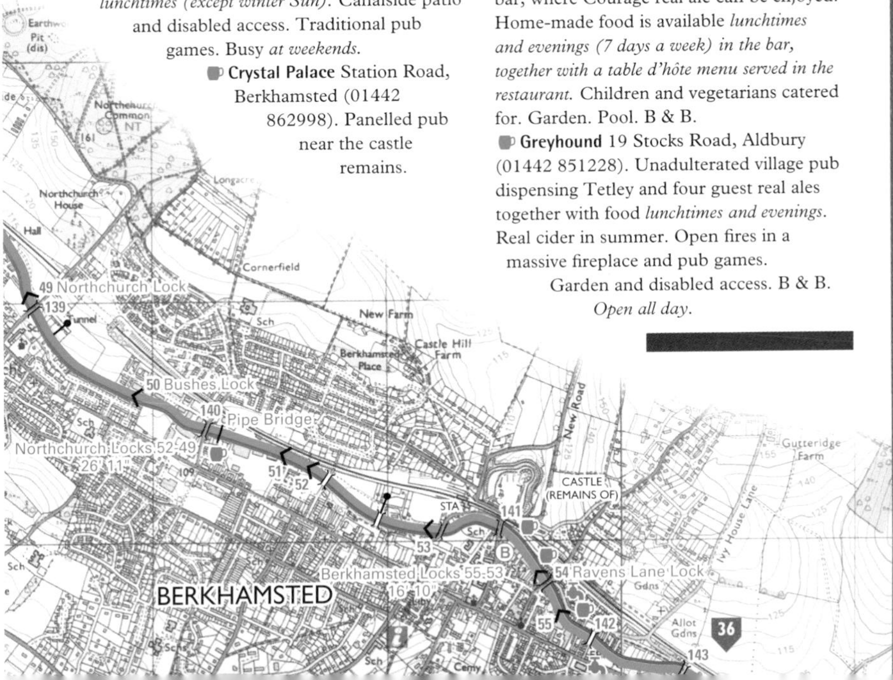

Marsworth

At the hamlet of Bulbourne are the BW workshops where to this day traditional wooden lockgate-making is carried out by a small team of craftsmen. Just to the west the old Wendover Arm joins the canal, constantly feeding water into the summit level. This arm no longer goes to Wendover, but it is still navigable for small boats as far as Little Tring and the Tringford pumping station. In 1989 the Wendover Arm Trust was established with the principal aim of restoring to navigation the full length of the Arm through to Wendover. Work is currently proceeding on the first stage, which is to restore a 550 yard length westwards from the present limit of navigation. An information box (opened with a BW key) containing leaflets about the arm and its restoration can be found on the mainline towpath at Bulbourne Junction, where there is also an attractively landscaped picnic and barbecue area. Back at Bulbourne Junction, the first of the Marsworth locks begin to wind down the hill past the reservoirs; at the bottom of the flight there is an interesting double-arched bridge, a sight often repeated between here and Stoke Bruerne 33 miles to the north. This type of bridge was built by the Grand Junction Canal Company in the expectation that the locks would later be paired – a programme that was never completed. One hundred yards north of the double bridge is Marsworth Junction, dominated by the BW workshops, where concrete piles were once manufactured. At the junction the main line bears round to the north east, while the Aylesbury Arm (a narrow beam canal) starts its fall west through the first of eight locks towards Aylesbury. Totally isolated and remote, it is one of the most peaceful stretches of canal in the country, passing through modest farmland with good views of the Chiltern Hills over to the east and, in the distance to the west, of tall new buildings in Aylesbury. The locks are 7ft wide, and the bridges too are narrow. This canal was once semi-derelict, but an energetic programme of dredging and lock repairing (spurred on by an enthusiastic canal society) restored it to a good navigable condition. The main line heads north east and continues its descent through Marsworth locks before entering the remote countryside beyond Ivinghoe.

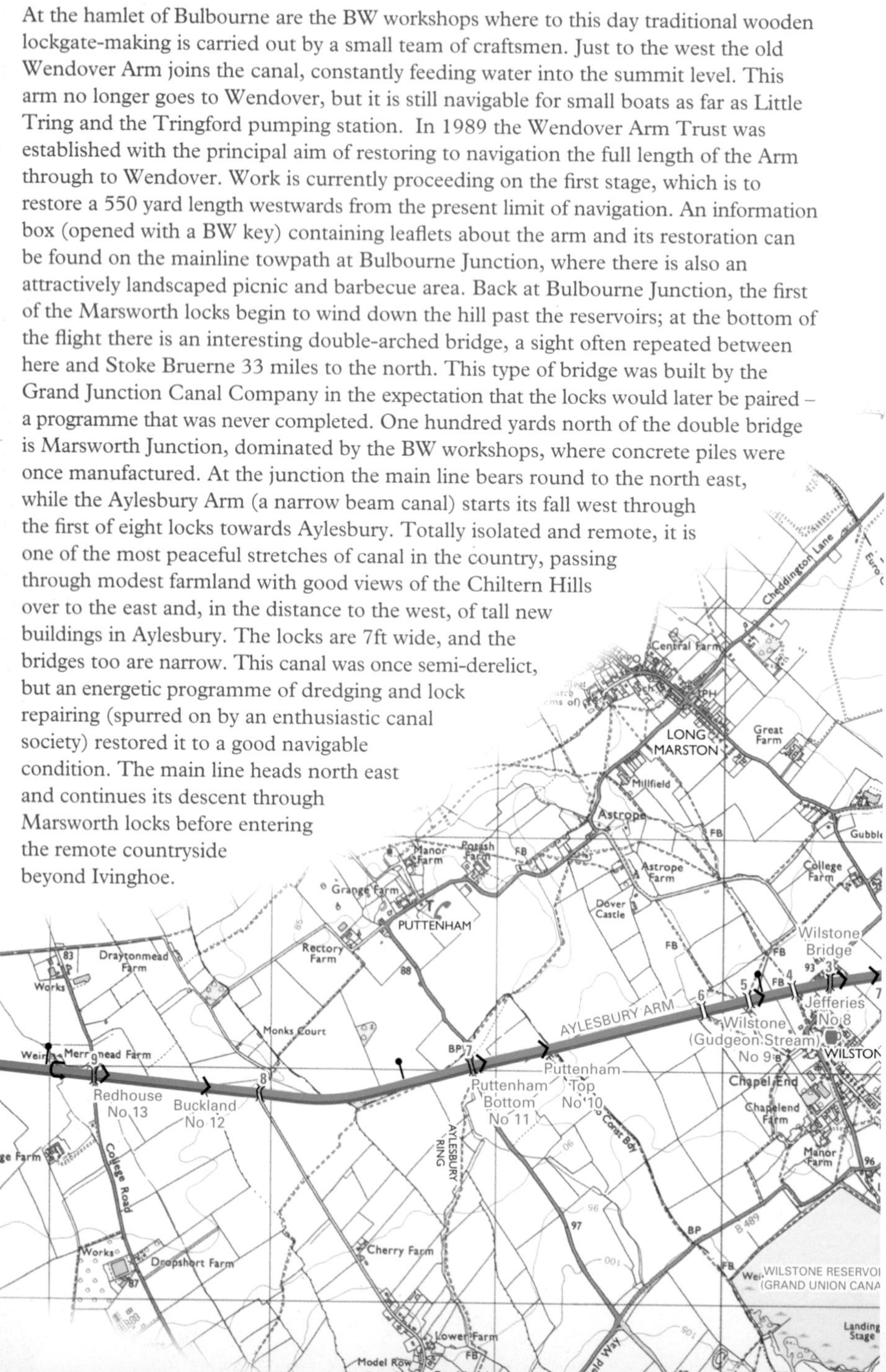

BOAT TRIPS
Grebe Canal Cruises
Pitstone Wharf, Cheddington (01296 661920). Trips *every weekend May–Sep, daily in school holidays.* Also private charter for up to 60 persons.

Bulbourne

Herts. Tel. Canalside settlement around the BW workshops which are a well-preserved example of early 19th-C canal architecture, with characteristic fanlights. To the north east is the long railway cutting built by Robert Stephenson in 1834–38, an engineering feat of the age.

Tringford Pumping Station At the present terminus of Wendover Arm. Built by the Grand Junction Canal Company to pump water up from the three reservoirs just down the hill, and from the 100-acre Wilstone reservoir over to the west. This water, plus the supply from springs in Wendover was – and still is – fed down the arm into the Tring summit level. Originally the pumping station housed big beam engines, but these were replaced in the 20thC by heavy diesels. Now quiet, smooth, electric motors perform this vital task, lifting some four million gallons of water each day. The system was recently overhauled, having been in constant use since 1929.

Tring Reservoirs South of Startops End (bridge 132) and beside Marsworth locks. Four reservoirs with many wildfowl and waterside birds, notably the Black Tern and the Great Crested Grebe. Also abundant marsh and water plants. This is a national nature reserve and public access is permitted along waymarked pathways.

Marsworth

Bucks. Tel. A quiet scattered village centred around the Grand Union Canal and the Aylesbury Arm. The Icknield Way, a Roman road, passes the village. Dunstable Downs rise to the south east, gliders are a common sight and occasionally a hot air balloon may be seen floating along in the sky.

Wilstone

Herts. PO, tel, stores. Quiet village running away from the canal to Wilstone reservoir, a national nature reserve.

Ivinghoe

Bucks. PO, tel, stores, garage. 1 mile east of bridge 123 or 126. An attractive although greatly expanded village, which centres round the large 13th- and 14th-C church, notable for its crossing tower and Jacobean pulpit. The main street, leading west from the church, contains the old town hall, partly 16thC. $^{1}/_{4}$ mile south of the village is Pitstone Green Mill, a post mill scheduled as an ancient monument.

Iron Age Hill Fort 1 mile north east of Ivinghoe, on top of Beacon Hill. The triangular hill fort encloses six acres: within this area stands a bowl barrow thought to date from the Bronze Age. There is a tumulus to the south and another to the east of Beacon Hill.

Cheddington

Bucks. PO, tel, stores, garage, station. 1 mile north of bridge 126. A residential area spread around the station, clearly a commuter development. The church contains a richly carved Jacobean pulpit. On the hills south of the village are the remains of a medieval field cultivation.

Mentmore House 1$^{1}/_{2}$ miles west of Horton Lock. A Tudor-style stone mansion built in the 1850s by Sir Joseph Paxton for the Rothschild family. Large plate glass windows, central heating and fresh air ventilation made the house advanced for its time, reflecting the ingenuity of the architect.

Mooring at Aylesbury (see page 44)

Boatyards

BW Bulbourne Workshops Bulbourne (01442 822261). Home of the maintenance yard and the lock gate making team. No services.
BW Tring Yard Marsworth (01442 825938).
Ⓑ **Grebe Canal Cruises** Pitstone Wharf, Cheddington (01296 661920). E Pump-out, gas, day boat hire, overnight mooring (by arrangement), long-term mooring, slipway, crane, boat sales and repairs, engine sales and repairs, wet dock, DIY facilities, books, maps and gifts, telephone, toilet. Café. *24 hr* emergency call-out. *Closed winter weekends.*

Pubs and Restaurants

Grand Junction Arms Bulbourne. Canalside at bridge 133. Family pub with a large garden and children's play area, serving Greenalls, Adnams and guest real ales together with bar meals *lunchtimes and evenings (not Mon).* Vegetarians catered for. Quiz *Wed,* music *Sun* and *weekend* barbecues. Darts. Mooring outside. *Open all day Sat & Sun.*
Charlotte Tea Rooms Startops End, Marsworth (01442 891708). Beside lock 39. Breakfasts, light meals, snacks, gateaux, tea and coffee and take-away menu served in an airy, downstairs extension to the old lock keepers cottage. *Open 08.00–20.00.* Vegetarian and children's menu. Attractive canalside gardens. There is also a **Bistro** *open 18.00-23.00* for booked meals only. Upstairs, adjacent to the canal, is a craft and gift shop which also sells *milk, basic provisions, coal and newspapers. Tel.*
White Lion Startops End, Marsworth (01442 822325). Canalside at bridge 132. A large pub serving Ruddles, Theakston and guest real ales. Meals are available *lunchtimes and evenings.* Canalside patio and moorings. Barbecues and entertainment on *summer Suns. Open all day.*
Angler's Retreat Startops End, Marsworth (01442 822250). Fuller's, Courage and Ruddles real ales in a homely pub tucked away below the White Lion. Bar meals available *lunchtimes and evenings (not Sun evenings)* and quiz on alternate *Mon.* Darts and dominoes. Beer garden, aviary and pets corner.
Half Moon Wilstone (01442 826410). A comfortable 17th-C pub, entered through a drunkenly, leaning front door and serving Flowers, Tetley's, Bass and Marston's real ales. Bar meals and snacks are available *lunchtimes and evenings (except Mon evenings):* the haggis is a speciality. Children's menu. Garden and traditional pub games.
Rising Sun Aston Clinton. South of bridge 9, at junction of B489 & A41. A roadside pub serving Courage and Worthington real ales and meals *L & D (not Sun evenings).* Children and vegetarians catered for. Garden. Quiz *Mon. Open all day.*
Red Lion Vicarage Road, Marsworth (01296 668366). Near bridge 130. A friendly (if you can ignore the ominous-looking stocks outside) village pub with an open fire and bars on two levels, dispensing Fuller'st real ale. Local information is displayed on a noticeboard in the public bar. Food is available *lunchtimes and evenings (except Sun and Mon evenings)* and there is a large garden. Traditional pub games. *Winter* skittles *first & third Wed in month.*
Duke of Wellington Cook's Wharf, Cheddington Road, Pitstone (01296 661402). Large, quiet and friendly pub, dating back 200 years. Adnams, Bateman, Greene King and guest real ales together with home-cooked meals *lunchtimes and evenings, 7 days a week.* Children's and vegetarian menus. Garden, children's playground and pub games.
Rose & Crown Vicarage Lane, Ivinghoe (01296 668472). In village, south east of bridge 123. Excellent food (*lunchtimes and evenings)* together with Adnams, Greene King and guest real ales make this lively local well worth seeking out, tucked away as it is opposite the church. Open fires and traditional pub games.

Aylesbury

Leaving the countryside, the canal enters the outskirts of Aylesbury, runs under the ring road and drops down through the last two locks into the town; boaters should be aware of the iron girder bridge 18, which is extremely narrow. Aylesbury basin itself is spacious and full of boats, although there is no longer a boatyard as such. However, there are moorings for visitors, and pubs nearby, and all the amenities of the town centre are a mere three minute walk away. The Aylesbury Canal Society hold a lease for the basin and offer facilities and a welcome for visiting boaters. Amongst their many activities they publish a comprehensive list, regularly updated, of all the laundrettes throughout the waterways system, within a reasonable distance of the navigation. This is obtainable from: Judy Clegg, c/o Canal Basin, Walton Street, Aylesbury, Bucks. Charge – for society funds. There is a useful bakery on Walton Street (next to the Ship), *open from 07.30*, selling bread and a range of pies, etc.

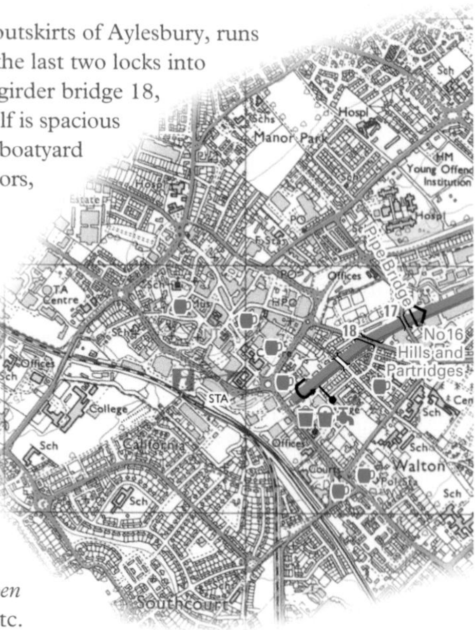

● **Aylesbury**
Bucks. MD Wed, Fri, Sat. PO, tel, stores, garage, laundrette, station, cinema. A busy market town where the 20thC has not taken over completely; the centre of Aylesbury is made up of a number of attractive squares, and the 13th-C church lies hidden in its secluded churchyard a short distance away. There are some interesting Georgian buildings too. The King's Head, dating from the 15thC and now no longer operating as a pub, has outstanding windows, gateway and courtyard, and Oliver Cromwell's chair in the bar.

Aylesbury Canal Arm It took 20 years for an arm to be built from the Grand Junction canal at Marsworth, through the 6 miles of remote countryside into the market town of Aylesbury. Negotiation and debate accounted for 17 years, the canal itself taking just three years to construct. During that time various proposals were put forward and many objections raised; in essence any scheme that required water from another navigation was strongly resisted. With the town lying in a geographical hollow it was inevitable that every proposal relied on 'borrowed' water for its success; and water was a scarce commodity much sought after by existing navigation authorities and mill owners alike. The most ambitious scheme was to link the Thames at Abingdon with the Grand Junction at Marsworth but this was vehemently resisted by the Thames Commissioners. When the canal actually reached Aylesbury in 1814 it halved the price of coal overnight and went on to be a successful means of transport for coal, agricultural produce and, on one occasion at least, emigrant paupers to the New World via Liverpool Docks. The inevitable railway competition eroded the waterway's profitability throughout the first half of this century and, but for an early hire boat operation in the town basin, together with the Aylesbury Canal Society's concerted efforts, the waterway might well have passed into extinction.

Buckinghamshire County Museum Church Street, Aylesbury (01296 331441). Illustrates county archaeology, geology and history, local crafts, costume, natural history. Also a collection of local prints and paintings together with loans from national galleries. Shop, café and garden. *Open Mon-Sat 10.00–17.00 & Sun 14.00–17.00.* Free.

Roald Dahl Gallery Church Street, Aylesbury (01296 331441). Part of the County Museum. Admission by timed tickets *(1 hour) on the hour so entrance is limited* – tickets can be booked by telephone in advance. *Opening is usually as per museum but can vary during term time.* Charge.

Buckinghamshire Railway Centre Quainton, Aylesbury (01296 655450). 6 miles north west of Aylesbury. Large site with miniature and full size steam railway, large number of static locomotive exhibits, gift and book shop, museum, picnic area and refreshment coach. *Open Sun & B. Hols; also Easter–Oct on Mon; Jun–Aug on Wed.* Charge. Bus from Aylesbury bus station.

Chiltern Brewery Nash Lee Road, Terrick, Aylesbury (01296 613647). The opportunity to join a tour of a traditional working brewery. Small museum, light refreshments *on Sat.* For tours please telephone to

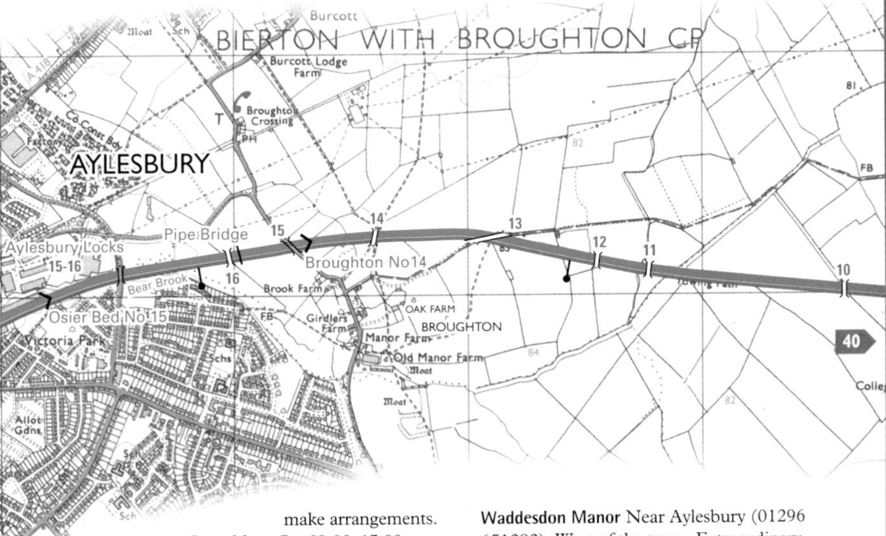

make arrangements. *Open Mon– Sat 09.00–17.00.* Bus from Aylesbury bus station.

Oak Farm Rare Breeds Park Broughton, Aylesbury (01296 415709). 1/4 mile south of bridge 15. Variety of farm animals – many from breeds no longer fashionable in the cold, hard world of agri-business – for children to see, handle and feed on an organically run farm. Picnic and play area, countryside walk and nature trail. *Open Easter–Aug, Wed–Fri 10.30–16.30 & Sun & B. Hols 10.30–17.30; Sep & Oct Sun 10.30–16.30.* Charge.

Civic Theatre Aylesbury (01296 86009). Contact for programme details.

Limelight Theatre Aylesbury (01296 431272). Contact for programme details.

Traveline (0345 382000). For full details of all local bus, train and coach travel. Excellent public transport network and inexpensive day rover tickets. The efficient rail service offers a painless way to visit the capital.

Waddesdon Manor Near Aylesbury (01296 651282). West of the town. Extraordinary French Renaissance-style château with sumptuous internal appointments (including paintings), marvellously landscaped gardens and licensed restaurant and wine shop all in the Rothschild mould, for whom it was created in the 1880s. Gardens, aviary, shops and restaurant *Open Mar–Dec, Wed–Sun 11.00–17.00 (18.00 when the house is open). House open Apr–mid Oct, Thu–Sat 12.30–18.00 & Wed in Jul & Aug. Also G. Fri & B. Hol Mon 11.00–18.30.* Charge – *timed tickets on a first come first served basis.* Recorded information on 01296 651211. Bus from Aylesbury bus station.

Tourist Information Centre 8 Bourbon Street, Aylesbury (01296 330559). *Open daily Apr–Oct 09.30–17.00 & Nov–Mar 10.00–16.30. Closed Sun except Jul & Aug open 10.00-16.00.* Note: six screen cinema and new swimming complex opening 2000 – contact Tourist Information Centre for further details.

Pubs and Restaurants

Ship 59 Walton Street, Aylesbury (01296 421888). Beside the canal basin. Greene King, Tetley's and guest real ales and *lunchtime* food in this popular pub. Outside seating and disabled access. Traditional pub games. Disco *Thu. Open all day Fri & Sat.*

Aristocrat 1 Wendover Road, Aylesbury (01296 415366). Turn left out of the basin, 1/4 mile. Fuller's real ales in a friendly, welcoming pub which serves food *lunchtimes and evenings.* Regular quizzes and music nights. Garden. Disabled access. Traditional pub games. B & B. *Open all day.*

Queen's Head 1 Temple Square, Aylesbury (01296 415484). Greenalls, Shipstone's and guest real ales together with food available *lunchtimes and evenings.* Outside seating. B & B.

Grapes Market Square, Aylesbury (01296 483735). Bare wooden floors and Victorian decor in a town centre pub dispensing Greene King real ale. *Lunchtime* bar snacks. *Open all day.*

Bell Hotel Market Square, Aylesbury (01296 489835). A traditional country town pub, serving John Smith's, Worthington and Flowers real ales and *lunchtime bar snacks.* Meals are available in the restaurant *L & D Mon–Thu.* Children and vegetarians catered for. *Open all day (not Sun).* B & B.

Linslade

Northwards from Marsworth the canal falls steadily away from Dunstable Downs and the Chilterns, leaving the hills as a backdrop to the west. As the hills give way to open grassland, the canal becomes more remote, a quiet, empty section that terminates in the peace of Grove Church Lock. Villages are set back from the canal, only Slapton, with its superb pub, being under 1 mile away. The main feature of the section is the locks, carrying the canal down from the Chilterns toward Leighton Buzzard and the Ouzel valley; these occur frequently, often in remote and attractive settings. The railway and the B488 run parallel to the canal to the west; there is a station at Cheddington. To the east the canal now runs parallel to the River Ouzel and, leaving the open fields behind, passes through the joined towns of Linslade and Leighton Buzzard, effectively acting as a boundary between them. Leighton Buzzard station is actually in Linslade. There is a useful supermarket north of bridge 114, on the towpath side.

- **Whipsnade White Lion** On Dunstable Downs, visible from the canal from around Horton and Slapton. The lion was cut in 1935 and is over 480ft long.
- **Slapton**
Bucks. PO, tel, stores. Compact residential village; the Perpendicular church contains several brasses of the 15th and 16thC.
- **Grove**
Bucks. An attractive group formed by the bridge, lock, lock cottage and the tiny church, a 14th-C chapel with a later bell turret.
- **Linslade**
Bucks. PO, tel, stores, garage, take aways, laundrette, station. Linslade is virtually a residential extension of Leighton Buzzard. Traces of the old village can just be found to the north, especially the church, near the canal, easily recognised by its battlements; the front and parts of the structure date from the 12thC. West of the church is a railway tunnel with an extraordinary neo-Gothic portal in grey brick, looking delightfully incongruous.

Ascott House 2 miles to the west, along the A418 from Linslade (01296 688242). Attractive, irregular timber-framed house built in 1606, with extensive additions made in 1874 and 1938. Collection of paintings, French and Chippendale furniture, oriental porcelain. Twelve acres of grounds and gardens containing rare trees. Gardens *open every Wed and last Sun in month, 14.00–17.00.*

Pubs and Restaurants

Carpenters Arms Slapton (01525 220563). North east of bridge 120. Superb 16th-C, thatched pub dispensing Haddenman real ales and excellent food *lunchtimes and evenings (not Sat lunchtimes).* Children and vegetarians catered for. Patio seating. A genuine conversational village local with the emphasis on food. Booking essential *evenings and Sun lunch.* The landlady runs an interesting second hand bookshop in the adjoining, redundant malthouse.

New Waterfront Linslade (01525 853288). Greene King real ale in a waterside bar beside bridge 114. Discos on *Fri. Erratic opening hours.*

Bedford Arms Linslade (01525 372103). By bridge 114. B & B.

White Horse Linslade (01525 372324). Between bridge 114 and the railway station, Linslade. Friendly one-bar local serving Greene King real ales together with home-cooked food *lunchtimes and evenings.* Pub games. *Sun afternoon* singsong. B & B.

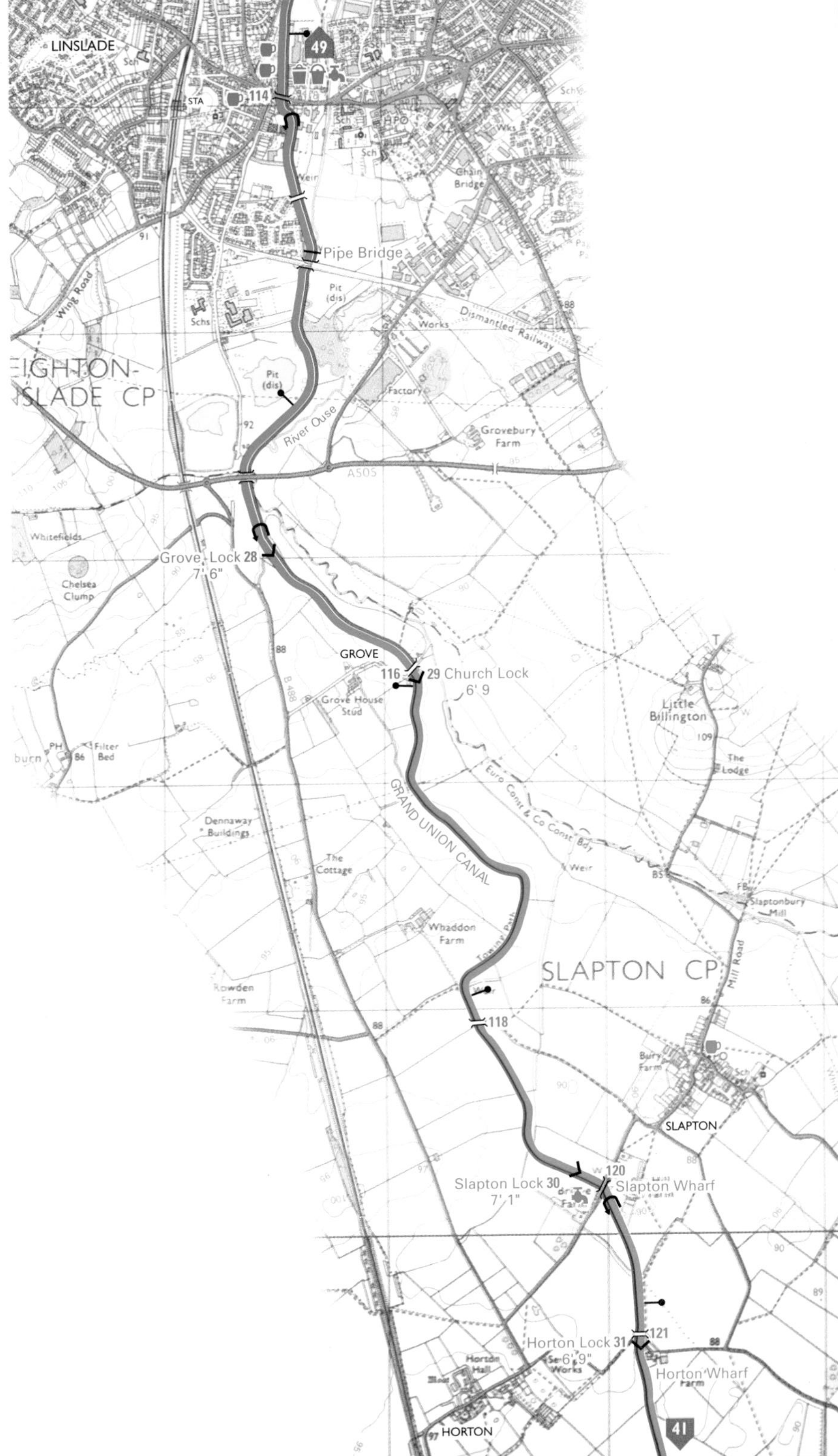
LINSLADE
49
114
STA
Pipe Bridge
Pit (dis)
Schs
Works
Dismantled Railway
Factory
Wing Road
River Ouse
Grovebury Farm
A505
Whitefields
Grove Lock 28
7' 6"
Chelsea Clump
GROVE
116
29 Church Lock
6' 9
Grove House Stud
B 488
Little Billington
The Lodge
Filter Bed
Dennaway Buildings
Euro Const & Co Const Bdy
GRAND UNION CANAL
The Cottage
Whaddon Farm
Weir
Slaptonbury Mill
Mill Road
SLAPTON CP
Rowden Farm
118
Bury Farm
SLAPTON
120
Slapton Lock 30
7' 1"
Slapton Wharf
Horton Lock 31
6' 9"
121
Horton Hall
Horton Wharf
HORTON
41

Soulbury

Leaving the twin towns of Linslade and Leighton Buzzard, the canal enters the valley of the Ouzel and meanders sharply, making the navigation itself seem like a river, which is rare on the Grand Union. Steep hills rise to the east and west, thickly wooded to the east. A low towpath hedge allows fine views of this beautiful valley. This section contains a good mixture of canal townscape and landscape, Leighton Locks having an attractive and well-kept lock house. The railway and the B488 continue to follow the canal to the west. As the valley widens, the canal continues its steady fall towards Bletchley, following the Ouzel closely. Flat meadows reaching to the west precede the approach to Bletchley. All the locks, the Soulbury flight of three, and one at Stoke Hammond, form an attractive canalscape, the double-arched bridges showing where the locks were once doubled. Remains of the supplementary locks can still be seen at Soulbury alongside the small pumping station that returns water back up the flight whenever necessary. There are a set of recycling bins on the towpath side at the bottom of the lock flight. The railway and the B488 run closely to the west of the canal.

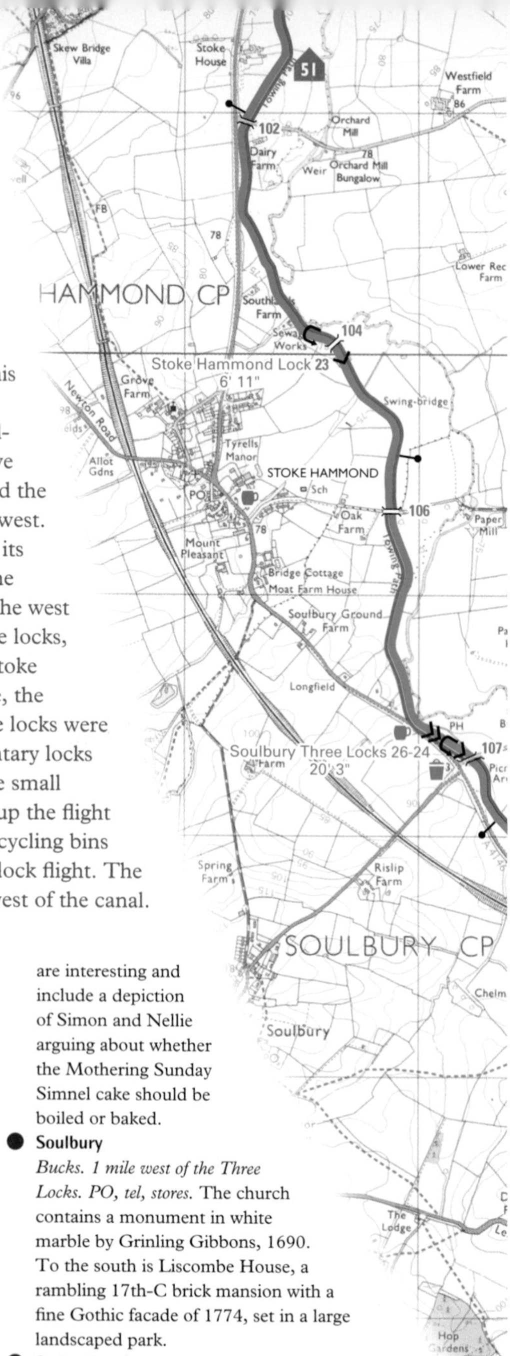

● **Leighton Buzzard**

Beds. PO, tel, stores, station, garage, cinema, take-aways. A picturesque market town with a superlative church. 17th- and 18th-C houses and half-timbered cottages are to be found in the streets leading to the Market Cross, which has stood for some 600 years in the centre of the town. There are also some fine 19th-C buildings; note particularly Barclay's Bank. In North Street stand the almshouses founded by Edward Wilkes in 1633 on condition that the bounds of the parish be beaten every Rogation Monday. The custom is still maintained, and on *23 May* a choir boy stands upon his head in front of the almshouses while the appropriate extracts from the donor's will are read.

All Saint's Parish Church Dates from 1288 and is notable for its 191ft tower and spire and the 15th-C wooden roof. It retains its ancient sanctus bell, 13th-C font, misericords, brasses and a medieval lectern. The medieval graffiti are interesting and include a depiction of Simon and Nellie arguing about whether the Mothering Sunday Simnel cake should be boiled or baked.

● **Soulbury**

Bucks. 1 mile west of the Three Locks. PO, tel, stores. The church contains a monument in white marble by Grinling Gibbons, 1690. To the south is Liscombe House, a rambling 17th-C brick mansion with a fine Gothic facade of 1774, set in a large landscaped park.

● **Stoke Hammond**

Bucks. PO, tel, stores, garage. Set above the canal to the west, the village overlooks the valley as it spreads untidily along the B488. The church, weighted down by its squat central tower, contains a decorative 14th-C font.

Boatyards

Ⓑ **The Wyvern Shipping Company** Rothschild Road, Linslade (01525 372355). D E by arrangement. Pump-out, gas, narrow boat hire, long-term mooring, dry dock, wet dock, boat repairs, books and maps, boat building and fitting-out, engine repairs (Lister only).

Pubs and Restaurants

Globe Inn Globe Lane, Linslade (01525 373338). Canalside, near bridge 11. Over £2½ million disappeared in 20 minutes during the Great Train Robbery, which happened close to the site of this old, low beamed pub. Marston's, Theakston, Fuller's and guest real ales are available, together with a wide range of food *lunchtimes and evenings, 7 days a week.* Canalside terrace. *Booking essential for meals.*

Three Locks Stoke Hammond (01525 272393). Adnams, Morland and Wadworth real ales in an attractively sited canalside pub. Bar meals available *lunchtimes and evenings.* Canalside terrace and moorings. *Open all day.*

Dolphin Stoke Hammond (01525 270263). West of bridge 106. Pleasant pub with an open fire. Boddingtons, Flowers and guest real ales and food available *lunchtimes and evenings, Mon–Fri.* Children's play area. Garden. Darts and dominoes.

BOAT TRIPS
Leighton Lady Canal Cruises Private charter and public trips *B. Hols and during Aug school holidays,* operating from bridge 114. Telephone 01525 384563 for further details.

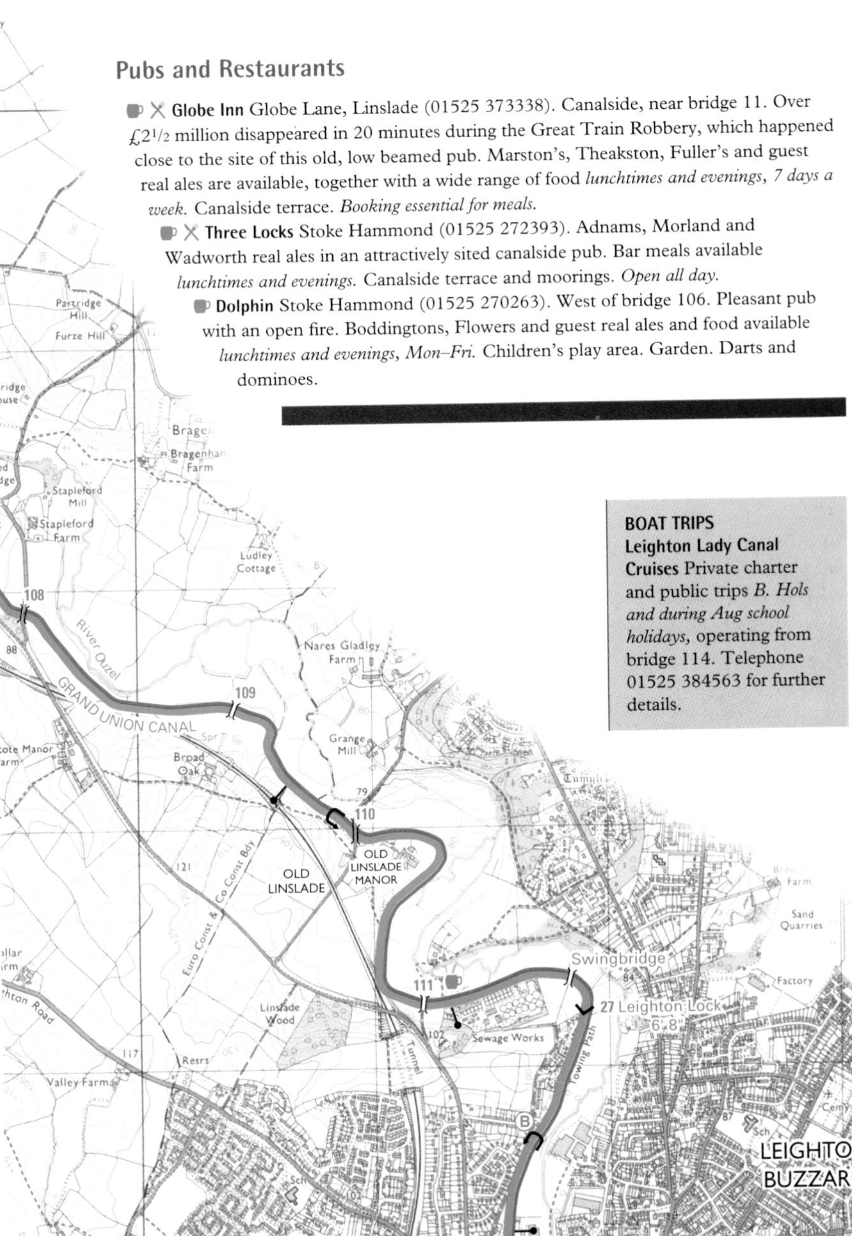

Fenny Stratford

The canal runs through open country, but to the south lie the suburbs of the rapidly expanding town of Bletchley, now part of the new city of Milton Keynes. There is a canal shop at Fenny Stratford Lock. Once north of the town the canal again meanders gently through villages, still following the course of the River Ouzel as far as Woolstone. There is only one lock on this section, but the old arched accommodation bridges abound. The main railway leaves the canal south of Bletchley, but another line, to Bedford, crosses at Fenny Stratford. There is a station close to the canal here. Through the whole of the Milton Keynes area to Wolverton the towpath is excellent – either gravel or tarmac.

● **Bletchley**
Bucks. MD Thu, Sat. PO, tel, stores, garage, station, cinema. This formerly agricultural and lace-making town is now a large, modern place that has swallowed up its neighbour, Fenny Stratford. A small part of the 12th-C St Mary's Church remains; much restoration and alteration has been done.

● **Fenny Stratford**
Bucks. PO, tel, stores, garage, laundrette, station. The town is now merged into Bletchley. The building of the red-brick church, 1724–30, was inspired by Browne Willis, the antiquarian; as a result it is an early example of Gothic revival. The old pump house is now a gift shop and cafeteria, run by handicapped youth – so why not call in and support them?

● **Simpson**
Bucks. PO, tel, stores. A main road village, much redeveloped as a suburb of Bletchley, but still retaining elements of independence. The church is mainly 14th-C; note the wooden roof and a monument by John Bacon, 1789. Beyond Woughton Park to the north is Walton Hall, the Open University.

● **Woughton on the Green**
Bucks. PO, tel, stores. The village is attractively scattered round a huge green flanked by the canal to the west. There are houses of all periods, mixed in a random but harmonious manner and presided over by the church built on a mound to the east.

Pubs and Restaurants

Bridge Inn 12-14 Watling Street, Fenny Stratford (01908 373107). B & T, Boddingtons and Wells real ales served in this canalside pub (bridge 96) with its own moorings and waterside terrace. Excellent food available *lunchtimes and evenings (not Sat & Sun evenings)* together with a range of regular entertainment: live music *Sat*; disco *Wed*; Karaoke *Fri & Sun*. Outside seating and pub games. *Open all day.*

Beacon Mount Farm Lake, Bond Avenue, Bletchley (01908 649025). A sports orientated place with six pool tables, a football pitch and tennis courts. Food is available *all day, every day.* Vegetarians and children catered for. Large garden. Music *at weekends.*

✕ **Plough** Simpson (01908 670015). By the aqueduct. Charles Wells real ale is available, and good value, home-made bar and restaurant meals are served *lunchtimes and evenings, (not Sun & Mon evenings). Sunday* carvery *12.00-18.00.* No smoking area. Vegetarian and children's menus.

✕ **Peartree** Milton Keynes (01908 691515). Beside Milton Keynes Marina. A Toby Inn serving Bass real ale and food *lunchtimes, evenings and all day Sun.* Children and vegetarians catered for. Patio seating. Live music *Fri.* B & B.

✕ **Parkside Hotel and Lane's Restaurant** Woughton on the Green (01908 661919). Courage real ale in a 200-year-old country hotel. Bar meals are available *lunchtimes and evenings, 7 days a week* and *L & D* are served in the restaurant *daily except Sat L & Sun D.* Children and vegetarians catered for. Special menus are offered for *Sun* lunch. Patio seating. B & B.

Ye Old Swan Woughton on the Green (01908 679489). Opposite the church. 17th-C tavern with Dick Turpin associations and Courage, Morland and guest real ales. Food is available *all day, every day.* Garden. Children welcome when eating.

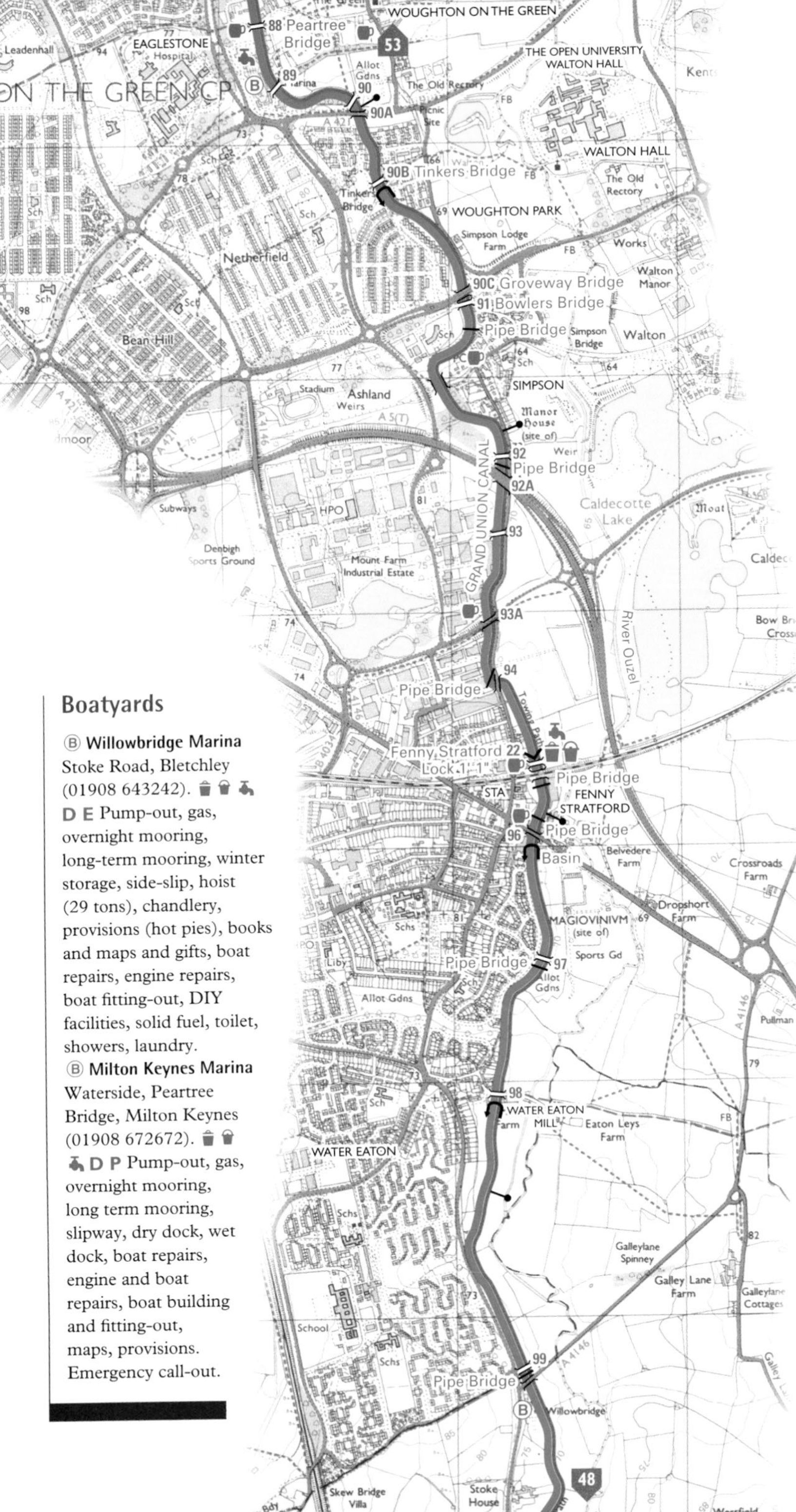

Boatyards

B **Willowbridge Marina** Stoke Road, Bletchley (01908 643242). **D E** Pump-out, gas, overnight mooring, long-term mooring, winter storage, side-slip, hoist (29 tons), chandlery, provisions (hot pies), books and maps and gifts, boat repairs, engine repairs, boat fitting-out, DIY facilities, solid fuel, toilet, showers, laundry.

B **Milton Keynes Marina** Waterside, Peartree Bridge, Milton Keynes (01908 672672). **D P** Pump-out, gas, overnight mooring, long term mooring, slipway, dry dock, wet dock, boat repairs, engine and boat repairs, boat building and fitting-out, maps, provisions. Emergency call-out.

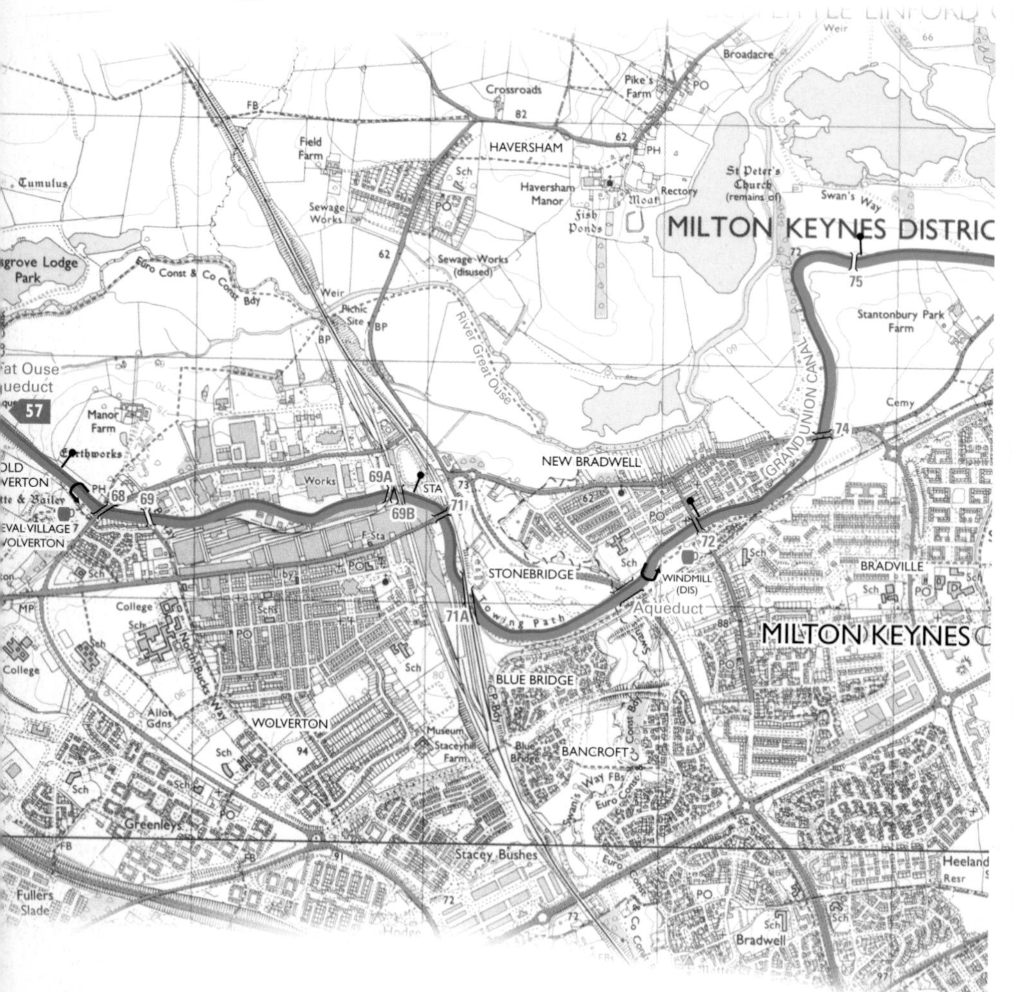

Milton Keynes

Continuing north west, and then at Great Linford turning sharply to the west, the canal runs through attractive, lightly wooded scenery that gradually gives way to hills and follows the Ouse valley, clinging to the south side. Either side, where once there were open fields, the new city of Milton Keynes has been built. Willen and Great Linford are well worth visiting. There are no locks, but a variety of bridges. By Great Linford Wharf there is a winding hole that marks the junction with the Newport Pagnell branch, closed many years ago. Immediately west of bridge 76, on the off-side, there is a tool hire centre selling gas. At New Bradwell the canal crosses a dual-carriageway on a splendid new aqueduct, completed in 1991. The canal continues westwards past industrial Wolverton, and then turns north west prior to crossing the Ouse valley by means of an embankment and aqueduct.

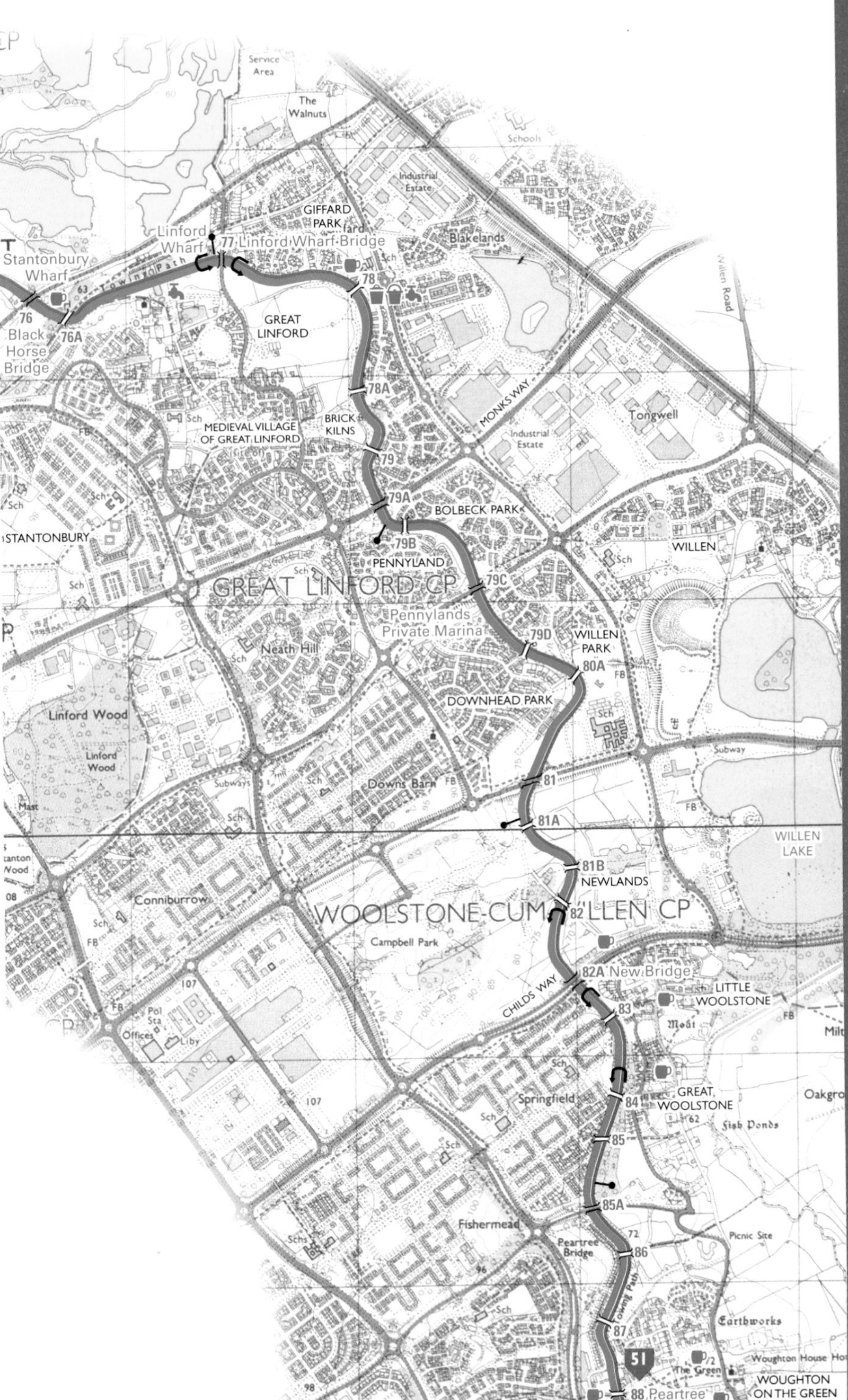
Service Area
The Walnuts
Schools
Industrial Estate
GIFFARD PARK
Linford Wharf
77 Linford Wharf Bridge
Blakelands
Stantonbury Wharf
63
76
Black Horse Bridge
76A
78
GREAT LINFORD
Willen Road
78A
MONKS WAY
Tongwell
BRICK KILNS
MEDIEVAL VILLAGE OF GREAT LINFORD
Sch
FB
Industrial Estate
79
79A
BOLBECK PARK
79B
PENNYLAND
STANTONBURY
WILLEN
GREAT LINFORD CP
79C
Pennylands Private Marina
Neath Hill
79D
WILLEN PARK
80A
DOWNHEAD PARK
Linford Wood
Subway
Subways
Downs Barn
81
81A
Mast
WILLEN LAKE
81B
NEWLANDS
Conniburrow
WOOLSTONE-CUM-WILLEN CP
82
Campbell Park
82A New Bridge
CHILDS WAY
LITTLE WOOLSTONE
83
107
Pol Sta
Offices
Liby
A4146
Moat
Springfield
84
GREAT WOOLSTONE
Oakgro
62
Fish Ponds
85
85A
Fishermead
Schs
72
Picnic Site
Peartree Bridge
86
96
Towing Path
Earthworks
87
51
Woughton House Ho
The Green
WOUGHTON ON THE GREEN
98
88 Peartree

● **Little Woolstone**
Bucks. A tiny hamlet with a pub and a garage. Great Woolstone is even smaller. Willen Lake recreation area is best approached from bridge 83.

● **Willen**
Bucks. 1/2 mile east of bridge 81. PO box, tel. A hamlet wholly dominated by the Wren church, which is well worth a visit. All the interior fittings are original, and the plaster work, pews, organ case and font should be seen. The 170-acre lake is a watersports centre, with sailing, canoeing, etc.

● **Milton Keynes**
Bucks. All services and a major shopping centre accessible by bus from bridge 82a. A typical new city development encompassing Bletchley and the scattered villages to the north. Work on the 22,000-acre area began in the early 1970s and the original population of 40,000 has grown to around 100,000. Strategically placed between Birmingham and the capital, close to the M1 and the main railway line, the Development Corporation has been successful in attracting many companies to the area. Some of the housing schemes are imaginative, and well endowed with green space and trees. Great emphasis is placed on the social and recreational needs of the population and in this respect the new city makes good use of the canal.
Tourist Information Centre Margaret Powell Square, 890 Midsummer Boulevard, Central Milton Keynes (01908) 558300.

● **Great Linford**
Bucks. PO, tel, stores. Great Linford is magnificent: a traditional village street running away from the canal, with a marvellous group formed by church, manor, farm and almshouses, all in rich golden stone. The 14th-C church right alongside the canal contains Georgian box pews and pulpit, and fine 19th-C stained glass. The almshouses are 17th-C with strong Dutch gables. The manor, symmetrical, dignified and elegant in a totally 18th-C way, completes the picture.

● **New Bradwell**
Bucks. PO, tel, stores, take-away. A Victorian railway town, built on a grid of extreme monotony and regularity. The church, by Street, 1858, is of interest, especially for its Victorian stained glass. The 19th-C Bradwell Windmill is now restored. Access from bridge 72 where there are good moorings.

● **Wolverton**
Bucks. MD Fri. PO, tel, stores, garage, station. Ignore the regularity of New Wolverton, and continue further west where the remains of the old village still survive among the trees. The Norman-style church was built in 1815, its large size perhaps anticipating the coming of the railway! By the church is the rectory with a handsome portal, built in 1729.

Pubs and Restaurants

Cross Keys Newport Road, Great Woolstone (01908 679404). Thatched village pub with an attractive garden, serving Charles Wells real ale and meals *lunchtimes and evenings.* Children's play area. Regular barbecues and quizzes.

X **Barge** Newport Road, Little Woolstone (01908 208891). Smart old pub with bar meals available *all day, 7 days a week.* Bass and Hancock's real ales. Children welcome. Garden. Log fires. *Open all day.*

X **Wayfarer Hotel** Milton Keynes (01908 675222). East of bridge 82a. Tetley's and guest real ale in a stylish new hotel on the shore of Willen Lake. Bar meals available *lunchtimes, evenings and all day Sun.* The restaurant is *open in the evenings only.* Children and vegetarians catered for. Terrace overlooking the lake. B & B. Disabled facilities.

X **Giffard Park** Milton Keynes (01908 210025). Canalside at bridge 78. A large modern pub, with bars on 3 levels, serving Flowers real ales together with a wide range of food. *Open all day, including Sun,* food is available *11.00–22.00.* Family room and children's play area. Canalside seating. Mooring.

X **Black Horse** Milton Keynes (01908 605939). Canalside at Black Horse Bridge. A popular pub with a choice of bars and open fires in the winter. Tetley's, Marston's and guest real ales are served, and there is a wide variety of reasonably priced food *lunchtimes and evenings.* Vegetarians and children catered for. Canalside seating, large garden, mooring. Quiz *Wed.*

X **New Inn** 2 Bradwell Road, New Bradwell, Milton Keynes (01908 312094). Canalside near bridge 72. Friendly, stone built pub and restaurant offering Wells, Adnams, Morlands and guest real ales and good value bar food *lunchtimes and evenings.* Garden with pets corner. *Open all day.*

Galleon Inn Old Wolverton (01908 313176). Refurbished pub, overlooking the canal, serving Tetley's and guest real ales. Food available *all day.* Children's menu. Canalside garden.

Yardley Gobion

Hills now begin to dominate the landscape to the west as the canal follows the course of the River Tove, an indication of the climb ahead up to Stoke Bruerne. After Wolverton the canal becomes more remote, with only Cosgrove exploiting it. The railway 1 mile to the east provides the only intrusion. There is plenty of canalscape; Wolverton Aqueduct, Cosgrove Lock ending the 11-mile Fenny Stratford Pound, Cosgrove Bridge and the disused and long abandoned Buckingham Arm branching away to the west (part is now a nature reserve, and a nature trail follows the disused canal). After Cosgrove and the old junction, the A508 runs parallel to the west. The canal leaves the low hills to the west and passes through open fields to Grafton Regis, where the hills reappear. A quiet, rural stretch, with only the noise of the railway to intrude. The villages lie set back to the west, but are easily approached. Accommodation bridges occur with even regularity, mostly old brick arches.

Stoke Bruerne Locks *(see page 58)*

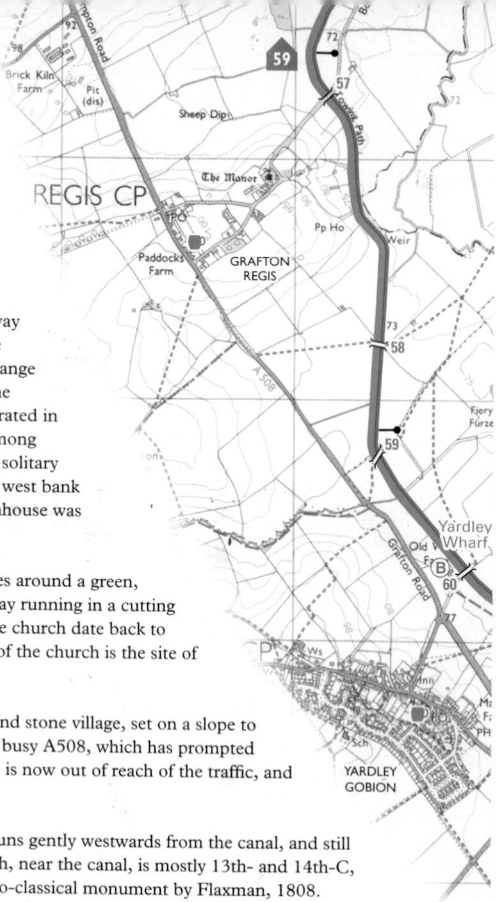

- **Great Ouse Aqueduct**
North of Old Wolverton the canal crosses the Ouse via an iron trunk aqueduct, a square cast iron trough carried on stone pillars. Built in 1811, it replaced a brick structure that collapsed in 1808. This in turn had replaced nine locks that enabled the Ouse to be crossed on the level, a system abandoned because of the danger of floods.
- **Cosgrove**
Northants. PO, tel, stores. The village climbs west away from the canal, its spread visually terminated by the wooded church. The best parts are by the canal: a range of warehouses, a curious pedestrian tunnel under the canal, and a splendid stone bridge charmingly decorated in the Gothic style, built in 1800. Its style is unique among canal bridges, and there is no obvious reason for its solitary splendour. The Georgian house that dominates the west bank by the lock is Cosgrove Hall; in 1958 a Roman bathhouse was discovered in front of the hall.
- **Castlethorpe**
Bucks. PO, tel, stores. A quiet village, thatched houses around a green, 1 mile north east of Thrupp Wharf. The main railway running in a cutting below the village is the only disturbance. Parts of the church date back to 1200, although the tower was built in 1729. North of the church is the site of a castle.
- **Yardley Gobion**
Northants. PO, tel, stores, off-licence. A small thatch and stone village, set on a slope to the west of the canal. The village is bypassed by the busy A508, which has prompted much new development. The church, built in 1864, is now out of reach of the traffic, and is once more serene.
- **Grafton Regis**
Northants. PO, tel, stores. A quiet stone village that runs gently westwards from the canal, and still preserves a strong manorial feeling. The large church, near the canal, is mostly 13th- and 14th-C, but contains a Norman font. There is also a fine Neo-classical monument by Flaxman, 1808.

BOAT TRIPS

Linda Cruising Company Cosgrove Wharf (07973 915652).Regular public cruises and day trips, private charter for entertainment or education on 40-passenger ex-working boat. Bar and shop on board.

Pubs and Restaurants

Barley Mow Cosgrove (01908 562957). By bridge 65. Courage and Theakston real ales and servery meals *lunchtimes and evenings, 7 days a week.* Canalside patio and children's play area. Children welcome when eating. Bar skittles, darts and table football. Mooring outside. *Open all day Sat & Sun in summer.*

X **Navigation** Thrupp Wharf, Cosgrove (01908 543156). Spacious and friendly pub, with open fires, serving a fine range of changing guest real ales. Families welcome. Bar food available *lunchtimes and evenings.* Balcony and canalside garden. Camping and moorings.

Coffee Pot Yardley Gobion (01908 542106). South of bridge 60. Tetley's and Flowers real ales together with bar meals available *lunchtimes and evenings.* Children and vegetarians catered for. Garden. Quiz *Thu & weekend* music.

White Hart Grafton Regis (01908 542123). On the busy A508, west of the canal from bridge 57. Greene King real ale and bar meals available *lunchtimes and evenings, including Sunday roasts.* Vegetarians catered for. Garden. *Closed all day Mon.*

Boatyards

Ⓑ **Cosgrove Marina** The Lock House, Cosgrove (01908 562467). D E Pump-out, overnight mooring, long-term mooring, winter storage, crane, boat sales and repairs, boat building and fitting-out, boat painting, engine sales and repairs (including outboards), solid fuel, toilets, telephone, groceries. *24 hour* emergency call-out.

Ⓑ **Baxter Boatfitting Services** Yardley Gobion (01908 542844). D E Pump-out, gas, overnight mooring, long-term mooring, winter storage, crane (1 ton), dry dock, wet dock, DIY facilities, chandlery, books and maps, gifts, boat building and fitting out, engine sales and repairs, boat repairs, solid fuel. *24 hr* emergency call-out (07860 643664). Also **Kingfisher Marina** (01908) 542293. Long-term mooring.

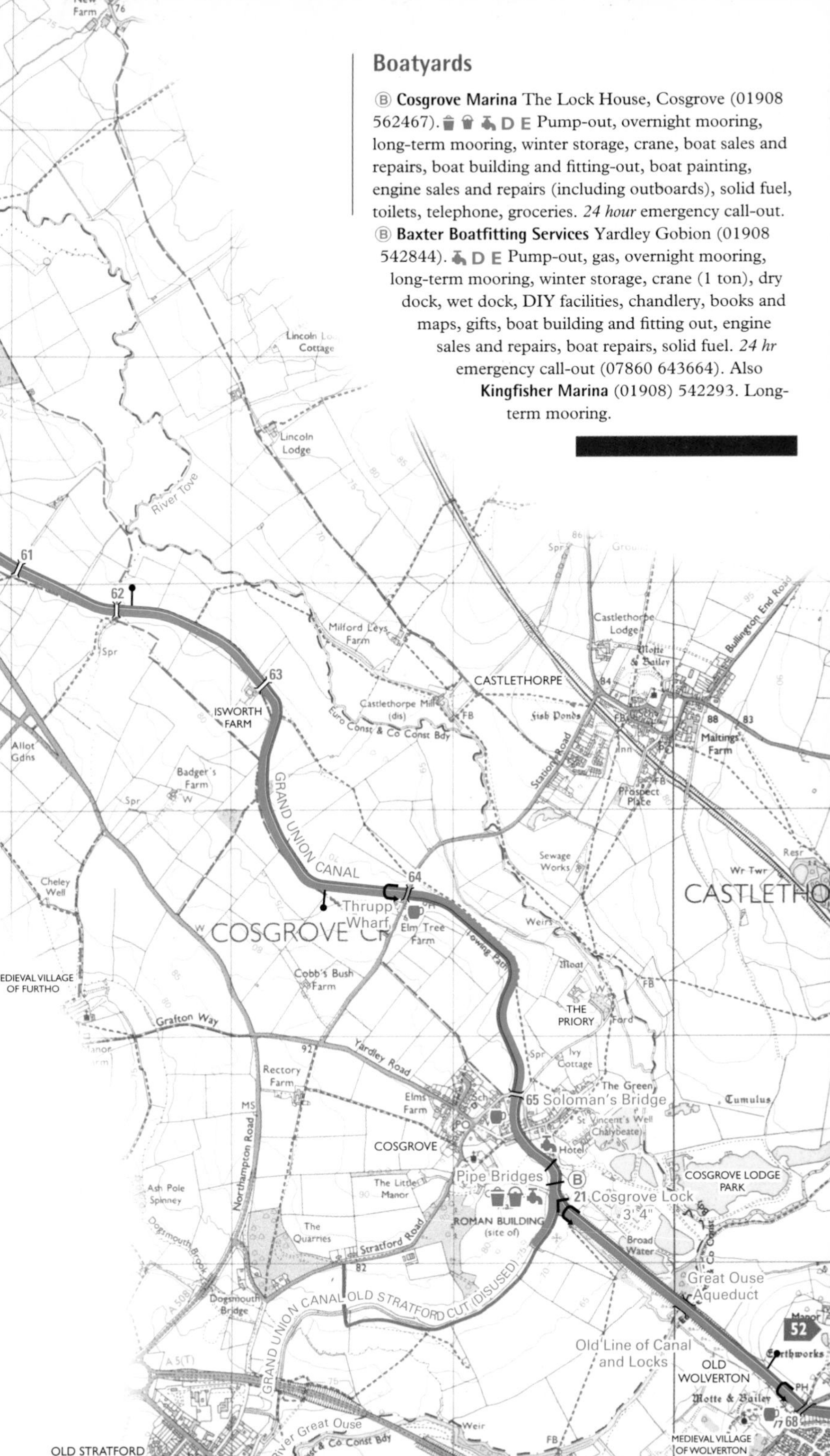

Stoke Bruerne

After Grafton Regis the River Tove joins the canal and then branches away to the west after 3/4 mile; there is a winding hole by this junction. At once the canal starts the seven-lock climb to Stoke Bruerne, via single wide locks. The A508 crosses after the second lock; there is a handy slipway nearby. As the village is approached the hills become more dominant, especially to the west and north west, anticipating Blisworth Tunnel. After the tunnel and the thickly wooded approach cutting, the hills recede to the west, and the canal, becoming wider but shallow at the edges, reaches Gayton Junction through open fields. The villages are very much on top of the canal, partly because of the landscape, and partly because of their importance to the canal; Stoke Bruerne is an ideal canal village. Beyond Stoke Bruerne Top Lock the level remains unchanged for several miles. A deep cutting leads to Blisworth Tunnel, the second longest in Britain still open to navigation. The Waterways Museum at Stoke Bruerne makes this altogether an exciting stretch. The main A43 used to cross in the middle of Blisworth but now passes further north, much to the relief of the inhabitants no doubt.

● **Stoke Park** Stoke Bruerne, Towcester (01604 862172). Approached via Stoke Bruerne, or along a footpath that leaves the canal at lock 20. The park is then 1/2 mile west of the canal. Built 1629-35 by Inigo Jones for Sir Francis Crane, head of the Mortlake Tapestry Works, the symmetrical façade with its flanking pavilions and colonnade made Stoke Park House (now demolished) one of the earliest Palladian or classical buildings in England. The pavilions and colonnade survived the fire, which virtually destroyed the mansion in 1886, and together with the gardens may be visited. *Open daily in Aug 15.00-18.00, otherwise by appointment.* Charge

● **Stoke Bruerne**
Northants. PO, tel, stores. Perhaps the best example of a canal village in this country. Built mostly of local Blisworth stone, the houses flank the canal, clearly viewing it as a blessing. To the west the hilly landscape warns of the approaching tunnel under Blisworth Hill. The Perpendicular church with its Norman tower overlooks the village, while the warehouses and cottages along the wharf have become a canal centre, greatly encouraged by the presence of the Waterways Museum. As a canalscape Stoke Bruerne has everything: a pub, locks, boat scales, a double-arched bridge, museum and canal shops and a nearby tunnel.
Waterways Museum Stoke Bruerne (01604 862229). Housed in a fine old stone warehouse, a unique collection brings to life the rich history of over 200 years of canals. Exhibits include a traditional narrow boat, boat weighing scales, a reconstructed butty boat cabin, steam and diesel engines, and extensive displays of clothing, cabinware, brasses, signs, models, paintings, photographs, and documents. Museum shop selling canal literature, maps, postcards, souvenirs and other ephemera. *Open summer, daily 10.00–18.00 inc B. Hols; winter, Tue–Sun 10.00–16.00. Closed Xmas Day and B. Day. Telephone to confirm opening times.* Charge.

● **Blisworth Tunnel**
At 3057yds long, Blisworth is the longest canal tunnel open to navigation in Britain (apart from Dudley, which is only open to electrically powered craft). The Grand Junction Canal was completed and opened in 1800 with the exception of this tunnel. The first attempt at excavation failed, and so a tramway was built over Blisworth Hill, linking the two termini. Boats arriving at either end had to be unloaded onto horse-drawn waggons, which were then pulled over the hill, and reloaded onto boats. A second attempt at the tunnel was more successful, and it opened on 25 March 1805. Originally boats were legged through. (Note the leggers' hut at the south end.) The British Waterways Board's £4.3 million restoration project was completed in 1984. There is no towpath, but the channel is wide enough to allow the passing of two 7ft boats, so keep to the right.
Boats over 7ft beam must give advance notice to the Waterways Office at Marsworth (01442 825938) so that craft can be prevented from entering the tunnel at the opposite end.

● **Blisworth**
Northants. PO, tel, stores, garage. A large brown stone village built around the old A43, it climbs up steeply from the canal, which passes through in a cutting shortly after leaving the tunnel. The church, mostly 14th-C, is just to the east of the canal, but appears to sit astride it.

Boatyards

Ⓑ **Blagrove** Wharf Cottage, Stoke Bruerne (01604 862174). **D E** Canal carriers, coal sales, B & B.

Ⓑ **Blisworth Tunnel Boats** Gayton Road, Blisworth (01604 858868). **D** Pump-out, gas, narrow boat hire, day hire craft, short-term mooring, long-term mooring, wet dock (with gantry for boats up to 50'), books and maps, gifts, boat and engine repairs, boat fitting-out and painting, solid fuel.

Ⓑ **Morley Canal Contractors** 2 Stoke Plain Cottages, Bridge Road (01604 862107/07808 859533). Canal carriers, towage, maintenance boats, waterside landscaping.

Pubs and Restaurants

Navigation Stoke Bruerne (01604 864988). Initially a pub, then a farmhouse and now converted into a busy family eating house and pub serving Mansfield real ales. Food available *all day in Summer* and *lunchtimes and evenings in winter, 7 days a week*. Elaborate indoor and outdoor children's play areas. Extensive garden seating beside the waterway. *Open all day.*

Boat Inn Stoke Bruerne (01604 862428). A bustling canalside pub (that has been in the same family since 1877) serving Marston's, Banks's, Fuller's, Timothy Taylor, Wadworth and Morland real ales, together with inexpensive snacks and bar meals *all day*. Vegetarians are catered for. Families are welcomed in the lounge and adjacent bistro. The restaurant is open daily (except Mon lunch) and offers a range of home-cooked English and international dishes all made from fresh produce, on a fixed price menu. Informal music sessions are encouraged. Canalside patio. Traditional pub games. Very much a local out of season.

The Old Chapel Restaurant and Coffee House Chapel Lane, Stoke Bruerne (01604 863284). Morning coffee, lunches, afternoon tea and dinner. Art and craft workshops and exhibition of traditional and contemporary two- and three-dimensional art. Garden dining. *Coffee House open Apr-Sep, daily 10.00-16.30; Oct–Mar, closed Mon. Restaurant open daily (except Oct-Mar, Mon) for L and Wed-Sat for D.*

Bruerne's Lock Restaurant Stoke Bruerne 01604 863654). Modern English cuisine with Mediterranean undertones. Light patio lunches available during the summer months. *L Tue–Fri & Sun; D Tue–Sat. Booking advisable.*

Royal Oak Blisworth (01604 858372). John Smith's, and as many as five rotating guest real ales in a traditional village local. Bar meals available *lunchtimes and evenings, 7 days a week*. Children welcome when eating. Garden and play area. Skittles. Quiz *Sun*.

BOAT TRIPS

Stoke Bruerne Boat Company Stoke Bruerne (01604 862107). *Daily trips on nb. Charlie Easter-Oct, and weekends all year.* Party bookings. Day hire boat *Skylark*.

Boat Inn Stoke Bruerne (01604 862428). *Weekend trips Mar–Nov on nb. Indian Chief.* Otherwise a wide range of party bookings on this 40-seater narrow boat with bar, snacks and disabled lift. Telephone for daily schedule.

Gayton Junction

At Gayton Junction the Northampton Arm of the Grand Union, opened in 1815, branches away to the north east. There is a useful provision shop – Stella's Canal Shop – behind the BW yard, *open every day until late.* The waterway falls steeply through 5 miles of open country to Northampton where it connects with the navigable River Nene and thus with Peterborough, the Fens and ultimately the Wash. There are no villages on the canal, and the main feature of interest

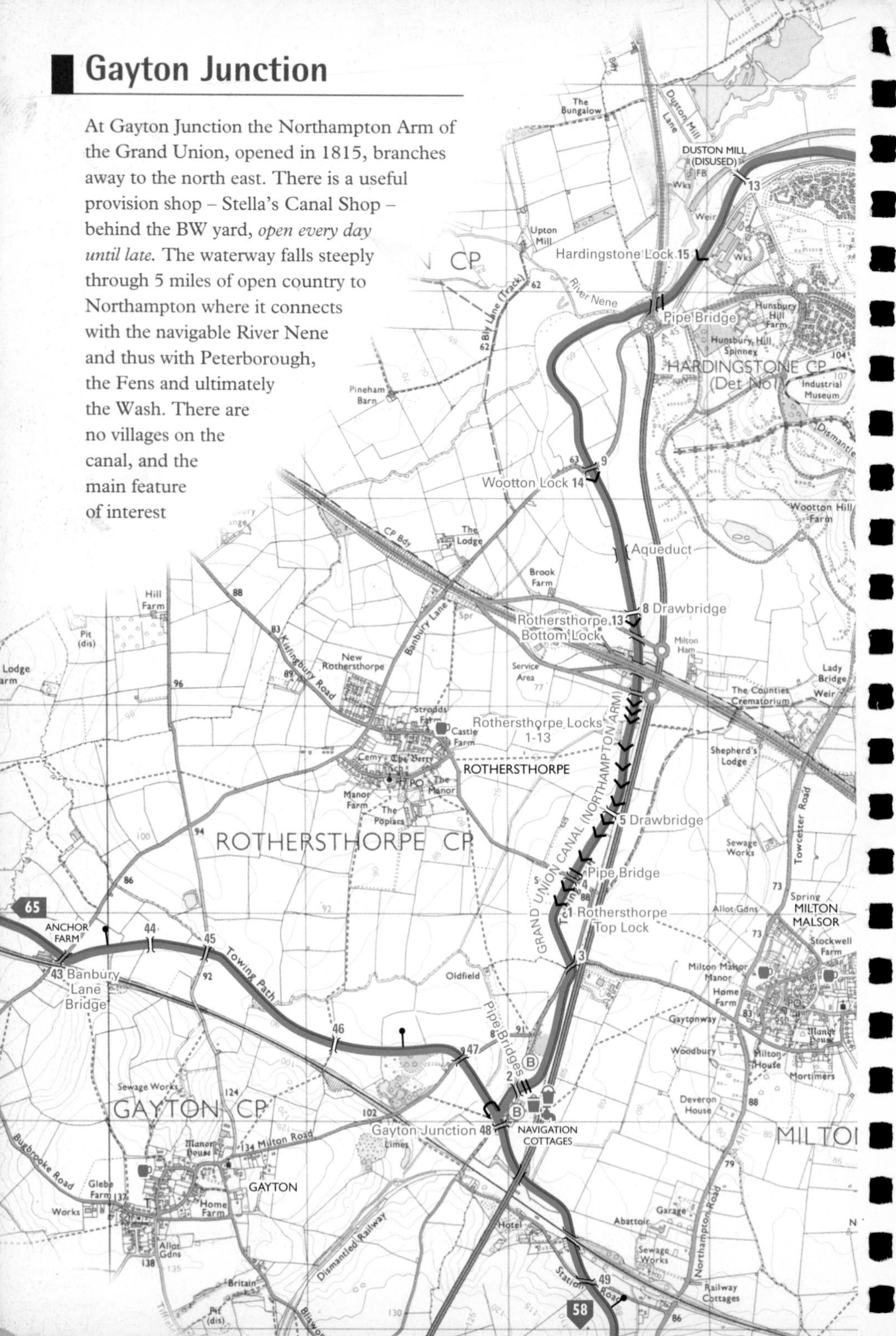

is the flight of 17 locks down to Northampton. Most of the long flight is visible from the top, as is Northampton in the distance. Several traditional drawbridges cross the canal, which look very pretty but are hard work to operate. Only the M1 bridge, a long concrete tunnel, interferes with the unchanged feeling of the arm. Swinging east after Hunsbury Hill, the canal leaves the open country behind as it approaches Northampton. Housing estates fringing the canal soon appear. The entry into the town passes factories, disused wharves and railway junctions before reaching Cotton End Wharf. Anyone considering stopping in Northampton is advised to pass through the bottom lock and into the Nene Navigation, where surroundings are more inviting.

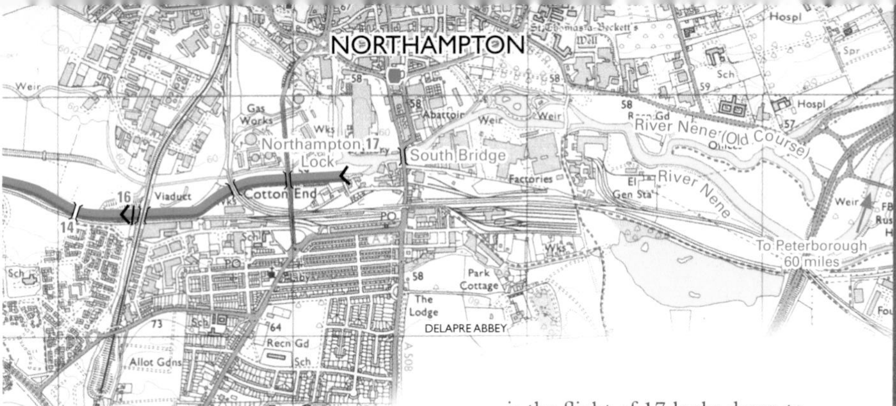

NAVIGATIONAL NOTES

The River Nene is a fully navigable river from Northampton down to the Wash. At Peterborough, which is 60 miles and 37 locks away, the river becomes tidal. It connects with the Middle Level Navigations and the Great Ouse and adjoining rivers. A licence to cover navigation on the river is obtainable from: Environment Agency, Anglian Region, Kingfisher House, Goldhay Way, Orton Goldhay, Peterborough, PE2 5ZR (01733 371811) or from the boatyards at Gayton.

Boatyards

Ⓑ **Grand Junction Boat Company** Blisworth (01604 858043). Adjacent to BW Blisworth Yard. Gas, slipway, engine sales and repairs, boat repairs, boat fitting-out, DIY facilities, chandlery. Emergency call-out.

Ⓑ **Alvechurch Boat Centre** Gayton Marina, Blisworth (01604 858685). On the Northampton Arm, 400yds from Gayton Junction. D E Pump-out, gas, narrow boat hire, overnight mooring, long-term mooring, boat sales and repairs, engine sales and repairs, boat fitting-out, wet dock, toilets, books and maps, gift shop. River Nene licences. Telephone.

Gayton

Northants. PO, tel, stores. Set on a hill to the west of the canal junction, the village seems to be composed of large, handsome stone houses, ranging in style from the 16th- to the 19th-C; trees among the houses increase the rural grandeur. The large church with its ornamented tower maintains the unity of the village.

Milton Malsor

Northants. PO, tel, stores. Attractive, meandering brick stone village, spreading east towards the 14th-C church. Around the church are several elegant stone houses of the 17th and 18thC, making an exploration on foot worth while. New houses have been well incorporated with the old.

Rothersthorpe

Northants. PO, tel, stores. A comfortable mixture of brick and stone built round a large square. The church contains a Tudor pulpit. To the west of the village is a large circular dovecot with 900 nesting places.

Northampton

Northants. MD Tue, Wed, Thu, Fri, Sat. All services. The centre of the town was destroyed by fire in 1675, and so little remains of Northampton's earlier industry. Only an archway of the 12th-C castle remains, one of the best-known Norman castles. Thomas Becket was tried here in 1164. There are several churches of interest, including a rare round Norman one of c.1110. The richly decorated Town Hall was built during the 19thC in the Gothic style and subsequently extended twice; most recently in 1992. The generous market square, dating from 1235, is flanked by a great diversity of façades, spanning the centuries and numbering more than 35.

Abington Museum Abington Park, Northampton (01604 31454). Period rooms, toys, bygones. Northampton lace, ceramics, natural history, military history and a snapshot of Northampton life exhibited in a 15th-C manor castle. Beautiful public park and museum shop. *Open Tue–Sun & B. Hol Mon 13.00–17.00.* Free. Partial disabled access. Toilets.

All Saints Church George Row, Northampton (01604 32194). Described as the finest 17th-C parish church outside London, the present church was reconstructed around the medieval tower, in 1860, after the great fire. Shop and refreshments. *Open daily 09.00–15.00 & 16.30–18.30 and for Sun services.* Donations. Toilets.

Battle of Northampton 10 July 1460 1/2 mile south of Northampton Lock, between Delapre Abbey and Hunsbury Hill. A significant battle in the Wars of the Roses in which the Lancastrian King Henry was defeated by Edward of York. Beaumont, Shrewsbury, Egremont and Buckingham were slain and many bodies floated in the River Nene.

Carlsberg Brewery 140 Bridge Street, Northampton (01604 234333). Guided tours *Mon–Fri 09.15 & 14.15 and all year by appointment only.* Free. No disabled access.

Central Museum and Art Gallery Guildhall Road, Northampton (01604 39415). Archaeology, antiquities, paintings, furniture and the finest collection of historical footwear in Europe, including Queen Victoria's wedding shoes and ballet shoes of Nijinsky. Museum shop. *Open Mon-Sat 10.00– 17.00 & Sun 14.00–17.00.* Free. Full disabled access. Toilets.

Cycle Hire Supabikes, 48 Kingsley Terrace, Northampton (01604 716984). By the day, weekend or week.

Delapre Abbey London Road, Northampton. 1/2 mile south of canal, on A50. A former Cluniac nunnery, founded in 1145, the Abbey underwent major alterations in the 16th and 17thC. The garden is *open May–Sep.* South of the Abbey park is Eleanor Cross, one of three surviving crosses set up by Edward I in 1290 to mark the last resting places of Queen Eleanor on her way to burial in Westminster Abbey from Harby in Leicestershire where she had died.

Derngate 19–21 Guildhall Road, Northampton (01604 24811). Presents a broad mix of theatre, ballet, opera, classical music, comedy, music and dance.

Grandad's Attics Drapers (furniture), Barrack Road, Northampton (01604 38935). A small museum, on two floors above a furniture shop, with eight rooms each depicting a different theme. *Open Mon–Sat 10.00–16.00.* Charge.

Northampton & Lamport Railway Pitsford & Brampton Station, Pitsford Road, Chapel Brampton, Northampton (01604 820327). A developing preserved railway with the aim of re-opening the line from Northampton to Market Harborough. Approximately 3/4 mile of track is currently operational and carrying passengers at their base at Pitsford Sidings; 5 miles out of Northampton. Shop, rolling stock, locomotives, restoration projects, memorabilia, etc. The Brampton Valley Way – footpath and cycleway – runs the full length of the proposed route, providing access for boaters. For up to date information telephone the *24 hr* number above.

Northamptonshire Ironstone Railway Hunsbury Country Park, Hunsbury Hill Road, Northampton (01604 890229). Steam/diesel passenger carrying railway, artefacts from the ironstone industry and locomotive restoration projects. Museum *open Sun & B. Hols 10.00–17.00.* Free. Railway *Apr–Sep*

Sun & B. Hols 14.00–17.00. Charge. Refreshments and toilets. Disabled access.
Roadmender 1 Lady's Lane, Northampton (01604 604603). Multi purpose arts and music venue.
Royal Theatre Guildhall Road, Northampton (01604 32533). A beautifully opulent Victorian theatre presenting a wide range of professional and amateur drama productions, pantomime, etc. Refreshments.
St Peter's Church Marefair, Northampton (01604 37783). A most distinguished Norman building with a wealth and variety of internal decoration. *Open by appointment by telephoning the above number (or 01604 844575/754491) 08.00–09.00 and 12.30–13.30.* Free.
Tourist Information Centre Mr Grant's House, St Giles Square, Northampton (01604 22677/233500). *Open Mon–Fri 09.30–17.00, Sat 09.30–16.00, Sun 12.00–16.00 (summer only).* Books, guides, gifts, travel shop *(opening times differ)* and a focal point for local guided walks. Telephone for further details.

Pubs and Restaurants

Eykyn Arms 20 High Street, Gayton (01604 858361). Traditional village local serving Mansfield, Wells and guest real ales together with *lunchtime* food. Outside seating and pub games. Camping. *Closed Mon lunchtimes.*

Greyhound Towcester Road, Milton Malsor (01604 858449). A fine village pub in 16th-C cottages, once occupied by workers from the brewery next door (now closed). An impressive refurbishment has achieved the remarkable: a convincing restoration with a genuine traditional cosy feel to it, reflecting the antiquity of the building. There is an open fire in the bar, where Theakston and John Smith's real ales can be enjoyed. An extensive and imaginative menu is offered *all day* and children and vegetarians are both well catered for. Large garden. *Open all day.*

Compass Green Street, Milton Malsor (01604 858365). Small 18th-C local serving Ruddles and two guest real ales, tucked away in a narrow village street. A traditional pub, unfettered by passing trade, where conversation, skittles and darts predominate. Small garden. *Open evenings only Mon–Fri & all day Sat & Sun.*

Chequers North Street, Rothersthorpe (01604 830892). Greene King real ales and bar meals available *lunchtimes and evenings, 7 days a week* in a cosy pub that willingly offers a taxi service to boaters phoning from Gayton Junction. Children and vegetarians catered for. Garden. Darts, dominoes, skittles and pool. *Open all day.*

Malt Shovel Tavern 121 Bridge Street, Northampton (01604 234212). A haven for beer and whisky drinkers alike, dispensing Banks's, Boddingtons, Castle Eden, Frog Island and guest real ales together with an excellent selection of malt whiskies. To complete the line-up there is a range of foreign, bottled beers and real cider. Food is available *lunchtimes and evenings.* Outside seating and pub games. Disabled access.

Moon On The Square The Parade, Northampton (01604 634062). Courage, Everards, Theakston and guest real ales dispensed in typical Wetherspoons surroundings. Food *available all day.* No smoking area and disabled access.

Victoria Inn 2 Poole Street, Northampton (01604 633660). Cosy, single-roomed, town pub dispensing Fuller's, Wadworth and guest real ales *from 16.00 (12.00 on Fri & Sat) onwards.* Traditional pub games. Quiz *Tue & Wed. Open all day Sun.*

Plough Bridge Street, Northampton (01604 230554). A large Victorian hotel, attracting the younger generation, offering Tetley's, Burton and guest real ales. Bar snacks. Music *most evenings.* B & B.

Lilly's Tea Room Tourist Information Centre, 10 St Giles Square, Northampton (01604 27778). Morning coffee, sandwiches, hot meals and snacks and afternoon tea. *Open Mon–Sat 10.00–16.00.* Disabled access.

Crown & Cushion 276 Wellingborough Road, Northampton (01604 33937). Moor at Becket's Park, below the Nene lock and walk north across the park, before taking the second main turning right. Banks's, Ruddles and John Smith's real ales in a superbly run establishment popular with a wide ranging clientele. Attractive garden with excellent children's play area. Traditional pub games. No food but worth the walk.

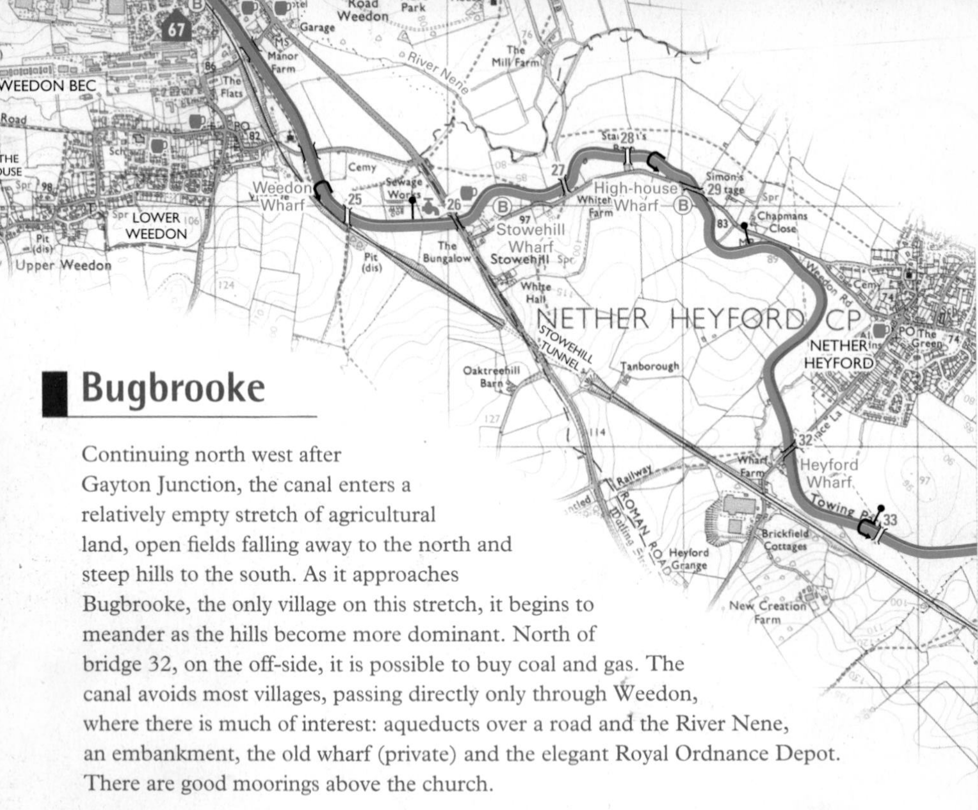

Bugbrooke

Continuing north west after Gayton Junction, the canal enters a relatively empty stretch of agricultural land, open fields falling away to the north and steep hills to the south. As it approaches Bugbrooke, the only village on this stretch, it begins to meander as the hills become more dominant. North of bridge 32, on the off-side, it is possible to buy coal and gas. The canal avoids most villages, passing directly only through Weedon, where there is much of interest: aqueducts over a road and the River Nene, an embankment, the old wharf (private) and the elegant Royal Ordnance Depot. There are good moorings above the church.

- **Bugbrooke**
  Northants. PO, tel, stores, garage.
- **Upper Stowe**
  Northants. Tel. Tiny village with an interesting **Craft Centre** (01327 340525) set in a series of listed farm buildings at the **Old Dairy Farm.** Everything from lace-making to woodturning, wrought iron-work to designer knitwear. Antiques, gifts and foods. *Open daily 10.00–17.30.* Free.
- **Nether Heyford**
  Northants. PO, tel, stores.
  Bridge 28 Nether Heyford, Weedon (01327 349171). Beside bridge 28. Canalside craft shop selling local crafts and works of art. Moorings and seating in the water gardens.
- **Weedon**
  Northants. PO, tel, stores, garage, take-aways.

Boatyards

Ⓑ **Bugbrooke Marina** Cornhill Lane, Bugbrooke (01604 832883). Overnight mooring (by arrangement), long-term mooring, boat sales and brokerage, toilets.

Ⓑ **Waterways Services** High House Wharf, Heyford Lane, Weedon (01327 342300). D E Pump-out, gas, long-term mooring, boat repairs, boat fitting-out, engine repairs, wet dock, toilets. Emergency call-out.

Ⓑ **Millar Marine** Stowe Hill Wharf, Weedon (01327 349188). D Pump-out, gas, craft, long-term mooring, boat and engine sales, chandlery, books, maps, gifts, solid fuel. *Open 7 days a week (Sun 10.00-16.00).*

Ⓑ **Stowe Hill Marine** Stowe Hill Wharf, Weedon (01327 341365). Long-term mooring, boat building and fitting-out, boat and engine repairs, dry dock, wet dock.

Ⓑ **Concoform Marine** The Boatyard, High Street, Weedon (01327 340739). Pump-out, gas, narrow boat hire, long-term mooring. *Closed Sun & Mon in summer, and winter weekends.*

Pubs and Restaurants

Wharf Inn Cornhill Lane, Bugbrooke (01604 832585). By bridge 36. A new pub serving Courage and Frog Island real ales and bar meals *lunchtimes and evenings seven days a week.* Moorings and canalside patio. Children welcome *until 19.00.* Quiz Mon.

Bakers Arms High Street, Bugbrooke. (01604 830865). Webster's and rotating guest real ales served in a traditional village local. This friendly pub has a large garden, skittles, pool and darts. Live music *alternate Sat and every winter Thu.* Quiz *Sun. Closed weekday lunchtimes (open at 17.00); open all day Sat.* No children inside.

Five Bells 14 Church Lane, Bugbrooke (01604 832483). Refurbished pub serving bar food *lunchtimes and evenings, 7 days a week.* together with Webster's, Marston's and guest real ales. Pool. Large play area and summer barbecues.

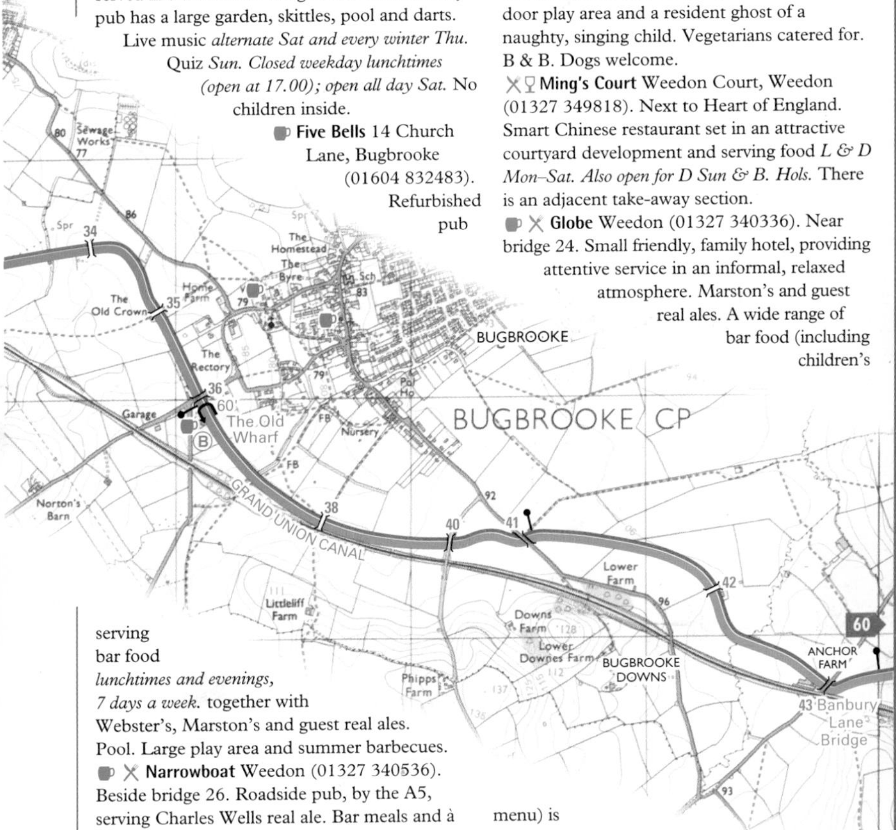

Narrowboat Weedon (01327 340536). Beside bridge 26. Roadside pub, by the A5, serving Charles Wells real ale. Bar meals and à la carte restaurant menu served lunchtimes and evenings. B & B in motel-type chalets. Canalside seating, mooring. *Open all day Sat.*

Plume of Feathers Weedon (01327 340978). West of Church Steps, at the aqueduct beside the church. Recently refurbished after serious flooding this pub has been transformed into a welcoming family establishment serving Flowers and Fuller's real ales. Home-cooked food is available *lunchtimes and evenings* and there is a large garden with children's play area.

Maltsters Weedon (01327 340175). Past the Plume of Feathers. Another victim of the floods, this 300 year old drinkers pub has been completely refurbished and now majors on serving an exciting range of real ales: five at any one time. Huge garden. Snooker, skittle alley, pool and table skittles. *Open all day.*

Heart of England Weedon (01327 340335). Near bridge 24. Recently extensively refurbished by Mansfield Brewery (and serving their range of real ales) this family pub, dating from 1740, offers meals *all day, every day.* Children's outdoor play area and a resident ghost of a naughty, singing child. Vegetarians catered for. B & B. Dogs welcome.

Ming's Court Weedon Court, Weedon (01327 349818). Next to Heart of England. Smart Chinese restaurant set in an attractive courtyard development and serving food *L & D Mon–Sat. Also open for D Sun & B. Hols.* There is an adjacent take-away section.

Globe Weedon (01327 340336). Near bridge 24. Small friendly, family hotel, providing attentive service in an informal, relaxed atmosphere. Marston's and guest real ales. A wide range of bar food (including children's menu) is available *all day, 7 days a week* and an appetising table d'hôte menu is served in the restaurant *L & D. Sunday lunches* are deservedly popular and are available to children half-price. Vegetarian options always available. Patio seating. Music *Mon.* B & B. *Open all day.* Disabled access.

Crossroads Hotel Weedon (01327 340354). Tetley's, Greenalls and guest real ales, bar food *lunchtimes and evenings (snacks available all day)* and an à la carte restaurant menu *L & D (all day Sun).* Children and vegetarians catered for. Large garden and tennis courts. B & B. *Open all day.*

Buckby Wharf

A quiet open stretch follows which gives way to the landscaped woods of Brockhall Park. This peace is short-lived, however, as soon several transport routes merge to produce a strange picture of three totally different means of transport running parallel. The old Roman road, Watling Street (A5), keeping as straight a course as possible through the hills; the canal, its junior by 1800 years, now looking more outdated than the Roman road; the London-Midland railway line and the 20th-C motorway complete this set of contrasts. Of all the thousands of travellers passing through this area every hour, it must surely be those who travel on the canal who enjoy its potential most as they compare the canal's dignity and quiet progress to the noise and rush of the roads and the railway. For most boaters it will act as a stimulous to steer for Whilton and Buckby Locks and the climb up to Norton Junction, accompanied as it is by attractive terraces of red-brick cottages. In one of these, by lock 8, there is a canal craft shop, whilst by lock 9 are the remains of Long Buckby Wharf. Opposite there is a useful farm shop selling fresh produce, groceries and home-made pies. All the locks have side ponds, now disused (with some filled in), and ivy leafed toadflax grows in the lockwalls. The system for pumping water back up the flight has been restored, using an electric pump. Above Buckby Locks is Norton Junction, where the Leicester Line branches off to the north (this is covered in *Book 3: Birmingham & the Heart of England*). The main line continues west towards Braunston.

● **Buckby Wharf**
Northants. PO box, tel, stores.

● **Whilton**
Northants. PO, tel, stores. 1 mile east of the canal at the end of a road that goes nowhere. Whilton is quiet and unchanged, especially at the east end. There are several fine stone houses, including a pretty Georgian rectory. At the locks there is a pottery – **Whilton Locks Pottery** (01327 842886) – specialising in raku and crystal glazed porcelain. *Open daily 09.00–18.00 but telephone before visiting.*

● **Brockhall**
Northants. PO box. A large, lightly wooded landscaped park climbs gently east away from the canal. In the centre a manorial brown stone village and church are still intact and remote despite the M1 roaring through the west end of the park. The Hall is Tudor in part, with fine 18th-C interiors; large trees screen it from the motorway. The **Heart of the Shires Shopping Village** (01327 349249) has been established in a courtyard of model farm buildings and amongst other things sells architectural antiques, furniture and also has a tea room. *Open Tue–Sat 10.00–17.00 & Sun & B. Hol Mon 11.00–17.00.* Free. Access from bridge 18.

Pubs and Restaurants

New Inn Long Buckby Wharf (01327 842540). Canalside, at Buckby Top Lock. Cosy alcoved free house, serving Marston's and Bass real ale and a range of inexpensive meals and snacks *all day, every day.* Children and vegetarians catered for. Canalside seating and patio. Moorings. Darts, dominoes and skittles. Music *Sun. Open all day.*

Stag's Head Watford Gap (01327 703621). Award winning restaurant with a lovely canalside rose garden. An extensive menu – ranging from bar snacks to table d'hôte and a wide à la carte selection – is available *L & D, 7 days a week.* The cuisine encompasses English, French and Portuguese dishes. Very much a family establishment with prices to match. Everards real ale. Occasional Portuguese food theme *evenings in winter.* Moorings.

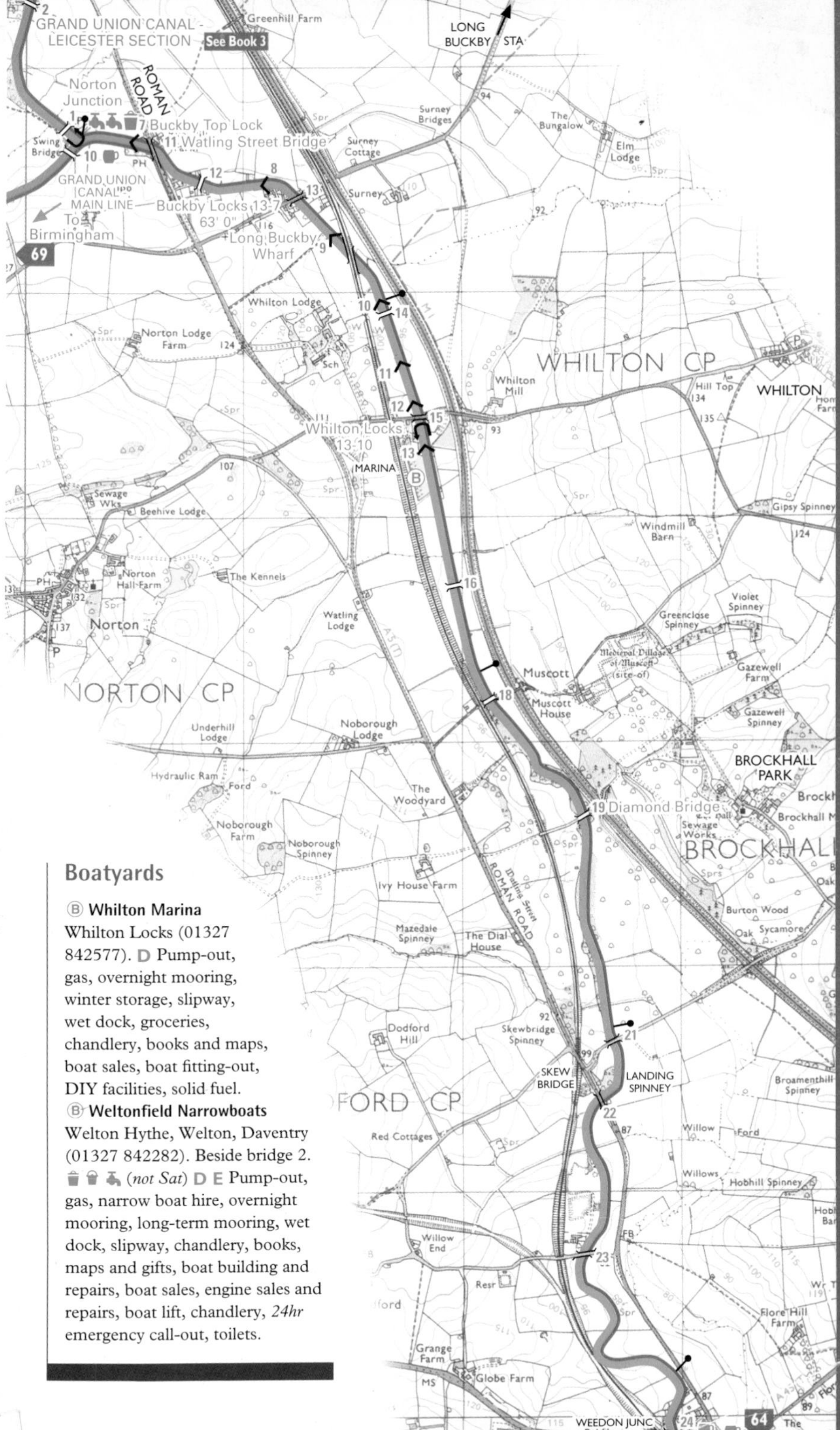

Boatyards

Ⓑ **Whilton Marina**
Whilton Locks (01327 842577). D Pump-out, gas, overnight mooring, winter storage, slipway, wet dock, groceries, chandlery, books and maps, boat sales, boat fitting-out, DIY facilities, solid fuel.

Ⓑ **Weltonfield Narrowboats**
Welton Hythe, Welton, Daventry (01327 842282). Beside bridge 2. (*not Sat*) D E Pump-out, gas, narrow boat hire, overnight mooring, long-term mooring, wet dock, slipway, chandlery, books, maps and gifts, boat building and repairs, boat sales, engine sales and repairs, boat lift, chandlery, *24hr* emergency call-out, toilets.

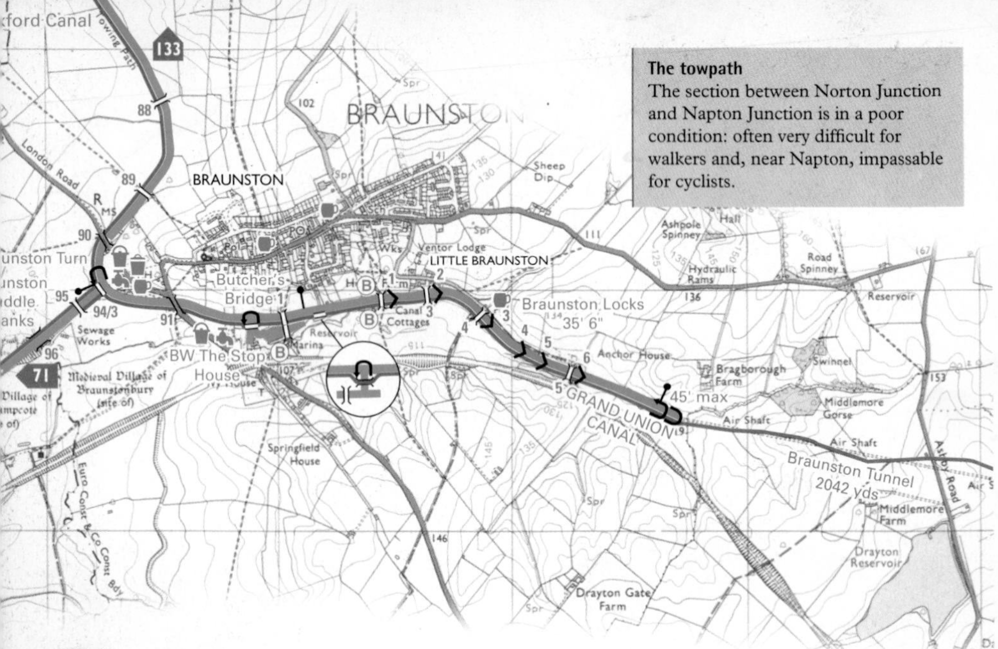

The towpath
The section between Norton Junction and Napton Junction is in a poor condition: often very difficult for walkers and, near Napton, impassable for cyclists.

Braunston

From Norton Junction to Braunston the canal runs westward through hills and wooded country, then into a wooded cutting which leads to Braunston Tunnel. There is a good track over the top of the hill, which passes the brick tops of the ventilation shafts. A cutting follows the tunnel, and then the landscape opens out although the hills stay present on either side. Long rows of moored craft flank the canal, although there is usually plenty of space to moor, and there is a fine selection of old buildings at Braunston. Note especially the iron side-bridge and the 18th-C dry dock. The arm in fact was part of the old route of the Oxford Canal before it was shortened by building a large embankment (Braunston Puddle Banks) across the Leam Valley to Braunston Turn. The entrance to this arm was thus the original Braunston Junction. The Waterway Office in the Stop House was originally the Toll Office between the Oxford Canal and the Grand Junction Canal.

Pubs and Restaurants

White Horse High Street, Welton (01327 702820). 3/4 mile from the canal at bridge 6. Webster's, Marston's, Courage and guest real ales. Bar meals and snacks served *lunchtimes,* with restaurant meals available *D every day and Sun L only.* Vegetarian options. Large garden.

Admiral Nelson Dark Lane, Little Braunston (01788 890075). By lock 3. Food *lunchtimes and evenings, every day (except Mon in winter)* John Smith's real ale. Canalside seating. Cottage crafts are sold nearby.

Wheatsheaf The Green, Braunston. A locals' pub with a warm atmosphere. Everards, Flowers, Wadworth's and guest real ales. Meals are served *18.30-22.00 daily*. Children welcome, and a garden with a barbecue.

Old Plough 82 High Street, Braunston (01788 890000). A fine pub dating from 1672, serving Ansells, Burton and guest real ales. Good food *lunchtimes and evenings every day*, with a vegetarian menu. Children are welcome, and there is a garden. Quiz every other *Sun.*

The Mill House Braunston (01788 890450). Once the Rose & Castle. Bass and Worthington real ale. Food *12.00–21.30 Mon–Sat (21.00 Sun)*. Children's room and fine canalside garden with swings. Overnight mooring for patrons.

NAVIGATIONAL NOTES

Braunston Tunnel – two boats of 7ft beam can pass in this tunnel, but wide beam boats *must get permission from BW* to arrange a passage. Telephone 01788 890666

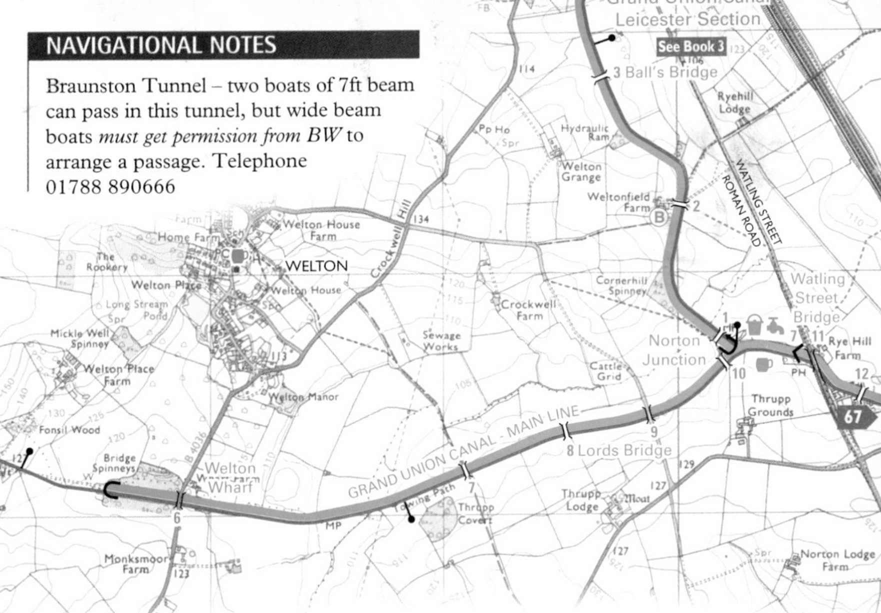

BOAT TRIPS

Rachael Operating from Braunston Marina, this licensed restaurant boat can accommodate 20 people. It makes regular *3-hour evening trips during the summer* on the Oxford Canal, and can also be chartered for *lunchtime* cruises. Telephone 07071 880784 for details.

The Rambler Operating from The Mill House (see below). Seating 12 people, this boat provides *lunchtime* cruises, *aftenoon* cream tea cruises, and *evening* trips to the Napton Bridge Inn *Fri-Sat*, plus *hourly trips each Sun, throughout the summer.* It is also available for private charter. Details from Braunston Cruises, 14 Countryside, braunston (01788 890373). Booking is essential.

Welton
Northants. Tel. The village climbs up the side of a steep hill, which makes it compact and attractive, especially around the church.

Braunston Tunnel
Opened in 1796, to bore through the Northamptonshire heights, the tunnel is 2042yds long. Its construction was hindered by quicksands, and a mistake in direction whilst building has given it a slight S bend.

Braunston
Northants. PO, tel, stores, butcher, fish & chips. Set up on a hill to the north of the canal. The village is really a long main street a little separate from the canal, with houses of all periods. A well known canal centre, it is no less significant today than when the Oxford and Grand Junction canals were first connected here. British Waterways reopened the Stop House as the local Waterway Office in 1990, and there is a small information room and gift shop within.

Boatyards

The Boat Shop (01788 891310). Started on board a boat moored at Braunston Turn, this is now a shop by Braunston Top Lock selling basic chandlery, coal, groceries, fruit and vegetables and canal ware, brass ware and much more. *Open mid-Mar–mid-Oct 08.00–20.00; rest of year 08.00–18.00.*

Ⓑ **Braunston Boats** Bottom Lock, Braunston (01788 891079). D Pump-out, gas, long-term mooring, winter storage, slipway.

Ⓑ **Union Canal Carriers** Canalside at Braunston Pump House, Dark Lane (01788 890784). D Pump-out, gas, narrow boat hire, dry dock, engine sales, boat and engine repairs.

Ⓑ **Braunston Marina** The Wharf, Braunston (01788 891373). Through the fine bridge dated 1834 and into an historic canal wharf. D E Gas, pump-out, overnight and long-term mooring, dry and wet dock, chandlery, boat building sales and repairs, engineering – all services. Toilets and showers, public telephone, chandlery, gift shop selling books and maps. Laundrette.

Napton Junction

The canal now passes through open countryside with a background of hills, and is very quiet and empty following all of the waterway activity around Braunston. The land is agricultural, with just a few houses in sight. There are initially no locks, no villages and the bridges are well spaced, making this a very pleasant rural stretch of canal running south west towards Napton Junction, on a length once used by both the Grand Junction Company and the Oxford Canal Company. As the Oxford Canal actually *owned* this stretch, they charged excessive toll rates in an attempt to get even with their rival, whose more direct route between London and the Midlands had attracted most of the traffic. At Napton Junction the Oxford Canal heads to the south while the Grand Union Canal strikes off north towards Birmingham. The empty landscape rolls on towards Stockton, broken only by Calcutt Locks. The windmill on top of Napton Hill can be seen from Napton Junction.

Boatyards

Ⓑ **Napton Narrowboats** Napton Marina, Stockton (01926 813644). D Pump-out, gas, narrow boat hire, overnight and long-term mooring, boat & engine repairs, toilets, chandlery, gifts.

Ⓑ **Calcutt Boats** Calcutt Top Lock (01926 813757). D Pump-out, gas, narrow boat hire, day boat hire, overnight mooring, long-term mooring, slipway, crane, dry dock, boat and engine sales and repairs, toilets, chandlery, solid fuel, breakdown service.

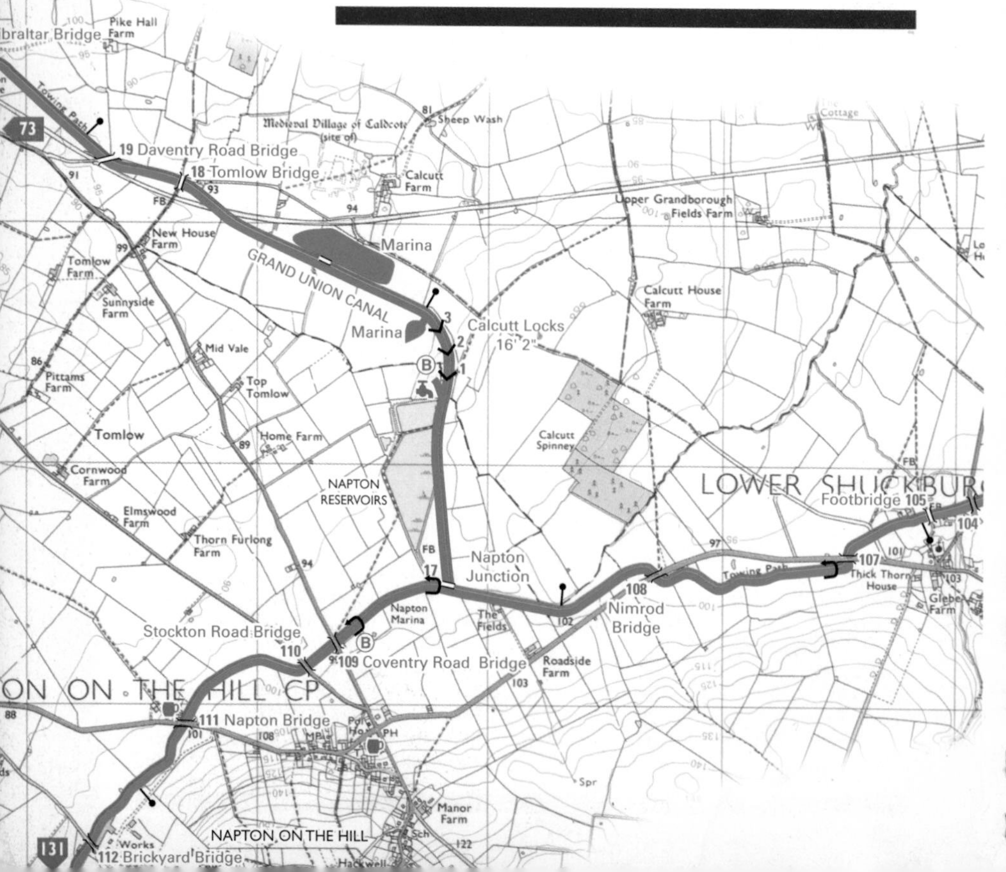

Pubs and Restaurants

Napton Bridge Inn (01926 812466). Canalside at bridge 111 on the Oxford Canal. Excellent food is served *lunchtimes and evenings every day,* with restaurant meals *L & D.* You can choose from steaks to fish to spicy pasta. Vegetarians are well looked after, and children are welcome. Flowers, Tetley's and a guest real ale are available. There is a pleasant garden with a children's play area, and often entertainment during *the summer months.*

Ye Olde Kings Head Napton-on-the-Hill (01926 812202). Just 200yds south of bridge 109. Marston's, Morland's plus seven constantly changing real ales and a wide range of bar and restaurant meals *lunchtimes and evenings every day (all day at weekends, when there is a Sunday carvery).* Children are welcome, there is a children's menu, and a large garden.

Old Olive Bush Flecknoe (01788 891134). A village pub serving meals *Tue-Sun evenings,* and bar snacks *lunchtimes Sat & Sun.* Vegetarian options, children welcome, and there is a garden. *Closed lunchtimes Mon-Fri.*

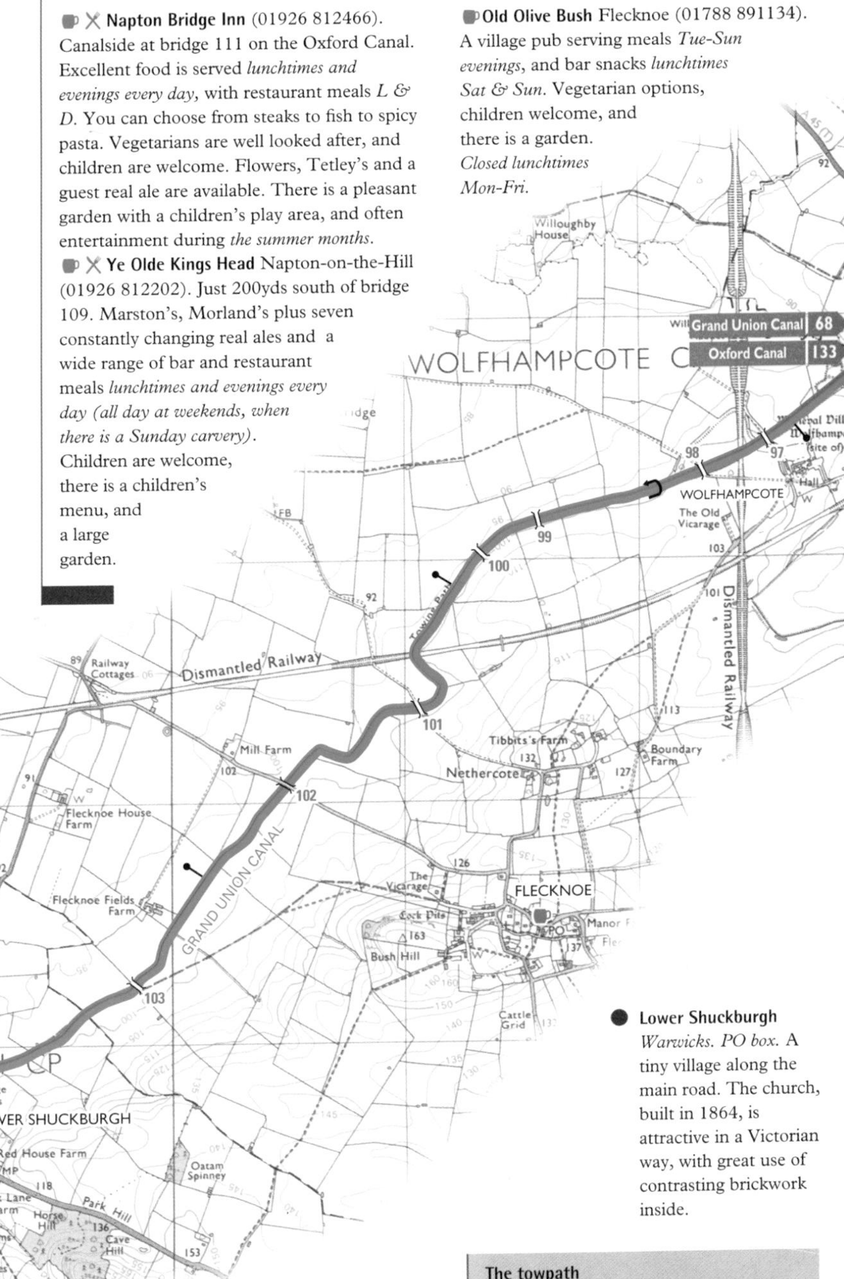

Lower Shuckburgh
Warwicks. PO box. A tiny village along the main road. The church, built in 1864, is attractive in a Victorian way, with great use of contrasting brickwork inside.

The towpath
The section between Napton Junction and Norton Junction is in a poor condition: often difficult for walkers and, near Napton, impassable for cyclists.

Stockton

Continuing west, the canal passes to the north of Stockton and descends Stockton Locks, where you will notice the remains of the old narrow locks beside the newer wide ones. Around here there is a change in landscape, with the hills coming much closer to the canal, broken by old quarries and thick woods along the south bank. The quarries produced blue lias, a local stone, and cement which was used in the construction of the Thames Embankment. Huge fossils have been found in the blue lias clay, which is the lowest layer from the Jurassic period. This section contrasts greatly with the open landscape that precedes and follows it. The canal passes Long Itchington, a village with a large number of pubs, including two on the canal, all the while flanked by open arable land backed on both sides by hills. This pleasant emptiness is broken only by further locks continuing the fall to Warwick. Of particular interest are the top two locks at Bascote, just beyond the pretty toll house, which form a staircase. Then once again the canal is in quiet, wooded, countryside.

● **Stockton**
Warwicks PO, tel, stores, fish & chips, Indian take-away. Stockton is a largely Victorian village in an area which has been dominated by the cement works to the west. St Michael's church is built of blue lias, quarried near Stockton Locks, although the tower is of red sandstone.

● **Long Itchington**
Warwicks. PO, tel, stores, garage. A large housing estate flanks the busy A423; the village proper lies a short walk to the north west, and is very attractive. Apart from several pubs there are houses of the 17th- and 18th-C, and impressive poplars around the village pond. St Wulfstan, who later became Bishop of Worcester, was born here in 1012.
Holy Trinity A largely 13th-C church whose tall spire was blown down in a gale in 1762, and replaced with a stump. Parts of the south aisle date from the 12thC, although the 13th-C windows are perhaps the building's best feature. There is a 14th-C screen.

Boatyards

Ⓑ **Blue Lias Marina** Stockton (01926 854976). By bridge 20. D Pump-out, gas, overnight and long-term mooring, winter storage, slipway, crane, boatbuilding, telephone, chandlery, solid fuel, DIY facilities.

Ⓑ **Warwickshire Fly Boat Company** Stop Lock Cottage, Stockton (01926 812093). By the Kayes Arm. D Pump-out, gas, overnight mooring, long-term mooring, winter storage, dry dock, boat and engine sales and repairs, boatbuilding, telephone, toilets, showers, chandlery, solid fuel, laundrette.

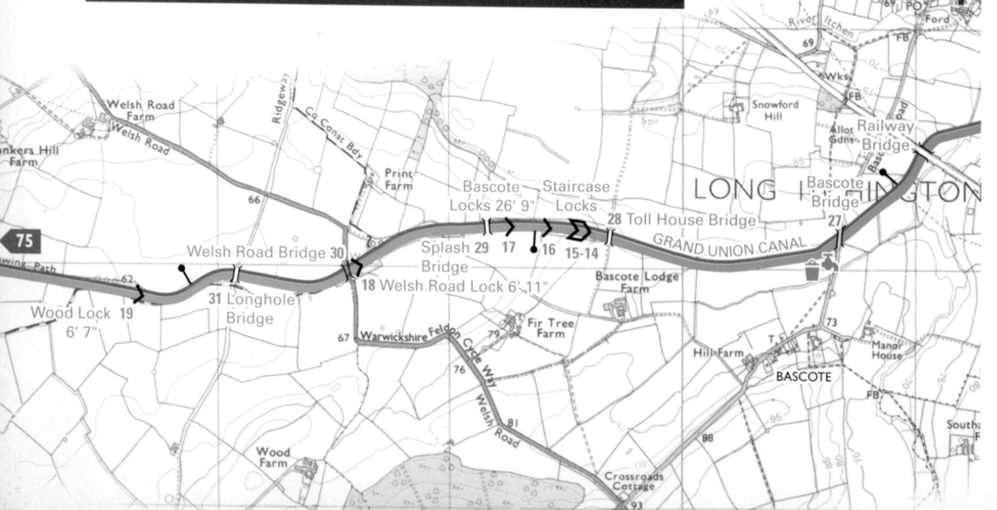

Pubs and Restaurants

Boat Birdingbury Wharf, Rugby Road (01926 812349). Canalside at bridge 21. A pleasant old pub with a fine canalside map, painted by Dusty Miller, around the top of the bar. Bass and guest real ales. Grills and bar meals *lunchtimes and evenings* with a vegetarian menu. Canalside garden with play area.

Blue Lias Stockton. (01926 812249). Canalside at bridge 23. A well kept and attractive pub, with a pleasant canalside garden with ponies, donkeys and rabbits. Be prepared for the uneven interior brickwork, which may look straighter when you have enjoyed one of the four real ales they regularly keep. Bar meals *lunchtimes and evenings every day*, with vegetarian choices. Live music *Sat evenings in summer.* Children are welcome.

✕ **Barley Mow** School Street, Stockton (01926 812713). Banks's, Bass and a guest real ale modernised pub. Bar meals *lunchtimes and evenings (not Mon)*, with a vegetarian menu. Outside seating on the green, opposite the church. Children welcome.

Two Boats Inn Southam Road, Long Itchington (01926 812640). Canalside at bridge 25. A good selection of real ale including Bass, Greene King and Hook Norton are available in this fine pub, built in 1743. At one time there was a forge and stables here for the boat horses. Bar meals and grills *lunchtimes and evenings* with vegetarian choices. Children welcome. Garden with fine views of the canal. Live music *Sat* with folk evening *first Sun in every month.*

Green Man Church Road, Long Itchington (01926 812208). Just past the church, this is a fine traditional country pub with a very low ceiling in the corridor. Bass and Tetley's real ale and bar meals *lunchtimes and evenings (but not Tue: bookings only for Sun)*, with a vegetarian menu. Family room and garden.

✕ **Harvester** Church Road, Long Itchington (01926 812698). Opposite the village store. Small, popular local serving Hook Norton and guest real ales. Bar and restaurant meals *lunchtimes and evenings,* with a selection of vegetarian dishes. Outside seating. Children welcome. Young Farmers meet here on *Wed evenings.*

Jolly Fisherman The Green, Long Itchington (01926 812296). A large pub overlooking the village green and pond. Garden. Queen Elizabeth I once stayed in the black and white timbered building opposite.

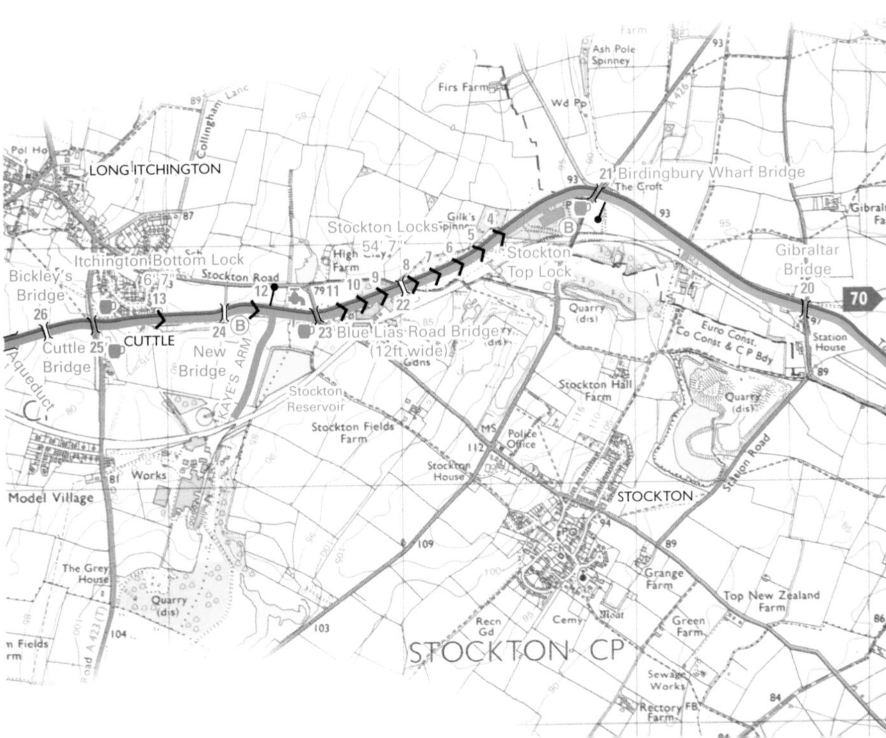

Royal Leamington Spa

The waterway makes its descent through the quiet Fosse Locks and continues west through attractive and isolated country to pass to the north of Radford Semele, where there is a fine wooded cutting. Emerging from the cutting, the canal joins a busy road for a short while, then carves a fairly discreet course through Leamington. Midway through the town the canal enters a deep cutting that hides it from the adjacent main road and railway. Leaving Leamington the canal swings north west under a main road and crosses the railway and the River Avon on aqueducts, to immediately enter the outskirts of Warwick. There are good moorings, shops and two Indian take-aways by bridge 40.

Pubs and Restaurants

Stags Head Welsh Road, Offchurch (01926 425801). A thatched 15th-C pub, serving Bass, Flowers and Tetley's real ale and food *lunchtimes and evenings daily*, with vegetarian options. Children welcome, and garden with swings. *Sun evening* quiz.

Old White Lion Southam Road, Kingshurst, Radford Semele (01926 425770). Greenalls, Marston's and Tetley' real ales, and meals served *all day every day*, with vegetarian options. Garden with play area. Occasional quiz nights. Children welcome in the restaurant.

The Fusilier Sydenham Drive, Leamington Spa (01926 336048). No real ale, no children, but dogs are welcome. Karaoke *Sat*, quiz and disco *Sun*. Lawn at the back. Fish & chips next door, and shops nearby.

Bridge Brunswick Street, Leamington Spa (01926 425674). Canalside at bridge 40. Bass and Whitbread real ale and bar meals *lunchtimes and evenings every day*, with vegetarian choices. Children welcome when dining. Big garden, barbecue and canalside terrace. Mooring for patrons.

Grand Union & JJs Restaurant 66 Clemens Street (01926 421323). At bridge 40, overlooking the canal. English dinner and à la carte menu. *D only, and a champagne Sun lunch.* Booking essential for the Grand Union, not essential for JJs.

The Tiller Pin Queensway, Leamington Spa (01926 435139). By bridge 43. M & B and Bass real ale. Food is available *lunchtimes and evenings Mon–Fri, and all day until 21.00 at weekends.* Children are welcome if you are having a meal. Large garden.

The Moorings (01926 425043). By bridge 43. Banks's, Marston's and Camerons real ale. Food available in bar or restaurant *all day every day*. Children are welcome. BBQs in *summer*. Mooring.

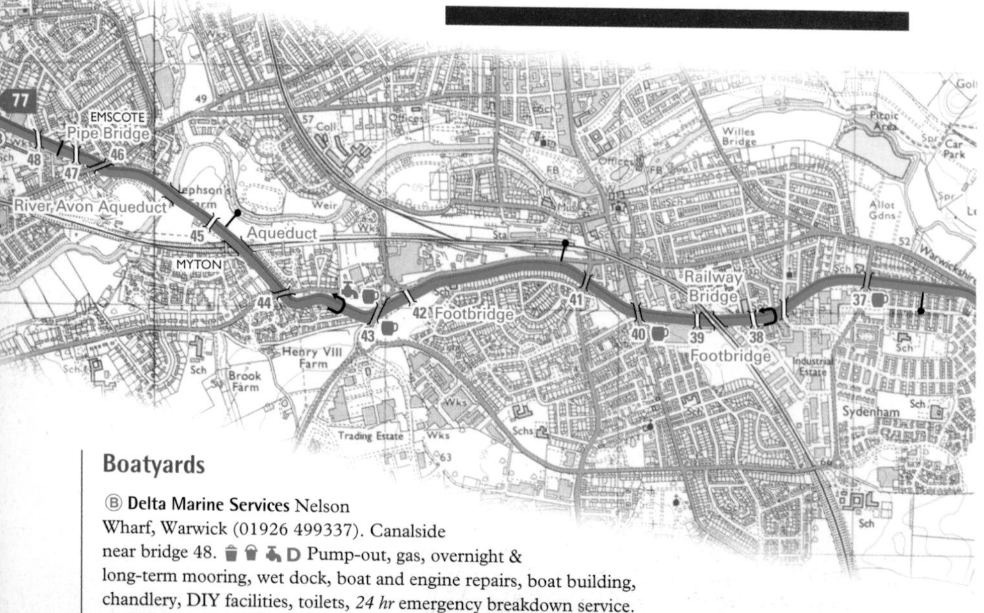

Boatyards

Ⓑ **Delta Marine Services** Nelson Wharf, Warwick (01926 499337). Canalside near bridge 48. D Pump-out, gas, overnight & long-term mooring, wet dock, boat and engine repairs, boat building, chandlery, DIY facilities, toilets, *24 hr* emergency breakdown service.

Offchurch

Warwicks. Tel. A scattered residential village reflecting the proximity of Leamington. It takes its name from Offa, the Saxon King of Mercia, reputedly buried near here. The church, with its tall grey stone tower, contains some Norman work. To the west lies Offchurch Bury, whose park runs almost to the canal. Originally this was a 17th-C house, but is has since been entirely rebuilt. The façade is now early 19th-C Gothic.

Radford Semele

Warwicks. PO, tel, stores, garage. A main road suburb of Leamington, Radford Semele takes no notice of the canal that runs below the village, alongside the River Leam and what was once the railway line to Rugby. Among the bungalows are some fine large houses, including Radford Hall, a reconstructed Jacobean building. The Victorian church of St Nicholas is set curiously by itself, seeming to be in the middle of a field.

Royal Leamington Spa

Warwicks. PO, tel, stores (by bridge 40), garage, station, cinema. During the 19thC the population of Leamington increased rapidly, due to the late 18th- and 19th-C fashion for spas generally. As a result the town is largely mid-Victorian, and a number of Victorian churches and hotels dominate it, several designed by J. Cundall, a local architect of some note who also built the brick and stone Town Hall. The long rows of villas, elegant houses in their own grounds spreading out from the centre, all express the Victorian love of exotic styles – Gothic, Classical, Jacobean, Renaissance, French and Greek are all mixed here with bold abandon. Since the Victorian era, however, much industrialisation has taken place.

Assembly Rooms, Art Gallery & Museum Royal Pump Rooms, The Parade, Royal Leamington Spa (01926 742700). British, Dutch and Flemish paintings of the 16th and 17thC. Also a collection of modern art, pottery and porcelain through the ages and a specialist series of 18th-C English drinking glasses. Victorian costumes and objects. *Open Wed, Fri & Sat 10.30-17.00, Tue & Thu 13.30-20.00, Sun 11.00-16.00. Closed Mon.* Free.

All Saints' Church Bath Street. Begun in 1843 to the design of J. C. Jackson, who was greatly influenced by the then vicar, Dr John Craig. It is of Gothic style, apparently not always correct in detail. The north transept has a rose window patterned on Rouen Cathedral; the west window is by Kempe. The scale of the building is impressive, being fully 172 feet long and 80 feet high.

Jephson Gardens Alongside Newbold Terrace, north of bridge 40. Beautiful ornamental gardens named after Dr Jephson (1798–1878), the local practitioner who was largely responsible for the spa's high medical reputation.

Tourist Information Centre Royal Pump Rooms, The Parade, Royal Leamington Spa (01926 742762).

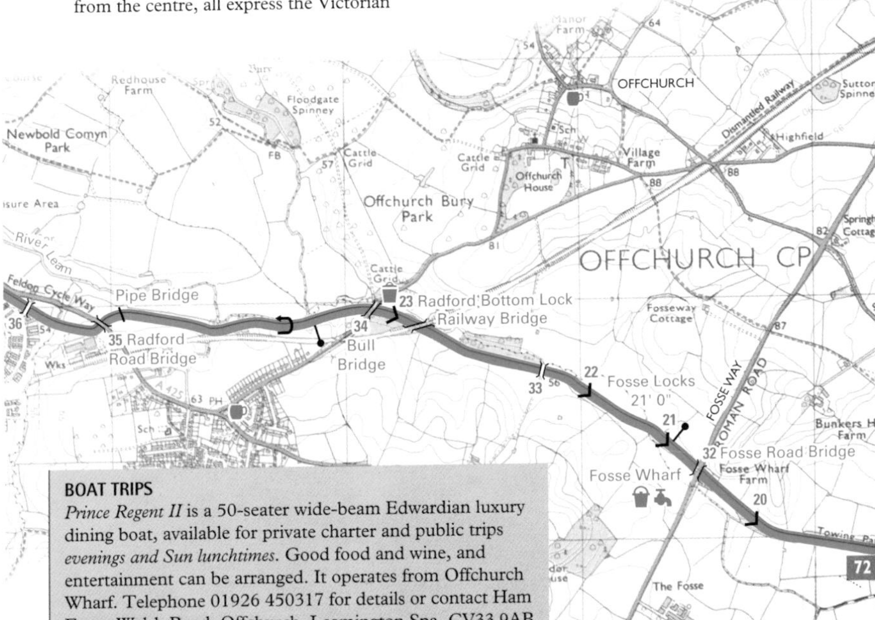

BOAT TRIPS

Prince Regent II is a 50-seater wide-beam Edwardian luxury dining boat, available for private charter and public trips *evenings and Sun lunchtimes.* Good food and wine, and entertainment can be arranged. It operates from Offchurch Wharf. Telephone 01926 450317 for details or contact Ham Farm, Welsh Road, Offchurch, Leamington Spa, CV33 9AB.

Warwick

The canal passes around the north side of central Warwick, so if you wish to visit the town centre, it is best to approach from bridge 49 (walking to the south for a little over half a mile), or from the Saltisford Canal Centre (see below). After climbing the two Cape Locks, the canal swings south to Budbrooke Junction, where the old Warwick and Napton Canal joined the Warwick and Birmingham Canal. A short section of the arm to the east of the junction has been restored, and has a winding hole, moorings and other facilities. To the west of the junction, beyond a large road bridge, is the first of the 21 locks of the Hatton flight, with its distinctive paddle gear and gates stretching up the hill ahead, a daunting sight for even the most resilient boatman. Consolation is offered by the fine view of the spires of Warwick as you climb the flight. There is a small shop selling maps and canalia between locks 45 and 46. On reaching the top, the canal turns to the west, passing the wooded hills that conceal Hatton village and Hatton Park. The canal then enters the wooded cutting that leads to Shrewley Tunnel.

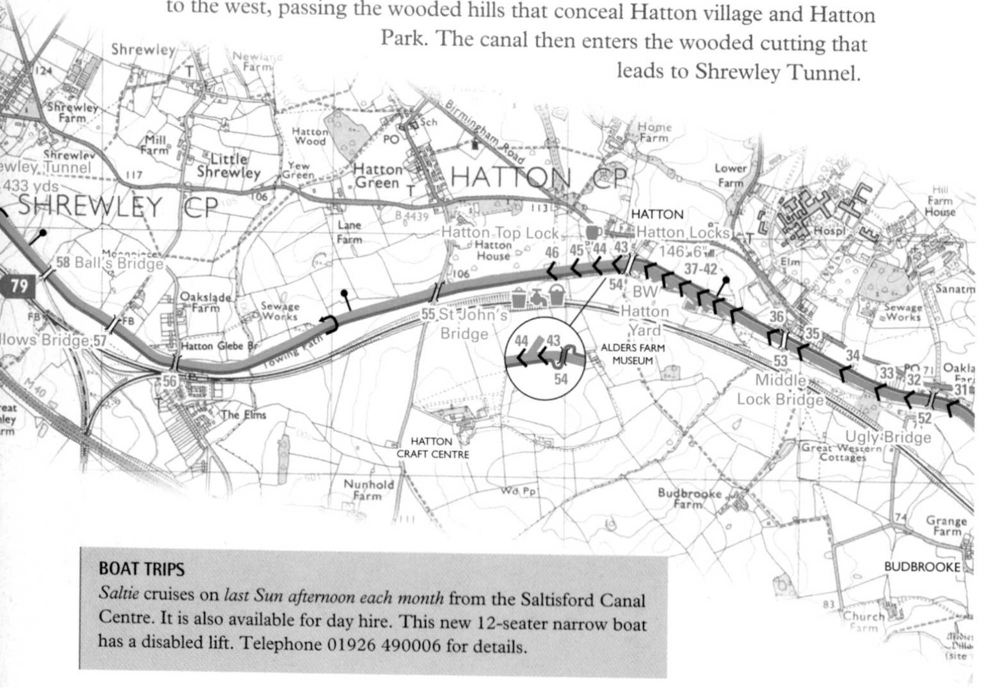

BOAT TRIPS

Saltie cruises on *last Sun afternoon each month* from the Saltisford Canal Centre. It is also available for day hire. This new 12-seater narrow boat has a disabled lift. Telephone 01926 490006 for details.

Boatyards

Ⓑ **Saltisford Canal Centre** Budbrooke Road, Warwick (01926 490006). Pump-out, day hire craft, overnight mooring, long-term mooring, telephone nearby, toilets, gifts, small laundrette. Gardens, picnic places, BBQ and snacks available. Small museum and information centre. An excellent place in its own right, with good access to Warwick.

Ⓑ **Kate Boats Warwick** The Boatyard, Nelson Lane, Warwick (01926 492968). D Pump-out, gas, narrow boat hire, overnight mooring, long-term mooring, boat and engine repairs, boatbuilding, telephone, toilets, chandlery.

Get Knotted Lower Cape (01926 410588). Next door to the Cape of Good Hope pub. Rope fender making specialist, plus general ropework and an expanding chandlery.

Ⓑ **Stephen Goldsbrough Boats** Hatton (01564 778210). Dry dock on the Hatton flight, boat painting and repairs, DIY facilities.

Warwick

Warwicks. MD Sat. All services. Virtually destroyed by fire in 1694 the town rose again, with Queen Anne styles now mixed with the medieval buildings which survived the blaze.

Warwick Castle Castle Hill (telephone 01926 406600 for information line). Built on the site of a motte and bailey constructed by William the Conqueror in 1068, the present exterior is a famous example of a 14th-C fortification, with the tall Caesar's Tower rising to a height of 147ft. The castle grounds were laid out by Capability Brown. *Open daily 10.00–17.30. Closed Xmas.* Charge. Programme of events *throughout the year.*

Collegiate Church of St Mary's Of Norman origin. The most striking feature of the rebuilt church is its pseudo-Gothic tower, built 1698–1704. Climb to the top to enjoy the view *(May–Sep, 10.00–16.00, weather permitting).* Church *open summer 10.00–18.00; winter 10.00–16.00.* Free (charge for tower).

Warwick County Museum Market Place (01926 412500). Housed in the Market Hall. Includes the Sheldon tapestry map of Warwickshire, which dates from 1588. *Open May–Sep, Mon–Sat 10.00–17.30, Sun 11.00–17.00.* Free.

Lord Leycester Hospital High Street (01926 491422). A superbly preserved group of 14thC timber-framed buildings. Chapel of St James, Great Hall and galleried courtyard. The Museum of the Queen's Own Hussars is also here. *Open Tue–Sun & B. Hol Mon 10.00–17.00 (closes 16.00 winter).* The newly restored gardens are *open during the summer.* Charge.

Oken's House & Doll Museum Castle Street (01926 412500). A superb collection of early dolls housed in one of the few timber buildings that survived the great fire. *Open Easter–Oct, Mon–Sat 10.00–17.00, Sun 13.00–17.00; Nov–Easter, Sat only 10.00–dusk.* Charge.

Tourist Information Centre The Court House, Jury Street, Warwick (01926 492212). Guided walks are arranged from here *during the summer.*

Hatton

Warwicks. A heavily wooded village.

Hatton Country World George's Farm, Hatton (01926 843411). South of bridge 55. Rare breeds, craft workshops and a children's play area. *Open daily 10.00–17.00 (closed Xmas).* Entrance to the Craft village is free, but a charge is made for the Farm Park.

Shrewley

Warwicks. PO, tel, stores. Best approached from the north-western end of the Shrewley Tunnel, through an exciting, but slippery, towpath tunnel.

Shrewley Tunnel 433yds long, the tunnel was opened in 1799 with the completion of the Warwick and Birmingham Canal. *This tunnel allows two 7ft boats to pass: keep to the right.*

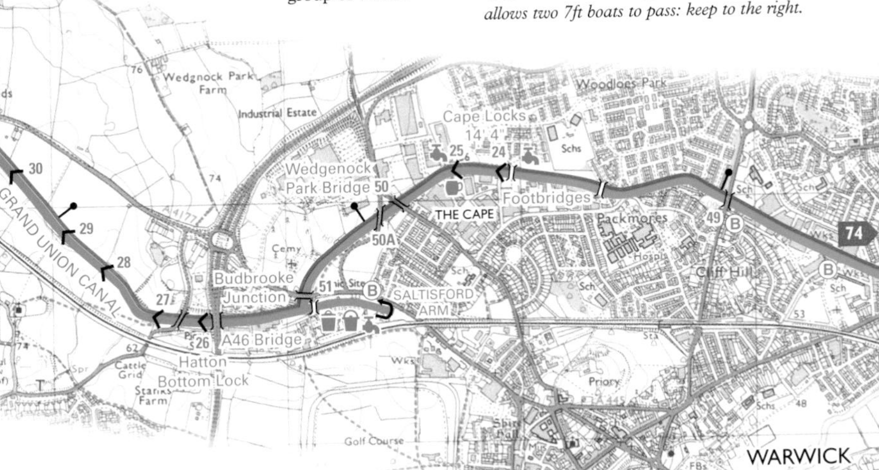

Pubs and Restaurants

There are many pubs and restaurants in Warwick which will repay exploration.

Cape of Good Hope Cape Locks, 66 Lower Cape (01926 498138). Good food is served *lunch- times and evenings every day,* and there are three regular real ales plus a guest. Lockside seating.

The Waterman Birmingham Road (A4177), Hatton (01926 492427). An excellent and extensive bar menu, with vegetarian choices, is available *lunchtimes and evenings every day* in this pub, which has a comfortable beamed bar and fine views over the Hatton flight. Bass, Tetley's and a guest real ale. Large garden. Children welcome. Regular live music.

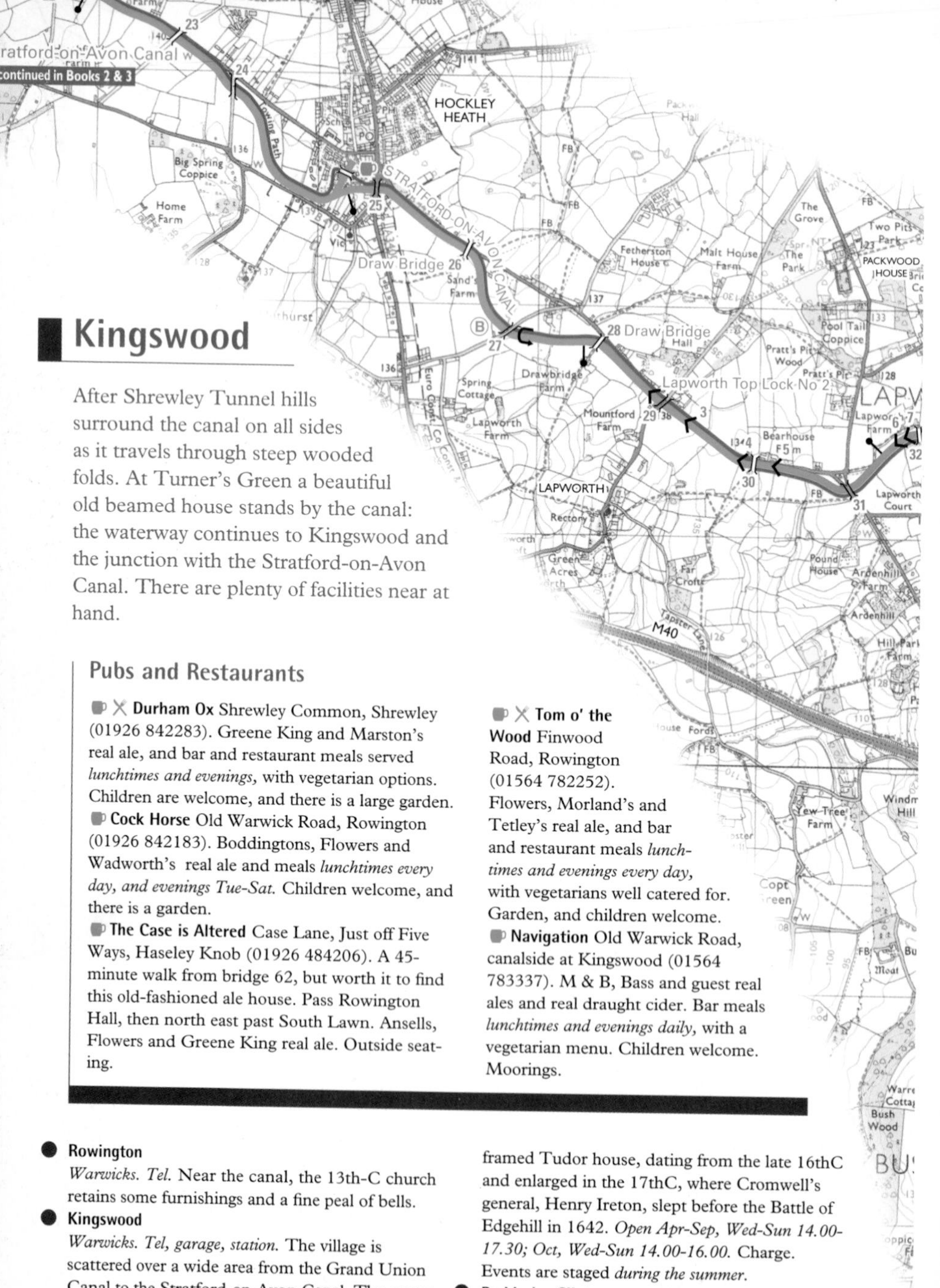

Kingswood

After Shrewley Tunnel hills surround the canal on all sides as it travels through steep wooded folds. At Turner's Green a beautiful old beamed house stands by the canal: the waterway continues to Kingswood and the junction with the Stratford-on-Avon Canal. There are plenty of facilities near at hand.

Pubs and Restaurants

Durham Ox Shrewley Common, Shrewley (01926 842283). Greene King and Marston's real ale, and bar and restaurant meals served *lunchtimes and evenings,* with vegetarian options. Children are welcome, and there is a large garden.

Cock Horse Old Warwick Road, Rowington (01926 842183). Boddingtons, Flowers and Wadworth's real ale and meals *lunchtimes every day, and evenings Tue-Sat.* Children welcome, and there is a garden.

The Case is Altered Case Lane, Just off Five Ways, Haseley Knob (01926 484206). A 45-minute walk from bridge 62, but worth it to find this old-fashioned ale house. Pass Rowington Hall, then north east past South Lawn. Ansells, Flowers and Greene King real ale. Outside seating.

Tom o' the Wood Finwood Road, Rowington (01564 782252). Flowers, Morland's and Tetley's real ale, and bar and restaurant meals *lunchtimes and evenings every day,* with vegetarians well catered for. Garden, and children welcome.

Navigation Old Warwick Road, canalside at Kingswood (01564 783337). M & B, Bass and guest real ales and real draught cider. Bar meals *lunchtimes and evenings daily,* with a vegetarian menu. Children welcome. Moorings.

- **Rowington**
  Warwicks. Tel. Near the canal, the 13th-C church retains some furnishings and a fine peal of bells.
- **Kingswood**
  Warwicks. Tel, garage, station. The village is scattered over a wide area from the Grand Union Canal to the Stratford-on-Avon Canal. The centre is a mile to the west, around the ambitious 15th-C church.

  Packwood House *NT property* (01564 782024). Hockley Heath, 2 miles west of bridge 66. Timber-framed Tudor house, dating from the late 16thC and enlarged in the 17thC, where Cromwell's general, Henry Ireton, slept before the Battle of Edgehill in 1642. *Open Apr-Sep, Wed-Sun 14.00-17.30; Oct, Wed-Sun 14.00-16.00.* Charge. Events are staged *during the summer.*
- **Baddesley Clinton**
  Warwicks. Tel, stores. The village is a mile from the canal at bridge 66, but nearer are the church and the hall, set amid parkland. The church is mostly 16th- and 17th-C.

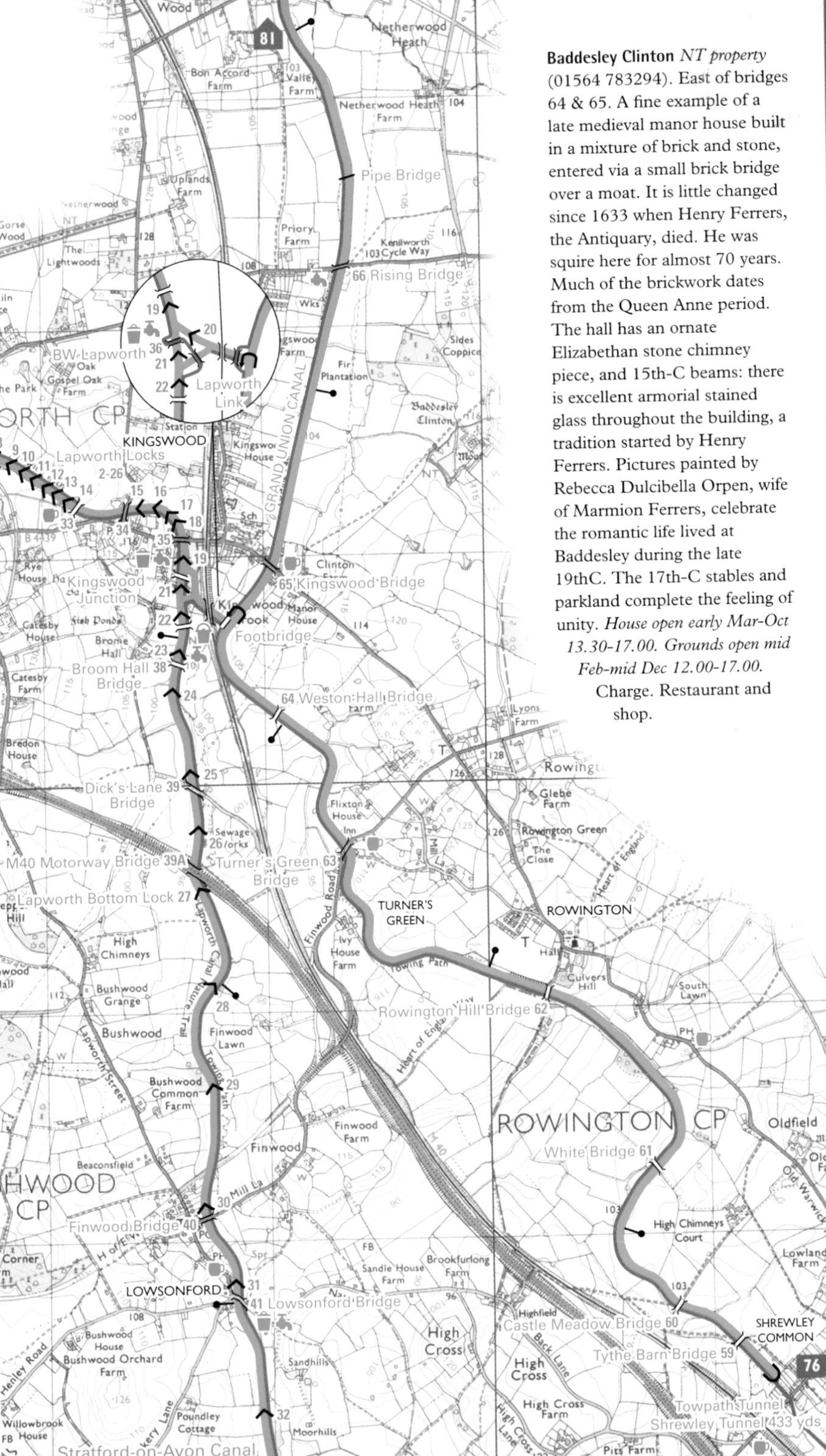

Baddesley Clinton *NT property* (01564 783294). East of bridges 64 & 65. A fine example of a late medieval manor house built in a mixture of brick and stone, entered via a small brick bridge over a moat. It is little changed since 1633 when Henry Ferrers, the Antiquary, died. He was squire here for almost 70 years. Much of the brickwork dates from the Queen Anne period. The hall has an ornate Elizabethan stone chimney piece, and 15th-C beams: there is excellent armorial stained glass throughout the building, a tradition started by Henry Ferrers. Pictures painted by Rebecca Dulcibella Orpen, wife of Marmion Ferrers, celebrate the romantic life lived at Baddesley during the late 19thC. The 17th-C stables and parkland complete the feeling of unity. *House open early Mar-Oct 13.30-17.00. Grounds open mid Feb-mid Dec 12.00-17.00.* Charge. Restaurant and shop.

Knowle

The canal now continues its northerly route, passing through countryside which is surprisingly peaceful. Knowle Locks introduce more hilly countryside again, and this green and pleasant land continues right through to Solihull, concealing the nearness of Birmingham. The flight of five wide locks at Knowle used to be six narrow ones, until the 1930 improvements: the remains of the old ones can still be seen alongside the new, together with the side ponds (originally built to save water). The locks are comparatively deep, and are well maintained and pleasantly situated. They are also the northernmost wide locks for many miles now, since all the Birmingham canals have narrow locks. Knowle is set back from the canal, but warrants a visit, especially to see the church. Continuing north west through wooded country, the canal passes under the M42 motorway and crosses the River Blyth on a small aqueduct.

● **Knowle**
W. Midlands. All services. Despite its proximity to Birmingham, Knowle still survives as a village, albeit rather self-consciously. A number of old buildings thankfully remain, some dating from the Middle Ages and including such gems as Chester House (now the library), which illustrate the advances in timber frame construction from the 13th to the 15thC. Have a look at the splendid knot garden around the back. Half a mile north of the village is Grimshaw Hall, a gabled 16th-C house noted for its decorative brickwork. There are good views of it from the canal.

Church of St John the Baptist, St Lawrence and St Anne Knowle. This remarkable church was built as a result of the efforts of Walter Cook, a wealthy man who founded a chapel here in 1396, and completed the present church in 1402. Prior to its building the parishioners of Knowle had to make a 6-mile round trip each Sunday to the church at Hampton-in-Arden. This involved crossing the River Blythe, an innocuous brook today, but in medieval times 'a greate and daungerous water' which 'noyther man nor beaste can passe wt. owte daunger of peryshing'. The building is built in the Perpendicular style, with a great deal of intricate stonework. There is much of interest to be seen inside, including the roof timbers, the original font and a medieval dug-out chest. Behind the church is the three-acre Children's Field, given to the National Trust by the Reverend T. Downing 'to be used for games'.

WE ARE THE OVALTINE-EES . . .

Dr George Wander founded the company which was to manufacture Ovaltine in Switzerland in 1864. Finding a ready market in England, the company established a factory at Kings Langley, beside what is now the Grand Union Canal. In 1925 they decided to build their own fleet of narrow boats to bring coal to this factory from Warwickshire. Their boats were always immaculately maintained, with the words 'Drink delicious Ovaltine for Health' emblazoned in orange and yellow on a very dark blue background. The last boat arrived at Kings Langley on 17 April 1959.

Pubs and Restaurants

Black Boy Warwick Road, at bridge 69 (01564 772655). A traditional pub, built in 1793, sporting a canalside garden with children's play area. Bass real ale and excellent bar meals with a choice of 72 main courses served *lunchtimes and evenings every day*. Vegetarian choices. Children welcome.

✕ **Wilsons Arms** Warwick Road, Knowle (01564 772559). A Toby Carvery pub which dates from the 16thC. The older part still retains much of its character. Bass and M & B real ale, and carvery served *lunchtimes and evenings every day*, with a vegetarian menu. Outside seating. Children welcome.

Heron's Nest (01564 771177). Canalside at bridge 75. A friendly pub serving Bass and M & B real ale. Bar meals *lunchtimes and evenings every day*. Children welcome. Garden.

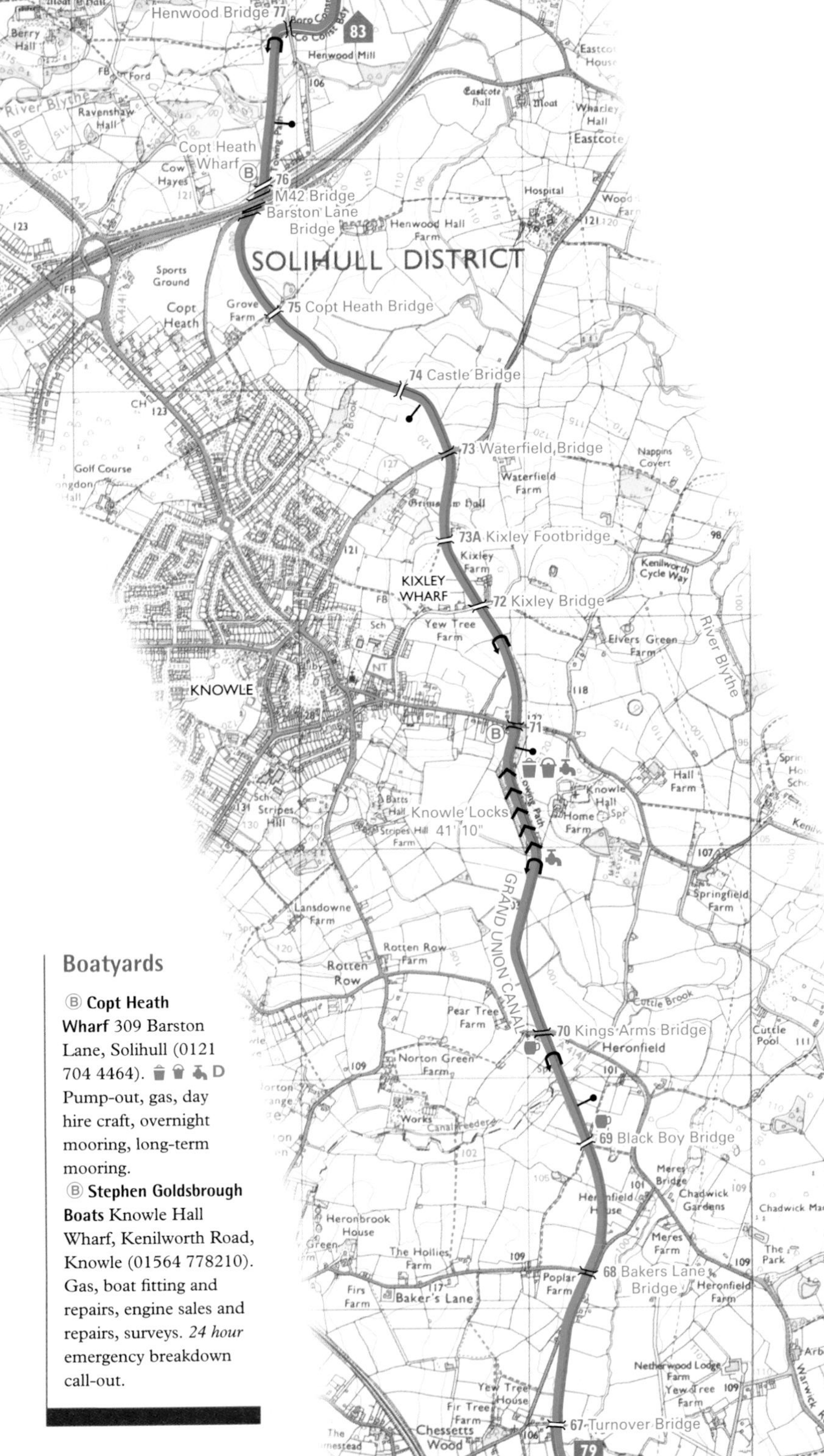

Boatyards

Ⓑ **Copt Heath Wharf** 309 Barston Lane, Solihull (0121 704 4464). D Pump-out, gas, day hire craft, overnight mooring, long-term mooring.

Ⓑ **Stephen Goldsbrough Boats** Knowle Hall Wharf, Kenilworth Road, Knowle (01564 778210). Gas, boat fitting and repairs, engine sales and repairs, surveys. *24 hour* emergency breakdown call-out.

Solihull

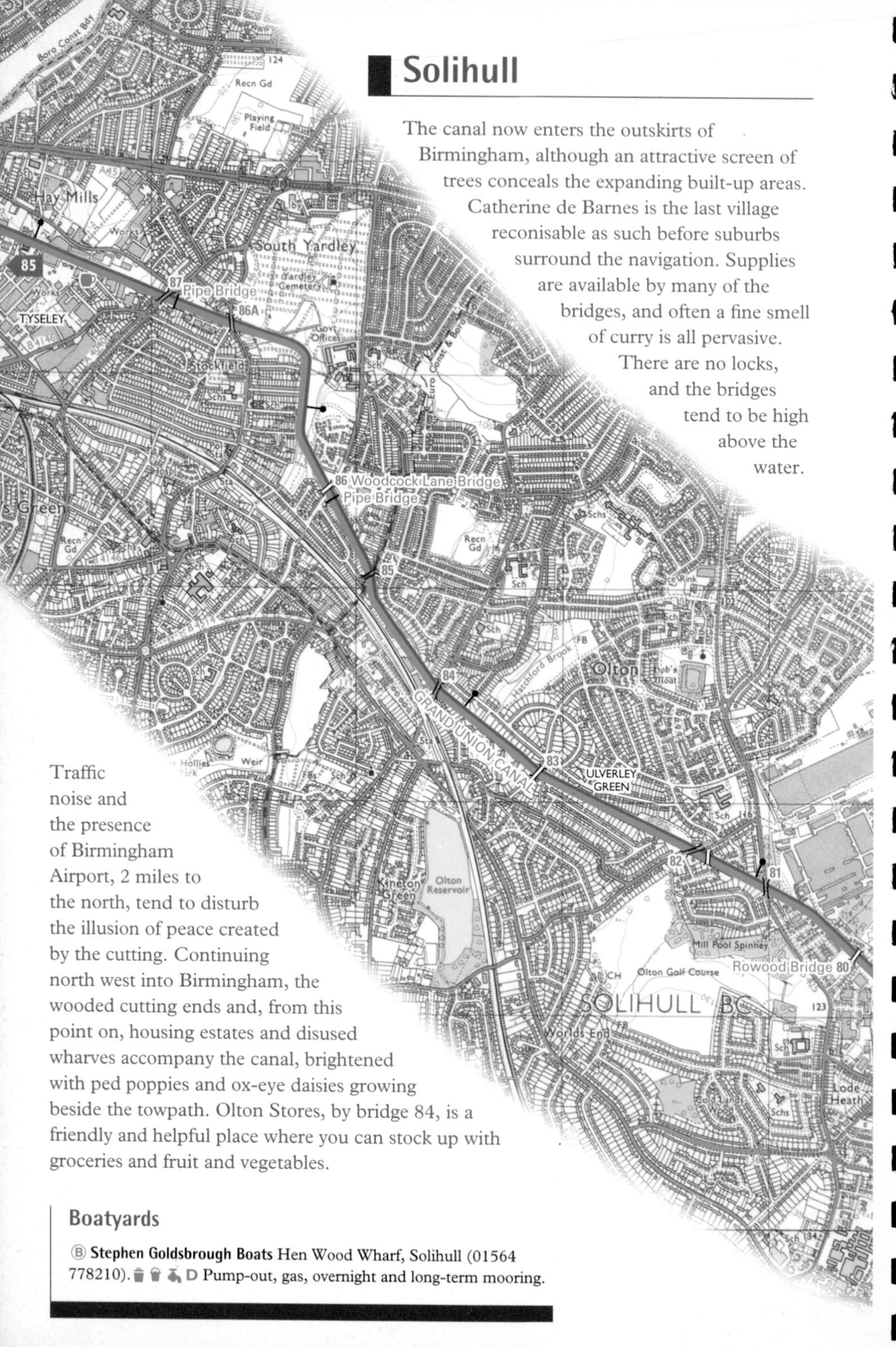

The canal now enters the outskirts of Birmingham, although an attractive screen of trees conceals the expanding built-up areas. Catherine de Barnes is the last village reconisable as such before suburbs surround the navigation. Supplies are available by many of the bridges, and often a fine smell of curry is all pervasive. There are no locks, and the bridges tend to be high above the water.

Traffic noise and the presence of Birmingham Airport, 2 miles to the north, tend to disturb the illusion of peace created by the cutting. Continuing north west into Birmingham, the wooded cutting ends and, from this point on, housing estates and disused wharves accompany the canal, brightened with ped poppies and ox-eye daisies growing beside the towpath. Olton Stores, by bridge 84, is a friendly and helpful place where you can stock up with groceries and fruit and vegetables.

Boatyards

Ⓑ **Stephen Goldsbrough Boats** Hen Wood Wharf, Solihull (01564 778210). D Pump-out, gas, overnight and long-term mooring.

- **Catherine de Barnes**
  W. Midlands. PO, tel, stores, garage. A higgledy-piggledy village far from the romanticism implied by the name. However, a convenient supply centre with easy access from the canal before the bulk of Birmingham begins to make its presence felt.
- **Elmdon Heath**
  W. Midlands. PO, tel, stores, garage. A suburb of Solihull useful for supplies.
- **Solihull**
  W. Midlands. PO, tel, stores, garage, cinema, station. A modern commuter development, with fine public buildings. What used to be the town centre, dominated by the tall spire of the parish church, is now a shopping area.

St Alphege Church Solihull. Built of red sandstone, it is almost all late 13th-C and early 14th-C. The lofty interior contains work of all periods, including a Jacobean pulpit, a 17th-C communion rail, 19th-C stained glass and a few notable monuments.

Tourist Information Centre Central Library, Homer Road, Solihull (0121 704 6130).

Pubs and Restaurants

Boat Inn Catherine de Barnes (0121 705 0474). A well-kept and friendly pub, offering real ale, together with bar meals *all day, every day*, including vegetarian dishes. Children are welcome, and there is a garden.

Longfellows English Restaurant Catherine de Barnes (0121 705 0547). *L Tue-Fri, D Tue-Sat.*

The Barge Stop Tyseley. Between bridges 87 and 88. Food served all day.

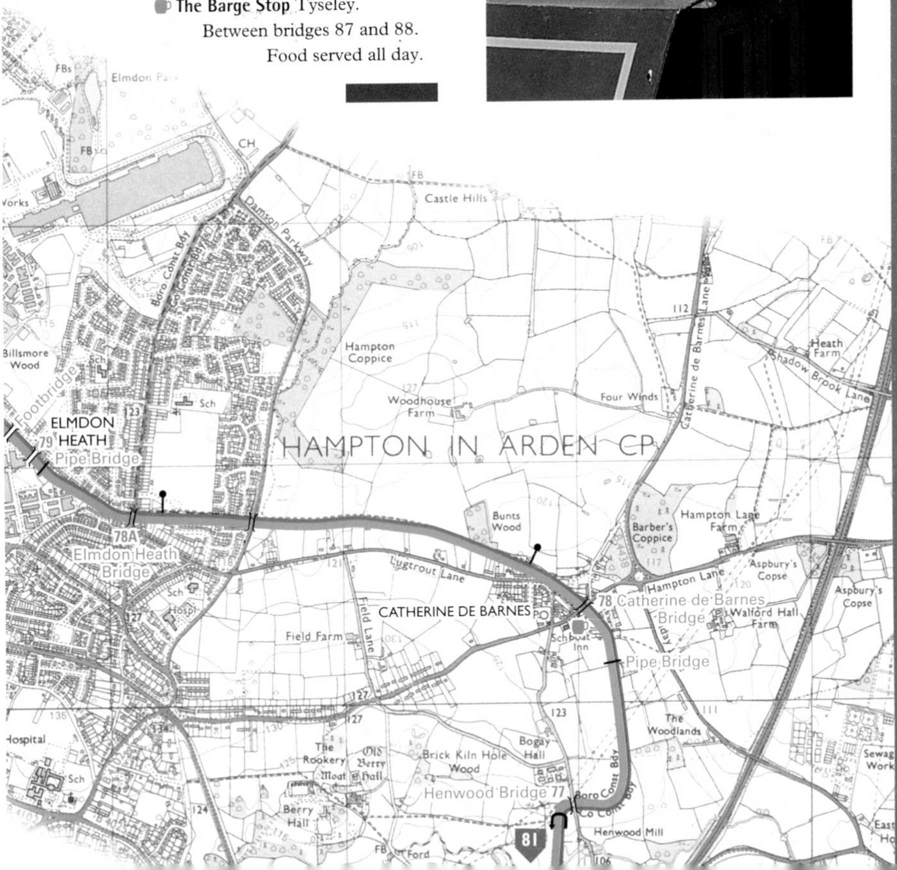

Birmingham

The canal curves past the large Energy from Waste plant and the Ackers Trust Basin before reaching Camp Hill Locks. These, and all the succeeding locks, are narrow. After passing through subterranean vaults formed by the criss-crossing of railway viaducts, Bordesley Junction is reached. Ahead, beyond the junction, the canal continues towards the Birmingham Canal Main Line, joining the Birmingham & Fazeley Canal at Aston Junction, passing a fine collection of old wharf buildings on the way. Heading north from Bordesley Junction, the Grand Union is accompanied by pleasantly transformed surroundings to join the Birmingham & Fazeley Canal at Salford Junction (see Book 3).

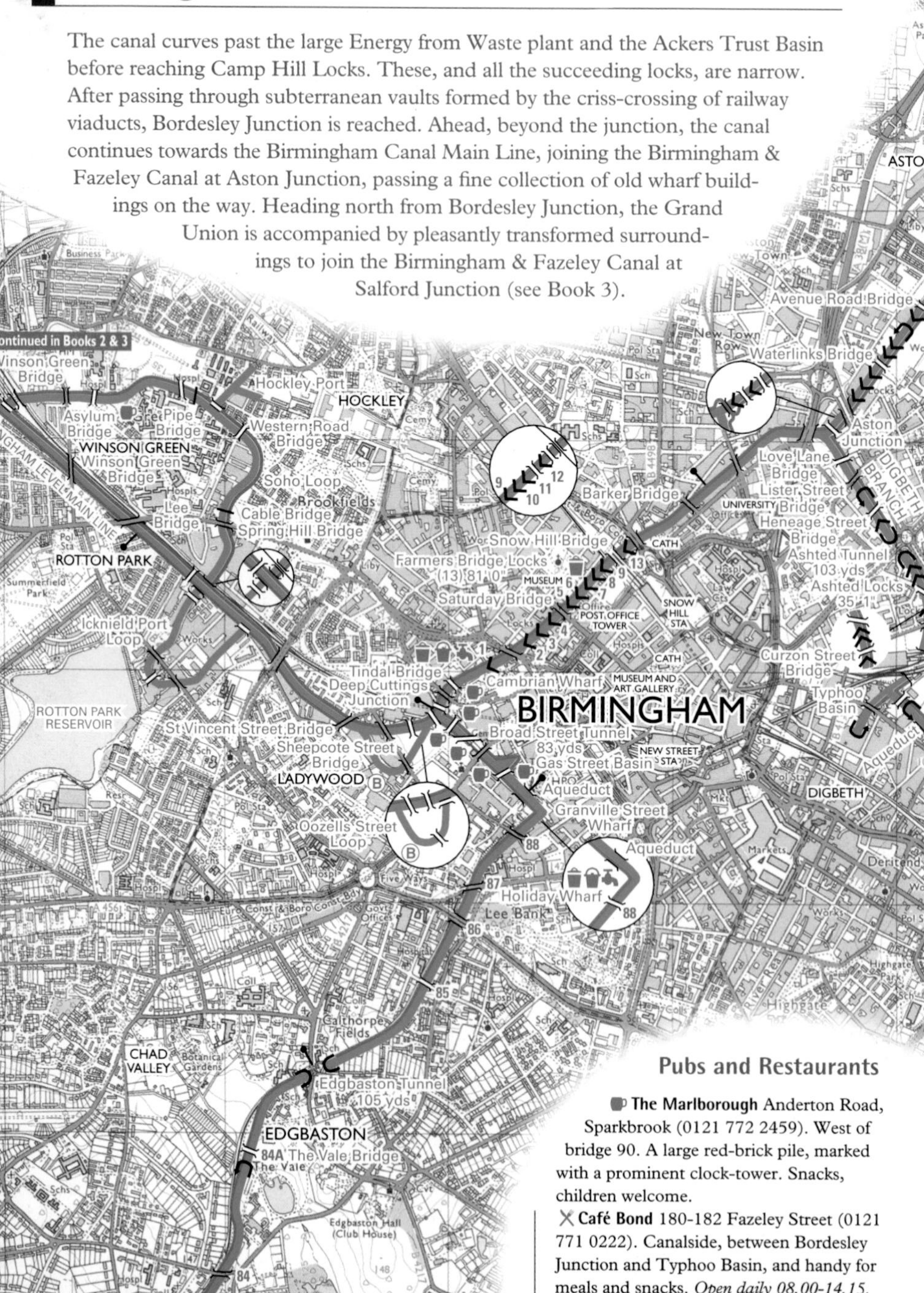

Pubs and Restaurants

The Marlborough Anderton Road, Sparkbrook (0121 772 2459). West of bridge 90. A large red-brick pile, marked with a prominent clock-tower. Snacks, children welcome.

Café Bond 180-182 Fazeley Street (0121 771 0222). Canalside, between Bordesley Junction and Typhoo Basin, and handy for meals and snacks. *Open daily 08.00-14.15.*

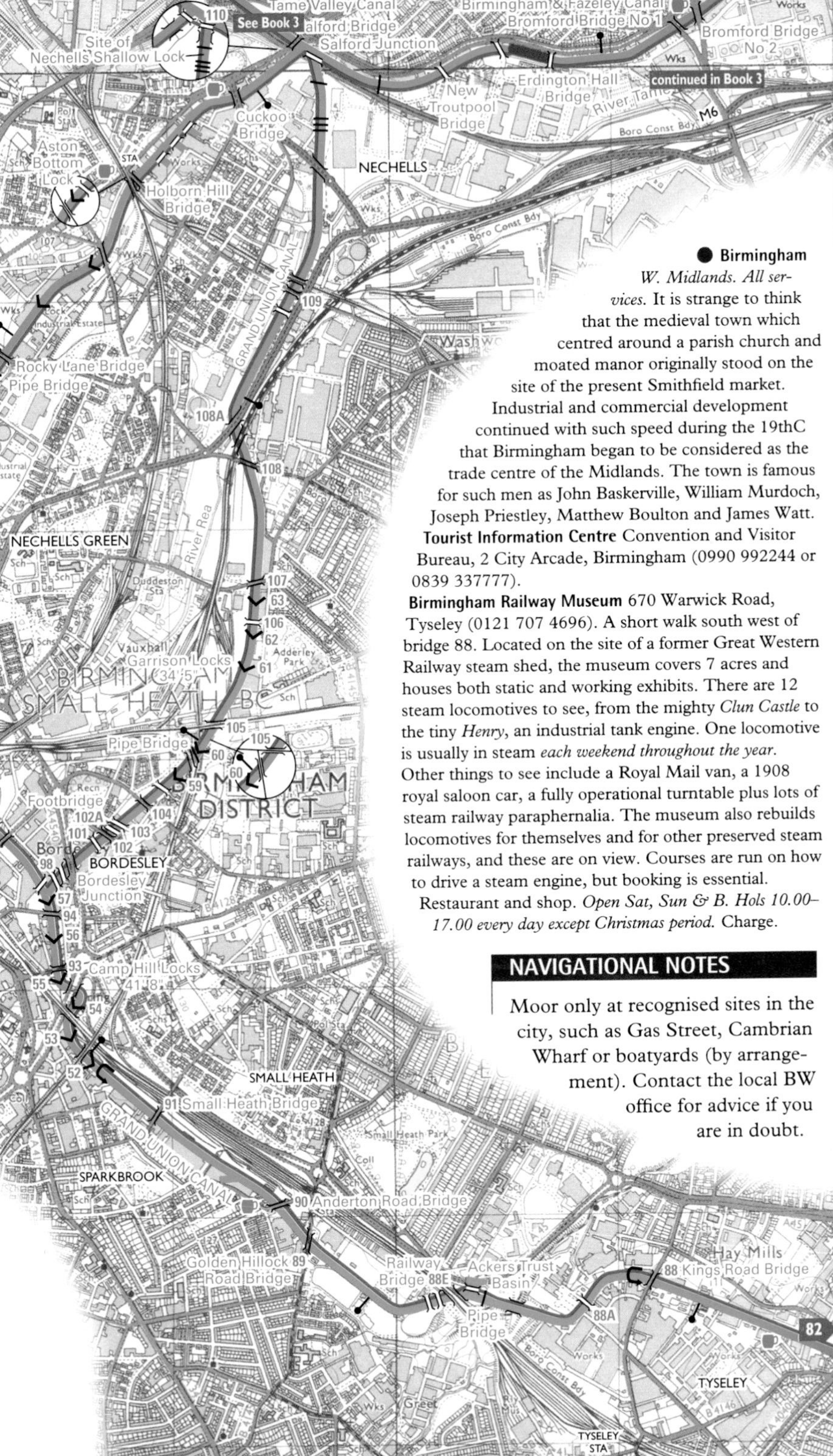

● **Birmingham** *W. Midlands. All services.* It is strange to think that the medieval town which centred around a parish church and moated manor originally stood on the site of the present Smithfield market. Industrial and commercial development continued with such speed during the 19thC that Birmingham began to be considered as the trade centre of the Midlands. The town is famous for such men as John Baskerville, William Murdoch, Joseph Priestley, Matthew Boulton and James Watt.

Tourist Information Centre Convention and Visitor Bureau, 2 City Arcade, Birmingham (0990 992244 or 0839 337777).

Birmingham Railway Museum 670 Warwick Road, Tyseley (0121 707 4696). A short walk south west of bridge 88. Located on the site of a former Great Western Railway steam shed, the museum covers 7 acres and houses both static and working exhibits. There are 12 steam locomotives to see, from the mighty *Clun Castle* to the tiny *Henry*, an industrial tank engine. One locomotive is usually in steam *each weekend throughout the year.* Other things to see include a Royal Mail van, a 1908 royal saloon car, a fully operational turntable plus lots of steam railway paraphernalia. The museum also rebuilds locomotives for themselves and for other preserved steam railways, and these are on view. Courses are run on how to drive a steam engine, but booking is essential. Restaurant and shop. *Open Sat, Sun & B. Hols 10.00–17.00 every day except Christmas period.* Charge.

NAVIGATIONAL NOTES

Moor only at recognised sites in the city, such as Gas Street, Cambrian Wharf or boatyards (by arrangement). Contact the local BW office for advice if you are in doubt.

LEE & STORT NAVIGATIONS

MAXIMUM DIMENSIONS

Lee Navigation

Bow to Hertford
Length: 84'
Beam: 16'
Headroom: 7' 3"

Low Bridges *check tides or flood conditions if close to maximum headroom between Limehouse and Old Ford. Also:*
Dicker Mill Bridge, Hertford 6' 10"
Folly Bridge, Hertford 6' 9"
All other bridges are in excess of 7' 9" at normal levels.

Stort Navigation

Length: 85'
Beam: 13' 3"
Headroom: 6' 9"
Draught: 3'

Low Bridges *check flood water conditions if close to maximum headroom at:*
Roydon Rail Bridge 7' 1"
Burnt Mill Bridge 7' 4"
Kecksey Rail Bridge 6' 10"
All other bridges are in excess of 7' 9" at normal levels.

NAVIGATIONAL NOTE

The pound between Limehouse Basin and Old Ford Lock, including the Bow Back Rivers, is semi-tidal and the level, speed and direction of flow will increase if the tide level on Bow Creek at Bow Locks exceeds 20' 4". *Extreme care is needed at this time. Always* check tide times and levels *before* navigating this section.

MANAGER

0207 286 6101

MILEAGE

Lee Navigation

LIMEHOUSE BASIN to
Old Ford Locks: $2^{3}/_{4}$ miles
Lea Bridge: $4^{3}/_{4}$ miles
Pickett's Lock: 10 miles
Enfield Lock: 13 miles
Waltham Abbey: 14 miles
Broxbourne: $18^{1}/_{2}$ miles
FEILDE'S WEIR (junction with River Stort): $20^{1}/_{2}$ miles
St Margaret's: $22_{1}/_{2}$ miles
Ware Bridge: 25 miles
HERTFORD, head of navigation, $27^{3}/_{4}$ miles

Locks: 19

Stort Navigation

FEILDE'S WEIR (junction with River Lee) to
Roydon station: $1^{1}/_{2}$ miles
Burnt Mill: $4^{1}/_{2}$ miles
Harlow Lock: $6^{3}/_{4}$ miles
Sawbridgeworth: $8^{3}/_{4}$ miles
BISHOP'S STORTFORD, head of navigation: $13^{3}/_{4}$ miles

Locks: 15

Parts of the River Lea (the spelling Lee defines the Navigation) were used as navigations in Roman times, and much of the river was navigable before the reign of Elizabeth I. The first legislation passed for the improvement of a navigation was for the Lee in 1425. In 1577 an early pound lock was built at Waltham Abbey, using two sets of mitred gates, a principle that became a standard feature of lock design. In the 17thC the Lee was established as a source of water supply for London, a role it still fulfils. The navigation was steadily improved throughout the 18th and 19thC, under the direction of various well-known engineers. During and immediately after World War I enlargements were carried out to allow 130-ton boats to reach Enfield, and 100-ton boats to Ware and Hertford. In the 1920s further improvements were carried out and in the 1960s locks were mechanised and duplicated. Timber had always been the main support of the Lee navigation, a trade that sadly does not survive today.
The Stort has never been a significant navigation commercially, and has not in fact carried any commercial traffic for some years. The navigation dates back to 1769 when the river was canalised to carry malt and barley as the main traffic. Sir George Duckett was the undertaker and first owner, and after his death the navigation passed through various brewery-associated hands until it was taken over by the Lee Conservancy in 1911. It would have prospered far more if the oft proposed but ill-fated schemes to build a canal from Bishop's Stortford to Cambridge and the Fenland waterways had ever succeeded.

LONDON'S OTHER WATERWAYS

Those who may wish to explore London's minor waterways, including the Bow Back Rivers, should obtain a copy of the *Briefing Notes for Navigating the Thames Tideway* prepared by the St Pancras Cruising Club, St Pancras Yacht Basin, Camley Street, London NW1 0PL (£3.50 as we go to press).

LEE VALLEY REGIONAL PARK

The concept of the Lee Valley Regional Park was developed in response to an increasing scarcity of land available for recreation, sport, entertainment and general enjoyment of leisure for the people of north and east London, Hertfordshire and Essex. The area designated to become the Lee Valley Regional Park was established by Act of Parliament in 1966.

It comprises some 10,000 acres stretching from East India Dock Basin, by the River Thames, up the valley to Ware in Hertfordshire. It has as its backbone the River Lea and the Lee Navigation, which in turn give access to the River Stort in the north of the park and, via the Hertford Union Canal and the Limehouse Cut, the Grand Union Canal in the south.

The park itself is a unique combination of purpose-built sports and leisure facilities strategically located within vast areas of countryside, urban green space and nature reserves. It provides for just about every leisure pastime imaginable – from organised sports to heritage sites, picnics and barbecues, bird watching and angling, and informal walks including, most notably, walks along the towpath and circular walks within the country park.

The River Lea and the navigation are ideal ways to access many areas of the park, which operates two marinas: one at Springfield in East London, and the other in the rural setting of Stanstead Abbots.

For more information contact:

Lee Valley Park Information Centre Abbey Gardens, Waltham Abbey, Essex EN9 1XQ (01992 702200, Web: www.leevalleypark.org.uk). *Open Easter–Oct, daily 09.30–17.00, Nov–Easter, Tue–Sun 09.30–16.30.*

Boat festival at Bishop's Stortford (see page 108)

Bow

Entrance to the River Lee Navigation can be made from:
the Regent's Canal via the Hertford Union Canal (*recommended*);
the Thames via Limehouse Basin and the Limehouse Cut;
the Thames direct up Bow Creek, and through Bow Locks.

The Hertford Union Canal is a short (1¼ miles) canal built in 1830 by Sir George Duckett (son of the Stort Navigation Duckett), and is often referred to as Duckett's Cut. It is a useful connection between the Regent's Canal and the Lee Navigation. It is straight, has three locks, and borders the attractive Victoria Park for most of the way. The route up into the River Lee from the Thames is through the lock into Limehouse Basin (1½ miles below Tower Bridge), then east along the Limehouse Cut to Bow Locks and Old Ford. The other entrance to the Lee Navigation is by way of Bow Creek, whose mouth is nearly 5 miles further down the Thames from the Limehouse Basin entrance.

The sinuous Bow Creek is a tidal river – it is in fact the mouth of the River Lee. It gives access for those in suitable craft to the backwaters bordering Stratford. Nearby is the Abbey Mills Pumping Station, a Gothic-Byzantine style building designed in 1868 by Bazalgette, who was also responsible for the Thames Embankments. The Three Mills at Bow still remain from the 18thC, although they were modified some years later. There is a handy supermarket to the west here. Hackney Marsh on the east bank of the canal is a footballer's delight: there are many pitches here, by the Lee Valley Sports Centre. As the river approaches Lea Bridge, it passes the Middlesex Filter Beds Nature Reserve: there is also pleasant parkland beyond the bridge.

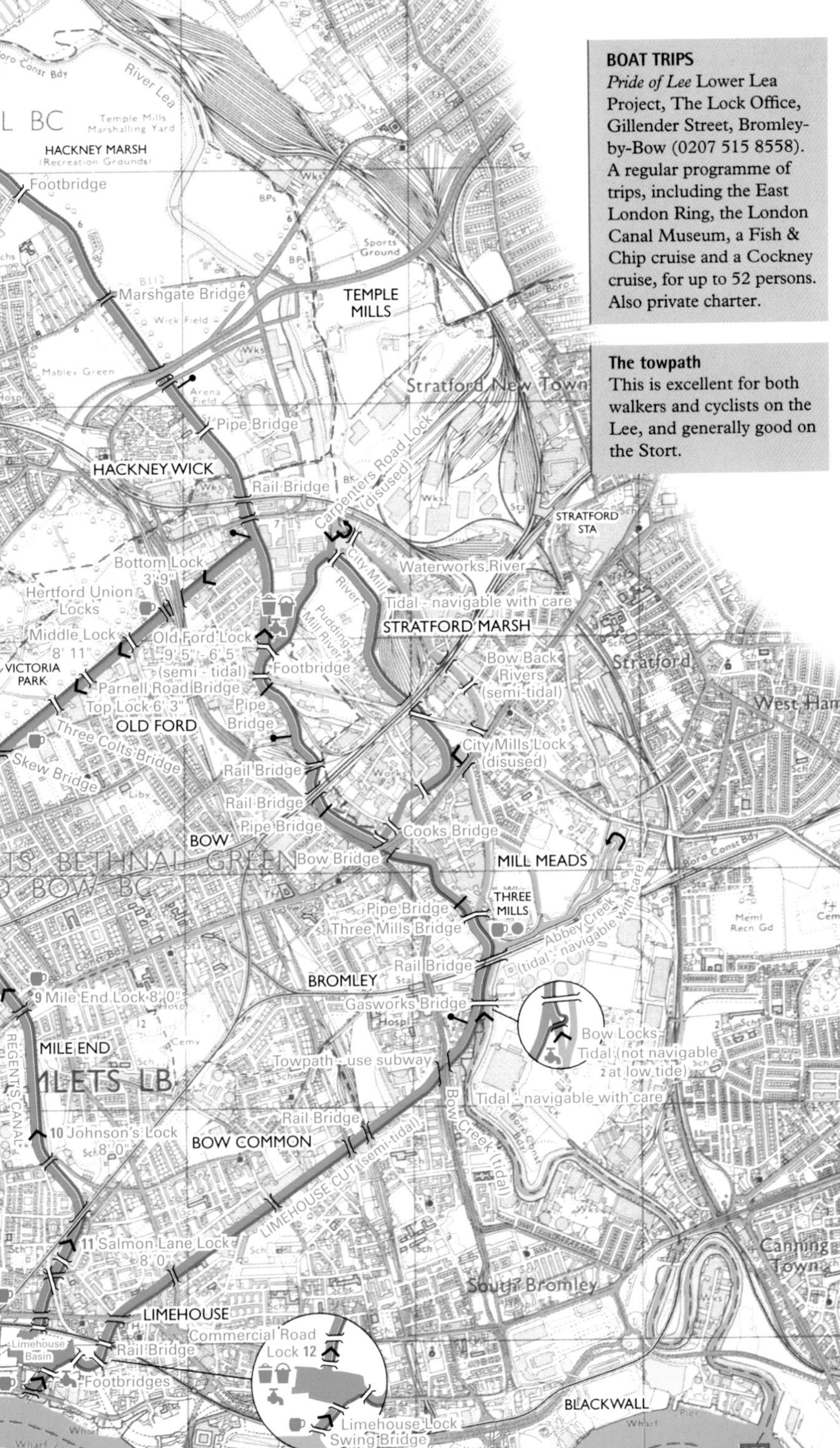

BOAT TRIPS

Pride of Lee Lower Lea Project, The Lock Office, Gillender Street, Bromley-by-Bow (0207 515 8558). A regular programme of trips, including the East London Ring, the London Canal Museum, a Fish & Chip cruise and a Cockney cruise, for up to 52 persons. Also private charter.

The towpath

This is excellent for both walkers and cyclists on the Lee, and generally good on the Stort.

NAVIGATIONAL NOTES

1 Limehouse Lock can accommodate craft 98' x 25' 4". It is *open summer, daily 08.00–18.00 (closes 16.00 winter)*. Telephone 0207 308 9930 to check opening times.

2 Passage through Bow Locks is subject to pre-booking and is dependent upon tide, *between 05.00–22.00 all year*. The locks can accommodate craft 88' x 18'. Bow Locks are not usually manned, and anyone wishing to pass through must notify the lock keeper *24hrs in advance* on 0207 987 5661 (24hr answer phone) or VHF channel 80. A leaflet giving full details of lock opening times is available from British Waterways, The Toll House, Delamere Terrace, Little Venice, London W2 6ND (0207 286 6101).

3 All locks on the River Lee between Old Ford and Rammey Marsh (except Picketts) are mechanised, and you will need a BW key and a windlass to operate them. There are instructions at each lock.

Boatyards

Ⓑ **Limehouse Basin Marina** 1 Northey Street, E14 (0207 537 2828). Administered by the Cruising Association. Pump-out, overnight moorings, long-term moorings, telephone, toilets, showers, laundry facilities. Bar and catering for marina users. BW licences, windlasses and lock keys.

The Bow Back Rivers Never a part of the Lee Navigation as such, this network of channels has, over the years, been the site of many mills. The main channels in the system are the Pudding Mill River, the City Mills River, Bow Back River, Waterworks River, Three Mills Wall River, Prescott Channel and the Abbey Creek. At the turn of the century these channels had largely fallen into disrepair and posed a potential flooding problem. During the 1920s, when unemployment was high, it was decided to instigate a rescue programme and, in 1930, the River Lee (Flood Relief) act was passed, allowing the building of new locks and the dredging of channels. Subsequently they again fell into disrepair, but recent dredging and refurbishment works have made them into an area worthy of exploration for those in *suitable, shallow-draught* craft. Cruising notes are available from BW or the St Pancras Cruising Club.

The House Mill Three Mills Lane, Bromley-by-Bow, E3 (0208 980 4626). One of two tidal mills on this site. The Domesday Survey recorded eight mills in the manor of Hame, now known as West Ham, and one of them would certainly have been here. During the medieval period the mill was ideally suited to provide flour to the bakers of Stratford-atte-Bow, who in turn baked bread for the City of London. In 1588, one of the two remaining mills on this site was described as a gunpowder mill. Purchased in 1728 by a Huguenot, Peter Lefevre, the mills worked in conjunction with a distillery, feeding the waste products to pigs. The House Mill was constructed in 1776 in the Dutch style by Daniel Bisson, on an artificial island, between two houses occupied by the miller and his family – hence the name. It is 80 feet long by 45 feet wide and bridges four mill races, and is probably the largest tidal mill in the country. The Clock Mill opposite was rebuilt in 1817, incorporating a clock dated 1753, and an earlier bell. A nearby windmill stood until 1840. The House Mill operated until 1940, and the Clock Mill until 1952, and both probably owe their survival to their integrated operation with a distillery. Taking advantage of the tidal flow in the River Lea, the mills had a head of 50 acres of water, allowing them to operate for about 7 hours during each tide. The House Mill fabric has been restored and work is in progress on the machinery. The site is well worth visiting. *Open late May–Oct, Sun 14.00–16.00; Mar-Dec, first Sun in month 11.00-16.00.* Charge. Special visits can be arranged for parties – telephone 0208 980 4626. The annual Three Mills Rally of Boats is held here on the *last weekend in June each year* – telephone 01992 702200 for details.

Middlesex Filter Beds Nature Reserve Near Lea Bridge (01992 702200). This disused water filtration plant right on the river bank now demonstrates stages of wetland succession, amidst industrial-archaeological artifacts and sculpture. *Open during school summer holiday, Mon–Fri 10.00–17.00; G Fri–end Sep, weekends & B Hols 10.00–18.00; Oct–Easter, weekends & B Hols 10.00–16.00.*

Tourist Information Centre Central Hall, Mare Street, Hackney E8 (0208 985 9055).

Pubs and Restaurants

Barley Mow Narrow Street, E14 (0207 265 8931). In the original Dockmaster's office, at the entrance to Limehouse Dock, with superb views up and down the River Thames, this splendid waterside pub serves Burton and Tetley's real ale and good food *lunchtimes and evenings every day*, with vegetarian options. The airy back bar is decorated with some interesting relics, including a turtle shell and rowing skiffs, and there are riverside seats. Children are welcome.

The House They Left Behind Ropemakers Fields, Limehouse, E14 (0207 538 5102). 1/4 mile east of Limehouse Lock. The only building left standing in a demolished terrace, this shored-up pub offers a warm and friendly welcome and serves an appetizing range of home cooked food *every day 11.00–23.00*, with vegetarian choices. Bass, HB and a guest real ale are available, and children are welcome. There is an outside seating area. Boules can be played, and there is live music *Thu*, and a DJ *Fri*.

The Still Café Three Mills Island (0208 215 3305). Situated in part of the old distillery complex, this café contains one of the original copper stills, and overlooks the river and the Clock Mill. Real ales, wine, coffee and home-made food. *Open Mon-Fri 09.30-23.00, Sat 11.00-23.00, Sun 11.00-19.00.*

Grapes Narrow Street, Limehouse, E14 (0207 987 4396). 1/4 mile east of Limehouse Lock. Beautifully kept one-bar pub behind an inviting traditional façade, where the balcony area overhangs the river. Charles Dickens lived upstairs, and based the Three Jolly Fellowship Porters, in *Our Mutual Friend (1865)*, upon this pub.They serve Adnams, Burton, Tetley's and a guest real ale. Bar meals and an upstairs fish restaurant are *available lunchtimes Mon–Fri and Mon–Sat evenings, with a Sun lunchtime roast*. There are always vegetarian choices. Skittles and other traditional bar games such as shove ha'penny can be played (ask at the bar). Children *over 14 years* are welcome.

Princess of Wales Lea Bridge Road, E5 (0208 533 3463). Waterside by Lea Bridge. Comfortable pub with a riverside garden, serving Young's real ale. Bar meals, ranging from steaks to sandwiches, served *lunchtimes and evenings (not Sun evenings)*, with vegetarian options. Darts and pin ball can be played.

Ship Aground Lea Bridge Road, E5 (0207 237 3314). Next to the Prince of Wales. Try this friendly city lunchtime pub for Courage real ale and meals *lunchtimes Mon-Fri*. Outside seating.

King's Head Mount Pleasant Hill, E5 (0208 806 4370). A riverside pub, with meals *usually available lunchtimes Mon-Fri*. Children are welcome, and there is a large garden.

The Clock Mill at Bow *(see page 88)*

Tottenham

The river now follows the wide sweeping course that is typical of this navigation. At Walthamstow, about a 1/4 mile north east of Springfield Marina, is the old Copper Mill, built c.1800, to process copper that was brought from the port of London along the Lee. Be wary of racing fours and eights, which emanate from the rowing club near the marina, and there are often groups of young people in canoes, but generally the river is quiet and business-like. Reservoirs to the east block off the view to one side with their high embankments, and the river begins to adopt the rather stark appearance that characterises it for several miles ahead. The reservoirs supply about 15 per cent of London's water, and are now used for sailing, fishing and bird watching. Above Tottenham Lock there are lots of moored craft.

Boatyards

Ⓑ **Lea Valley Marina – Springfield** Springhill, Clapton (0208 806 1717). D Pump-out, gas, overnight and long-term mooring, winter storage, slipway, boatbuilding, boat and engine repairs, toilets, showers. Cruising club and bar.

Pubs and Restaurants

King's Head Mount Pleasant Hill, E5 (0208 806 4370). A welcoming riverside pub serving Bass and guest real ales, with meals *from midday onwards,* with vegetarian choices. Children are welcome, and there is a large garden, with a listed walnut tree. Garden bar in *summer,* and occasional music *Thu-Sat evenings,* with R&B on *Sun.*

Anchor and Hope High Hill Ferry, Upper Clapton (0208 806 1730). A tiny riverside pub with one bar, amidst towering blocks of flats, serving Fuller's real ale. Children are welcome and there is waterfront seating and moorings.

Robin Hood Tavern High Hill Ferry, Upper Clapton (0208 806 4134). A family pub overlooking the marshes, serving Courage real ale. Meals are available *all day every day, with a Sunday roast.* Children welcome, and outdoor play area, garden and barbecue *B. Hols and summer weekends.* Mooring.

Narrow Boat Reedham Close, Tottenham (0208 808 5680). 1/4 mile south of Tottenham Lock. Canalside pub incorporated into a row of modern maisonettes, serving a range of guest real ales. Bar meals are served *lunchtimes until 19.00,* with vegetarian options. There is a sheltered riverside garden where barbecues are occasionally held *in the summer.* Children are welcome *for meals only.*

The Water's Edge (0208 365 1289). By Stonebridge Lock. Children are welcome, and there is a patio. Occasional entertainments, such as on Guy Fawkes night, but nothing regular.

Walthamstow Reservoirs An SSSI alongside the east bank of the navigation and an important part of London's water supply, controlled by Thames Water. Access is allowed only for bird watching or fishing by permits obtained from Thames Water, 2 Forest Road, Tottenham, N17 (0208 808 1527). There is a variety of land and water birds, including great crested grebes and yellow wagtails, as well as two thriving, long-established heronries on islands in reservoirs 1 and 5. The stock of fish in the reservoirs is being steadily increased and the reservoirs where fishing is permitted may vary each year; details can be obtained from Thames Water.

Walthamstow Marsh Nature Reserve (01992 702200). 1/2 mile upstream from Lea Bridge, on the east bank. Now an SSSI, this is the last remnant of the once extensive riverside marshes. A V Roe flew his 'yellow terror', the first all-British built and piloted aeroplane, from here in 1909.

NAVIGATIONAL NOTES

It is not advisable to venture up any of the side creeks feeding into the river – they are usually heavily silted up and are not open to navigation.

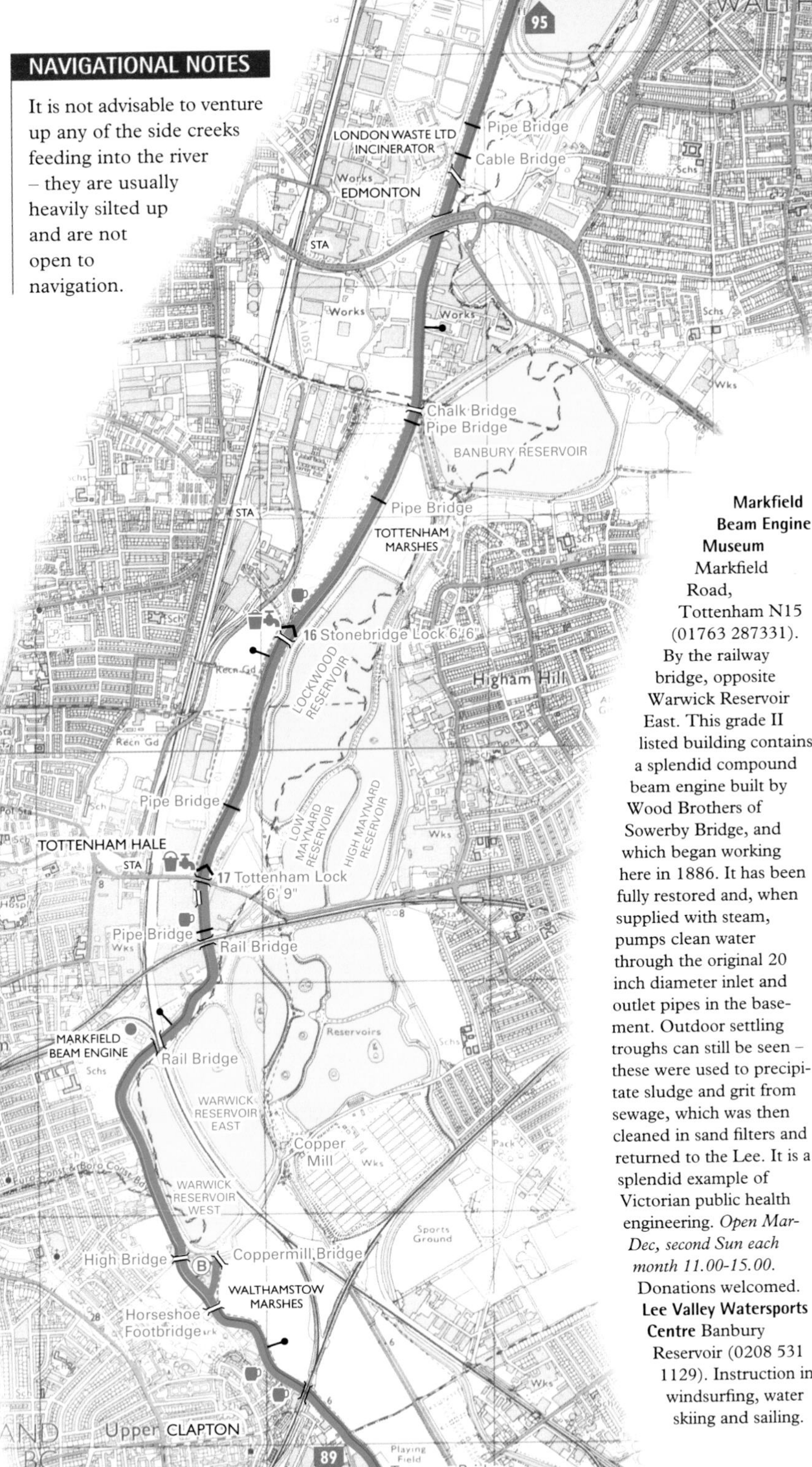

Markfield Beam Engine Museum Markfield Road, Tottenham N15 (01763 287331). By the railway bridge, opposite Warwick Reservoir East. This grade II listed building contains a splendid compound beam engine built by Wood Brothers of Sowerby Bridge, and which began working here in 1886. It has been fully restored and, when supplied with steam, pumps clean water through the original 20 inch diameter inlet and outlet pipes in the basement. Outdoor settling troughs can still be seen – these were used to precipitate sludge and grit from sewage, which was then cleaned in sand filters and returned to the Lee. It is a splendid example of Victorian public health engineering. *Open Mar-Dec, second Sun each month 11.00-15.00.* Donations welcomed.

Lee Valley Watersports Centre Banbury Reservoir (0208 531 1129). Instruction in windsurfing, water skiing and sailing.

Enfield

The navigation now maintains a direct course, passing Pickett's Lock, where the Lee Valley Park Authority has built a large covered leisure and sports centre, as well as a golf course, multi-screen cinema and restaurant. The King George & William Girling reservoirs accompany the navigation, lying behind high embankments to the east; so do ever-present power lines, which stride along as purposefully as the river. Ponders End Locks provide canal interest in this rather bleak area, with a handy wine merchant situated in a converted warehouse on Columbia Wharf, close by, and a pub in a listed former pumping house just north of the bridge. The river then passes a series of disused loading bays and the wharves of forgotten factories, the visible manifestation of the switch from water transport to road. In summer poppies and comfrey on the riverside brighten the scene as the attractive brick buildings and dry-dock of British Waterways Enfield Yard appear. Enfield Lock, accompanied by a handsome house dated 1889, signals the end of nearly 4 miles of reservoirs: beyond a fine riverside terrace the landscape at last starts to open out.

King George's Reservoir An SSSI managed by Thames Water, 2 Forest Road, Tottenham, N17 (0208 808 1527). Vast numbers of wintering ducks, including goldeneye and goosander may be seen here, along with some 30,000 gulls. There is no access to William Girling Reservoir, to the south.

Lee Valley Leisure Centre Pickett's Lock, Edmonton (0208 345 6666). All sorts of sports activities, including squash, yoga, swimming, golf and many others. Sauna, solarium, caravan and camping site. *Open daily.*

● **Enfield**

Middx. All services. Interesting features in this town include the Church of St Andrew in the market place, where the chancel window is 13th-C, and Gentlemen's Row, which probably dates from the early 18thC, and is completely preserved from numbers 9 to 23. Charles Lamb (1775–1834), the essayist who devoted his life to his rather unstable sister Mary, and who is perhaps best known for his *Essays of Elia*, stayed at no. 17 in 1827. To the north is Forty Hall, built in 1632 for Sir Nicholas Raynton, Lord Mayor of London.

Pubs and Restaurants

Navigation Inn (0208 804 7788). Just north of Ponders End Locks. A Beefeater pub serving Boddingtons, Marston's and Wadworth's real ale, and restaurant and bar meals *lunchtimes and evenings every day*. There are always vegetarian choices. Children are welcomed, and can amuse themselves in the 'discovery room', or play in the garden.

Greyhound (01992 764612). A fine corner local serving McMullens real ale. Bar meals are available *Mon–Fri lunchtimes and evenings and Sat afternoons*. If meals are required *on Sun, book a week in advance*. There are always vegetarian choices. Children are welcomed, and there is an outside patio area. Occasional entertainment. Mooring nearby.

SLAVING AWAY

Commercial traffic on the Lee Navigation has ebbed away over the years. During the mid-1950s horse drawn lighters were still journeying as far as Hertford, but this trade is, alas, no more. By 1980 commercial traffic extended no higher than the Enfield Rolling Mills at Brimsdown, with just one tug, the *Vassal*, regularly at work on the river. Powered by a 120hp Gardener diesel engine, she would typically tow a train of two lighters loaded with timber from Bow to Hahn's Wharf at Edmonton. Considerable skill was demonstrated by the skipper, who would propel the first of the train of lighters into a lock under its own momentum, pulling his tug aside at the very last moment. Now trials are in progress with a view to restoring commercial navigation, with tugs being used to tow rubbish container barges between Old Ford and Edmonton.

Boatyards

BW Enfield Yard Ordnance Road, Enfield Lock (01992 764626). BW keys, windlasses and licences. *Open Mon–Fri 08.00–12.00.*

Waltham Abbey

Passing under the busy M25 motorway, the navigation reaches Waltham Town Lock, where there is a handy café. This marks the start of more open country. Those who cruise the Lee between mid-June and mid-April will also discover that this river is very popular with anglers. Please take care to disturb them as little as possible. Waltham Abbey is a fine old town where the ancient abbey, an architectural gem, looks down unperturbed on attractively pedestrianised, but usually busy, streets. To the north the navigation runs into a massive water parkland, the River Lee Country Park, based upon the worked out gravel pits. The lakes are used for fishing, sailing, and as nature reserves. The green chain thus formed now acts as an important wildlife corridor and migration route for birds. Waltham Common Lock is soon followed by Cheshunt Lock and Aqueduct Lock. Duck and geese eggs are sold close-by. A flurry of glasshouses and Nazeing Marsh mark the approach to Broxbourne.

Pubs and Restaurants

Old English Gentleman Waltham Town Lock, Highbridge Street (01992 712714). Canalside pub with a garden serving *lunchtime (not Sun)* bar meals. Children are welcome. Quiz nights and live music.

Welsh Harp Market Square, Waltham Abbey (01992 711113). A traditional town pub. Bar meals available *lunchtimes*, with vegetarian menu. Children are welcome.

Angel Sun Street, Waltham Abbey (01992 718671). A cosy and friendly pub serving McMullen real ale. Good bar meals are served *lunchtimes and evenings*, and vegetarians are catered for. Children are welcome, and there is a garden. Regular entertainment with theme nights, discos, live music and singalongs.

Queens Arms Market Square, Waltham Abbey (01992 768902). Serves Courage, Young's and several guest real ales, along with bar meals *lunchtimes every day*. Children are welcome and there is a garden with barbecues *in the summer*.

Red Cow West of Cheshunt station, Windmill Lane (01992 789701). Well appointed pub serving Bass and Greene King real ale, along with bar meals. Children are welcome and there is a garden. Occasional entertainment with live music.

Maltsters Arms West of Cheshunt station, Windmill Lane (01992 631369). A smart pub serving McMullen real ale. Bar meals are served *lunchtimes and evenings* and vegetarians are catered for. Children are welcome *for meals*. There is outside seating and entertainment with quiz nights, pool and darts.

Waltham Abbey

Essex. MD Thu, Sat. PO, tel, stores, station. The history of the town goes back to before the Norman Conquest when King Harold chose it for development as a centre of learning and religious instruction. The local museum is in Sun Street.

Abbey Church Founded in 1030 as a collegiate church of secular canons. In 1184 it was nominated a mitred abbey and was soon one of the most prosperous and important in the country. Today's building is largely 19th-C, but the Norman nave and aisles still stand. The south chapel is 14th-C and the west tower 16th-C. The Jesse window at the east end is a fine example of Burne-Jones work, executed in 1861. Within the abbey grounds and just outside to the north are several interesting archaeological remains. The Information Centre here provides information, maps, guides, exhibitions and a gift shop. *Open Easter–Oct, daily 09.30–17.00; Nov–Easter, Tue–Sun 10.00–16.00.*

Waltham Abbey Tourist Information Centre Sun Street (01992 652295). Friendly and helpful service, with details of special events at the abbey and elsewhere in the park.

Waltham Cross

Herts. PO, tel, stores, station, cinema. The Eleanor Cross, 1 mile west along the A121, is one of the 12 crosses (of which only three survive) erected by Edward I to commemorate the resting places of his dead queen, Eleanor of Castile, on her last journey from Leicestershire, where she died, to Westminster Abbey. The Cross was built in 1291, but was greatly restored in Ketton stone in the 19thC.

Cheshunt
Herts. PO, tel, stores, station, takeaway. The Church of St Mary's was built in 1418–48 by the then rector of Cheshunt and is an example of the Perpendicular style. Of Cheshunt House not much remains: only one wing of a courtyard house. The former Royal Gunpowder Mills are being developed as a heritage museum.

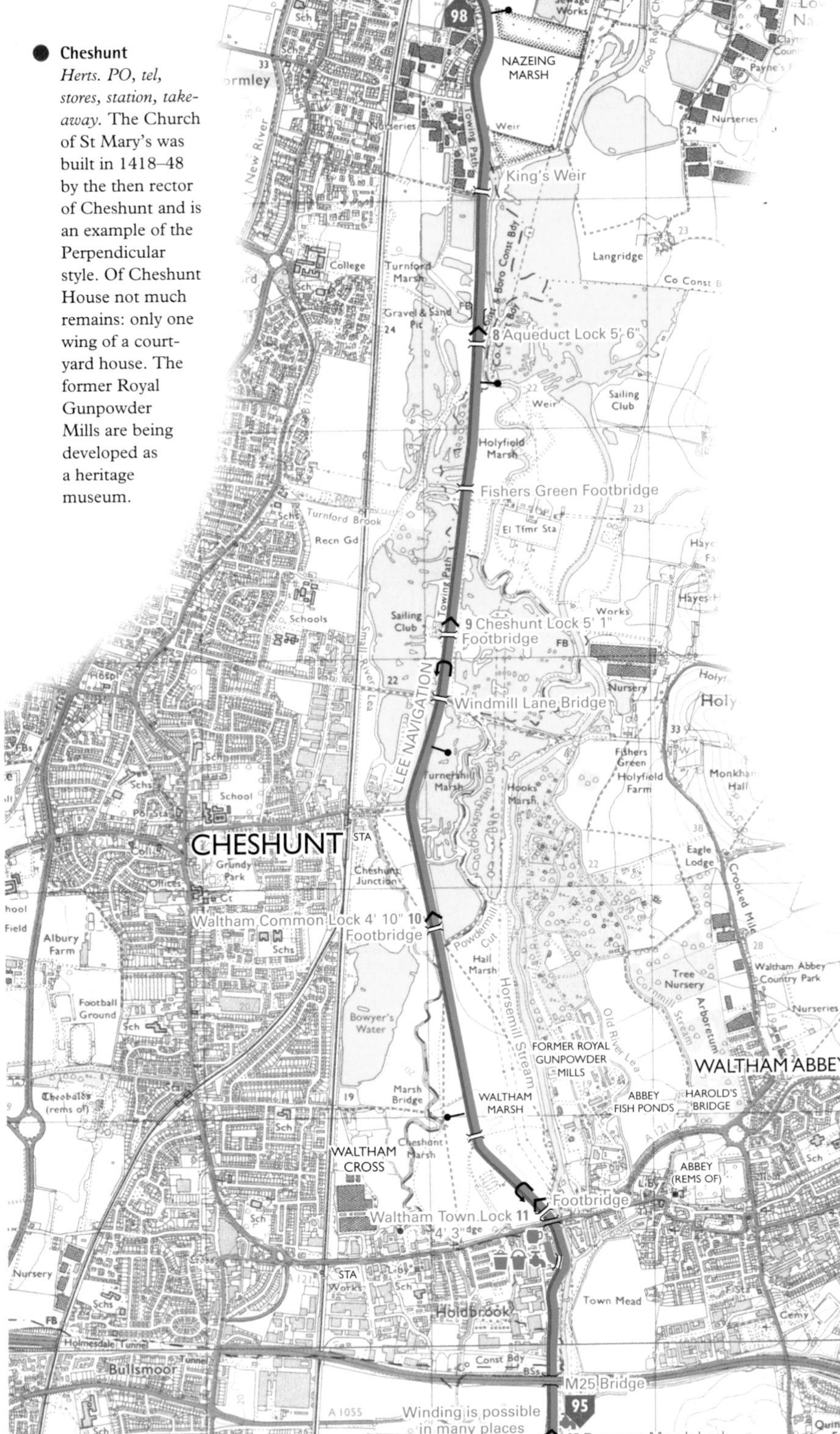

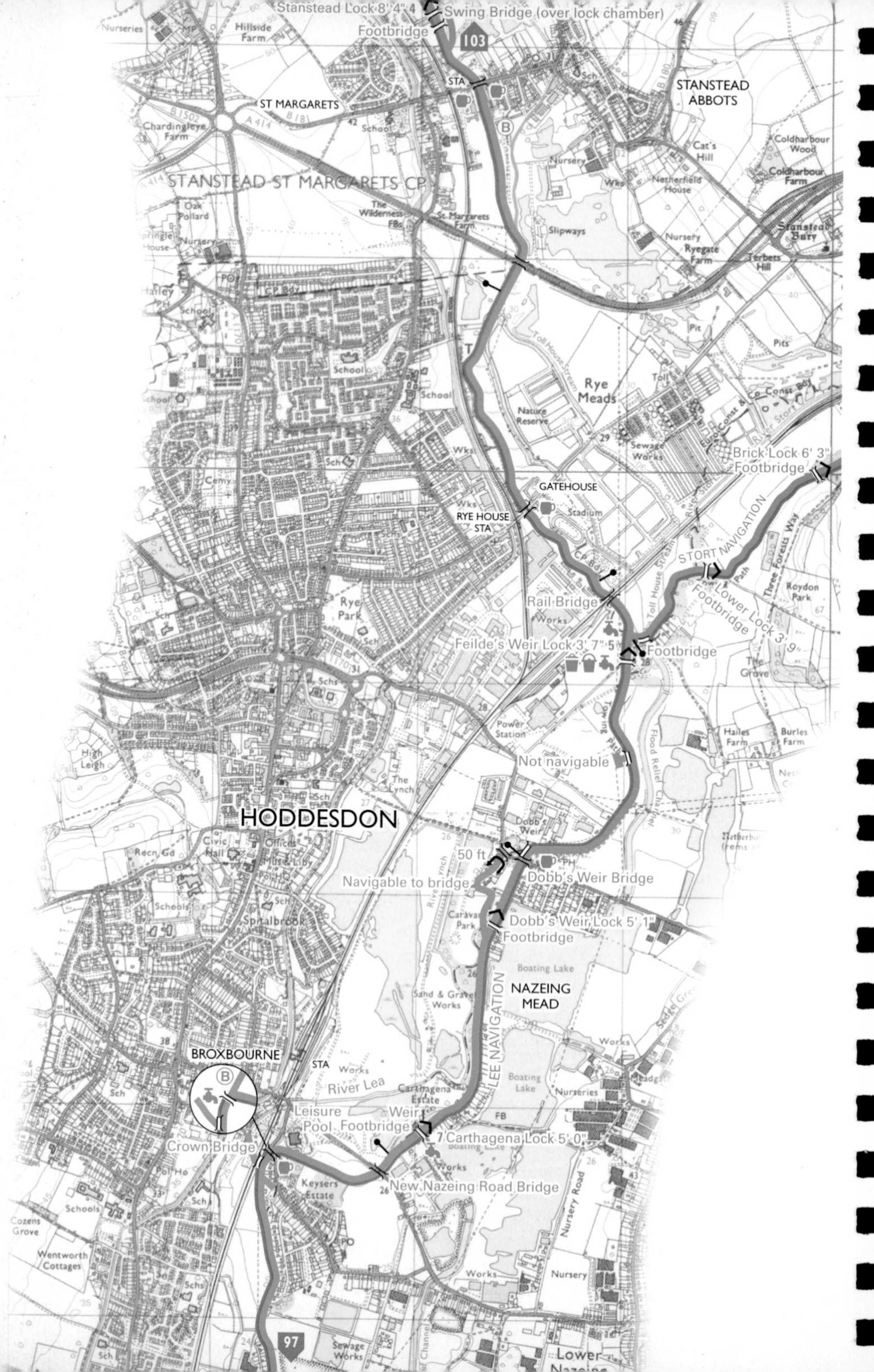
Stanstead Lock 8' 4" 4
Swing Bridge (over lock chamber)
Footbridge
103
STANSTEAD ABBOTS
ST MARGARETS
STANSTEAD ST MARGARETS CP
Rye Meads
Brick Lock 6' 3"
Footbridge
GATEHOUSE
RYE HOUSE STA
STORT NAVIGATION
Lower Lock 3' 9"
Footbridge
Rail Bridge
Feilde's Weir Lock 3' 7" 5
Footbridge
Not navigable
HODDESDON
50 ft
Dobb's Weir Bridge
Navigable to bridge
Dobb's Weir Lock 5' 1"
Footbridge
NAZEING MEAD
LEE NAVIGATION
BROXBOURNE
River Lea
Leisure Pool
Weir
Footbridge
Carthagena Lock 5' 0" 7
Crown Bridge
New Nazeing Road Bridge
97

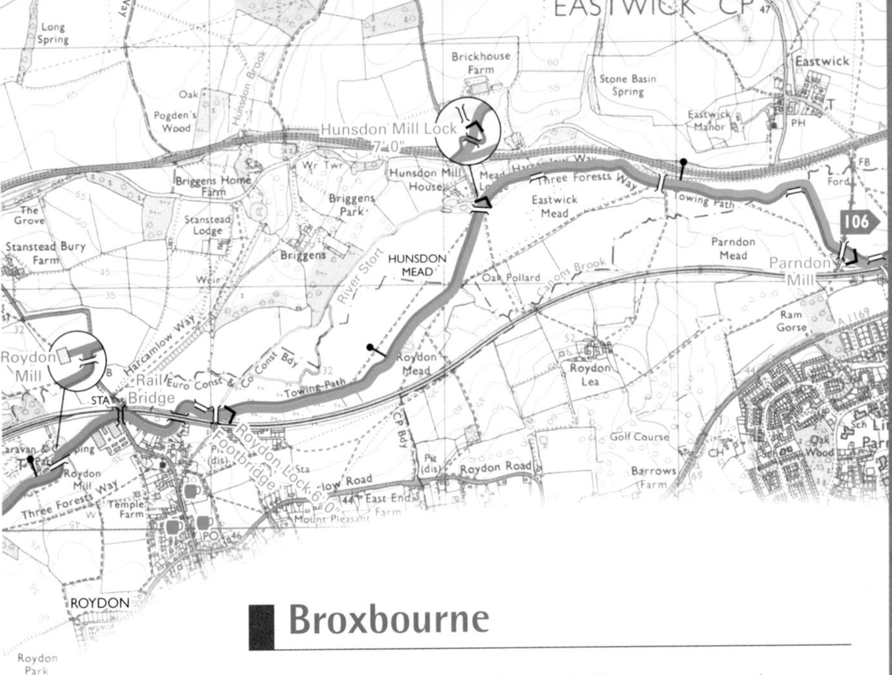

Broxbourne

The river turns sharply to the east in Broxbourne, passing a busy boatyard, a pub and a large leisure centre and swimming pool. Pretty flowers on the bridge announce the presence of Carthagena Lock: above here the Lee takes on a life of holidays rather than the workman-like demeanour it carried several miles downstream. At Feilde's Weir the beautiful Stort Navigation flows in from the north east, while the Lee continues north, passing a go-kart track, and Rye House gatehouse, before reaching Stanstead Abbots and St Margarets, attractive old villages with all useful facilities. The river is now smaller and shallower, and the pylons, which have relentlessly dogged its course since the outskirts of London, at last recede.

The Stort is instantly different from the Lee: narrow, winding, totally rural along almost its entire length, and very beautiful. There is no longer any commercial traffic on this river which, with its winding course and locks slightly narrower than those on the Lee, became financially uncompetitive long ago. Water mills are seen at some of these locks: the attendant clapboarded buildings are a handsome feature of this navigation. Low bridges are also common, and when the river is swollen by excessive rain water, the headroom under the them is even further reduced.

From Feilde's Weir, the Stort follows a line of hills past Lower Lock and Brick Lock, with its attractive but curious cottage dated 1830, to Roydon. Roydon Mill is now the centre of a large caravan site, and contains a useful grocery and laundry facilities – southbound boats should turn left under the bridge before the mill. Roydon village itself stretches up a hill away from the river, which is crossed by the railway on an extremely low bridge (less than 6ft headroom) and followed by Roydon Lock. East of Roydon the river flows through quiet water meadows to Hunsdon Mill Lock, with Hunsdon Mead Nature Reserve to the north – an enchanting area.

NAVIGATIONAL NOTES

1 Boaters should be extremely careful when ascending Stanstead Lock: the top paddles are, unusually, on the *gates*: the unexpected rush of water into the lock chamber can cause great harm to the unwary, as can the swing bridge *over* the lock, which should be swung out of the way.
2 Locks on the Stort are 13ft wide, and cannot take two narrow boats side-by-side.
3 Exercise care with top paddle gear on the Stort. Some of them face the water.
4 Beware canoes and water activity below Burnt Mill Lock.

BOAT TRIPS
Lady of Lee Valley and *Adventuress* 80- and 58-seater boats which run scheduled *summer* cruises, and are also available for private charter. Telephone 01992 466111 for details.

● **Broxbourne**
Herts. PO, tel, stores, station. Its name means 'a stream frequented by badgers', and it is very much at its best by the river. The church is entirely 15th-C and 16th-C, and in the High Street there are several timber-framed 17th-C Georgian brick houses.
Lee Valley Leisure Pool Old Nazeing Road, Broxbourne (01992 446677). A fine facility offering swimming, fitness suites, saunas and steam baths. *Open for various periods daily – telephone and check.*

● **Hoddesdon**
Herts. MD Wed. PO, tel, stores, station. The northerly continuation of Broxbourne, and indistinguishable from it. The town lies to the west of the railway. St Monica's Priory was the manor house of Marmaduke Rawdon from 1622. A clock tower stands in the centre of the town from where the two main streets of Hoddesdon begin. There is a large carnival on the *second Sat in September.*

● **Stanstead Abbotts & St Margarets**
Herts. PO, tel, stores, garage, station. Picturesque villages with the Church of St James particularly interesting because of its 15th-C open timber south porch and 16th-C brick north chancel chapel. Stanstead Bury, about a mile east of the bridge, was originally a 15th-C manor house, and dates from 1752.
The Rye House Plot During the reign of Charles II, Rye House was owned by Richard Rumbold, an ex-officer of the Parliamentarian army. It was here that he and a group of other discontented conspirators decided to ambush the King and his son James, heir to the throne. The plot failed miserably because the royal party passed by sooner than expected, and many of the traitors were put to death. William Henry Teale bought the Rye House estate during the reign of Queen Victoria, and turned it into a Pleasure Park. Alas Rye House itself is no more, but you can see the nearby:
Rye House Gatehouse (01992 702200). Built in 1443 for Sir Andrew Ogard, a Danish nobleman, and an excellent example of early English brickwork. An exhibition inside illustrates the conspiracy. *Open Easter-Sep, Sun & B. Hols, and daily during summer school holidays 11.00–17.00.* Nominal charge.
Amwell Quarry Nature Reserve near Stanstead Abbots. Although this is owned by the St Albans Sand & Gravel Co and there is no public access, there are excellent views from the boundaries. Consisting of farmland, woodland and gravel pits, it is one of the best places in the country to see smew, which are here in winter.

● **Roydon**
Essex. PO, tel, stores, station. Roydon Mill is the headquarters of a large residential and holiday caravan site. The pleasantness of the village itself is enhanced by the bold modern housing estate on the waterfront. The church is small but attractive and dates from the 13thC. The village is at its best around the triangular green, where Georgian and clapboarded houses mingle with willow trees. There are three fine pubs just along the road. Note the shield of Sir George Jackson, later Duckett (the originator of the Stort Navigation) on the lock cottage at Brick Lock.
Roydon Mill Park (01279 792777). Right by the river. Visitors may visit the park and enjoy the facilities, which include a children's playpark and the Riverside Club, with bars, a snooker table and regular entertainment. Charge for temporary membership. *Open 08.30-17.30 (leave at dusk).*
Hunsdon Mead Essex Wildlife Trust, South Green Road, Fingrinhoe, Colchester (01206 729678). A 68-acre reserve which has been kept for 600 years under the Lammas system, whereby farmers graze their cattle in late summer, following a hay cut in July. Over 100 species of plant have been recorded here, including green winged orchid and adder's tongue fern; small mammals are numerous. During the winter the mead floods, and large flocks of lapwing and golden plover may be seen. It is naturally important that at all times when visiting you keep to the paths, walking in single file if necessary.

Boatyards

Ⓑ **Lee Valley Marina** South Street, Stanstead Abbotts (01920 870499). D Pump-out, gas, overnight and long-term mooring, winter storage, slipway, crane, engine sales, boatbuilding, boat and engine repairs, telephone, toilets, showers.

Ⓑ **The Lee Valley Boat Centre** Old Nazeing Road, Broxbourne (01992 462085). D Pump-out, gas, narrow boat hire, day hire craft, slipway, café.

Pubs and Restaurants

Crown Inn Old Nazeing Road, Broxbourne (01992 446893). A well-kept pub, with garden and children's play area overlooking the river, serving Bass and Fuller's real ale. Bar and restaurant meals available *lunchtimes and evenings, with* vegetarian and children's menus. Regular entertainment with quiz nights, and *summer* fun events in the garden.

Fish and Eels Dobbs Weir Road, Broxbourne (01992 440029). A fine old riverside pub with a large garden beside the river, wide at this point with lots of waterlilies, and the weir opposite. Tetley's, Marston's and Morland's real ales are available, and bar meals, including steaks, are available *lunchtimes and evenings* from a small though varied and inexpensive servery menu. Vegetarian choices. Bar snacks are available *all day*. Children are welcome.

The Rye House Rye Road, Hoddesdon (01992 465151). An attractive riverside pub serving Theakston's and Courage real ale. Food always available *11.00–21.00* with vegetarian options. Children are welcome and there is a shady garden with play area.

Jolly Fisherman 8 Station Road, St Margarets (01920 870125). A mellow and friendly riverside pub, with a fine garden, serving McMullen and a guest real ale. Meals are served *lunchtimes and evenings every day*. Vegetarians are catered for, and children are welcome.

New Inn High Street, Roydon (01279 792225). A cosy and beamy village pub serving Ansells, Greene King and Tetley's real ales. Meals are available *lunchtimes, and evenings Tue–Sat*, and there are vegetarian choices. Children are welcome *until 21.00*, and there is a large garden. Occasionally live music or discos.

Crusader High Street, Roydon (01279 792161). A formal-looking pub offering food in the bar or in a separate dining area *lunchtimes and evenings*, with vegetarian options. McMullen real ale. Children are welcome *for meals*. There is outside seating in the summer.

White Hart High Street, Roydon (01279 792118). A small and cosy pub where bar and restaurant meals are served *lunchtimes and evenings (not Sun evenings) every day*. Greene King real ale is served. Children are welcome in the restaurant and there is an outside seating area for the family.

White Horse High Street, Roydon (01279 793131). A friendly and inviting pub at the top of the village, known locally as the Top House. The old-world interior has low beams, horse brasses and an inglenook fireplace, surrounding a bar serving Courage real ale. An imaginative menu is served in the bar or restaurant area *lunchtimes* and *evenings Wed–Sat*, with vegetarian options.

UNLOCKING THE RIVER

What was probably the first pound lock with mitred gates in England was built at Waltham Abbey in 1577. It was graphically described in *A Tale of Two Swans* by Vallans, 1590:

'Among them all a rare devise they see
But newly made, a waterworke: the locke
Through which the boates of Ware doe passe with malt.
This locke contains two double doores of wood
Within the same a cesterne all of Plancke
Which onely fils when boates come there to passe'.

Hertford

Leaving Stanstead Lock, the navigation runs dead straight for $1^1/_2$ miles to the north west, flanked by beautiful green, uncluttered water meadows contained by the nearby wooded hills. A lovely old branch railway line once ran from Stanstead Abbots to Buntingford – it now forms part of the Amwell Walkway to Easneye Woods. There is a pretty cottage at Hardmead Lock before the river turns west into Ware, the granary of London, where the river bisects this fine old town. There are some remarkable 18th-C gazebos along the river front and Ware Lock is surrounded by flower beds. This lock is the only one on British Waterways run by Thames Water, as the offtake of the New River is in the pound above. Above this lock, the river wanders along one side of the valley, with water meadows on one side and wooded parkland on the other.
The river enters Hertford via a deep lock accompanied by a pretty 19th-C lock cottage, and passes a basin used for pleasure boat moorings and an attractive bow-windowed riverside terrace, just before a fine pub.

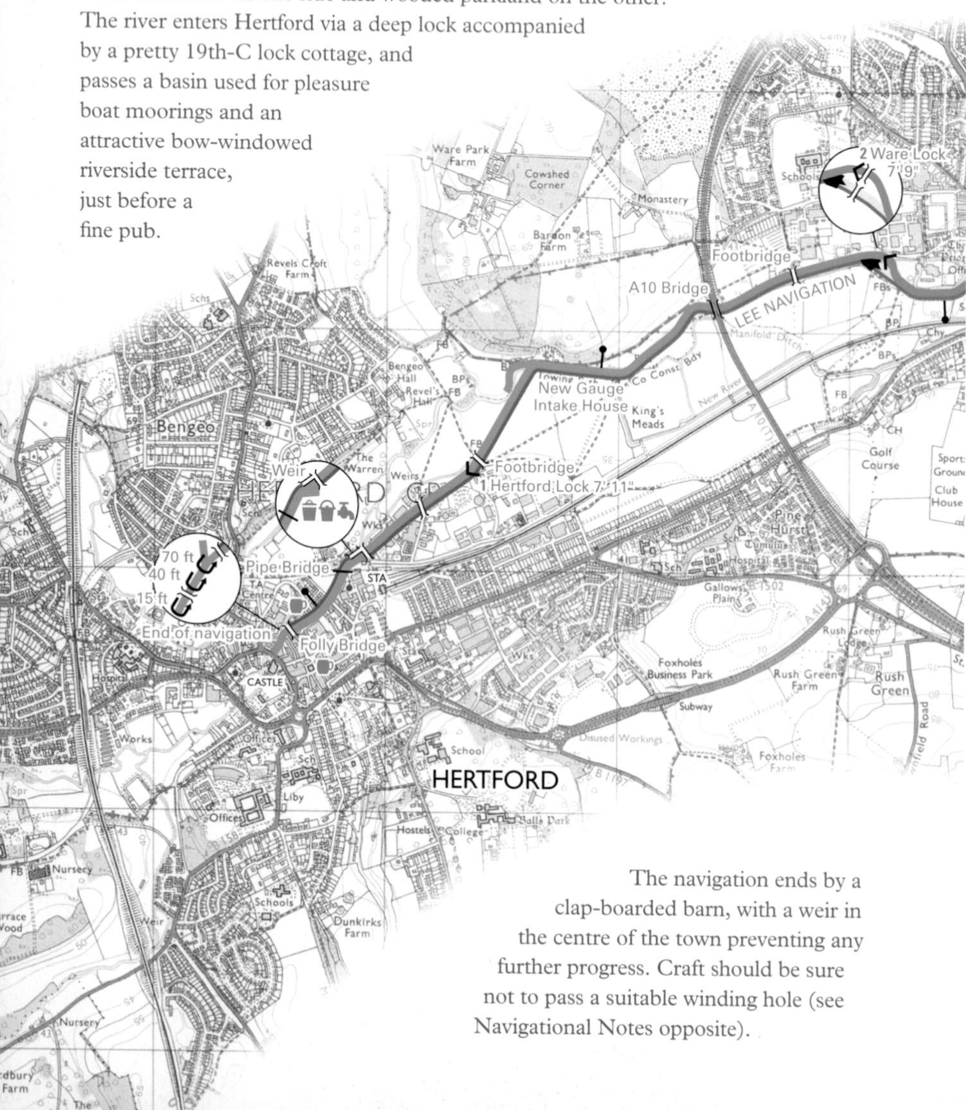

The navigation ends by a clap-boarded barn, with a weir in the centre of the town preventing any further progress. Craft should be sure not to pass a suitable winding hole (see Navigational Notes opposite).

Boatyards

Ⓑ **Lea Valley Narrowboat Co.** Lock Keeper's Cottage, Stanstead Lock, Amwell Lane, Stanstead Abbots (01920 870068). D Pump-out, gas, overnight and long-term mooring, boat sales, boat and engine repairs, chandlery. The company also maintain moorings at the basin in Hertford.

NAVIGATIONAL NOTES

Winding in Hertford: craft over 40 ft long should turn immediately above Folly Bridge; craft up to 40 ft long should turn immediately below Mill Bridge; craft up to 15 ft long may turn just above Mill Bridge.

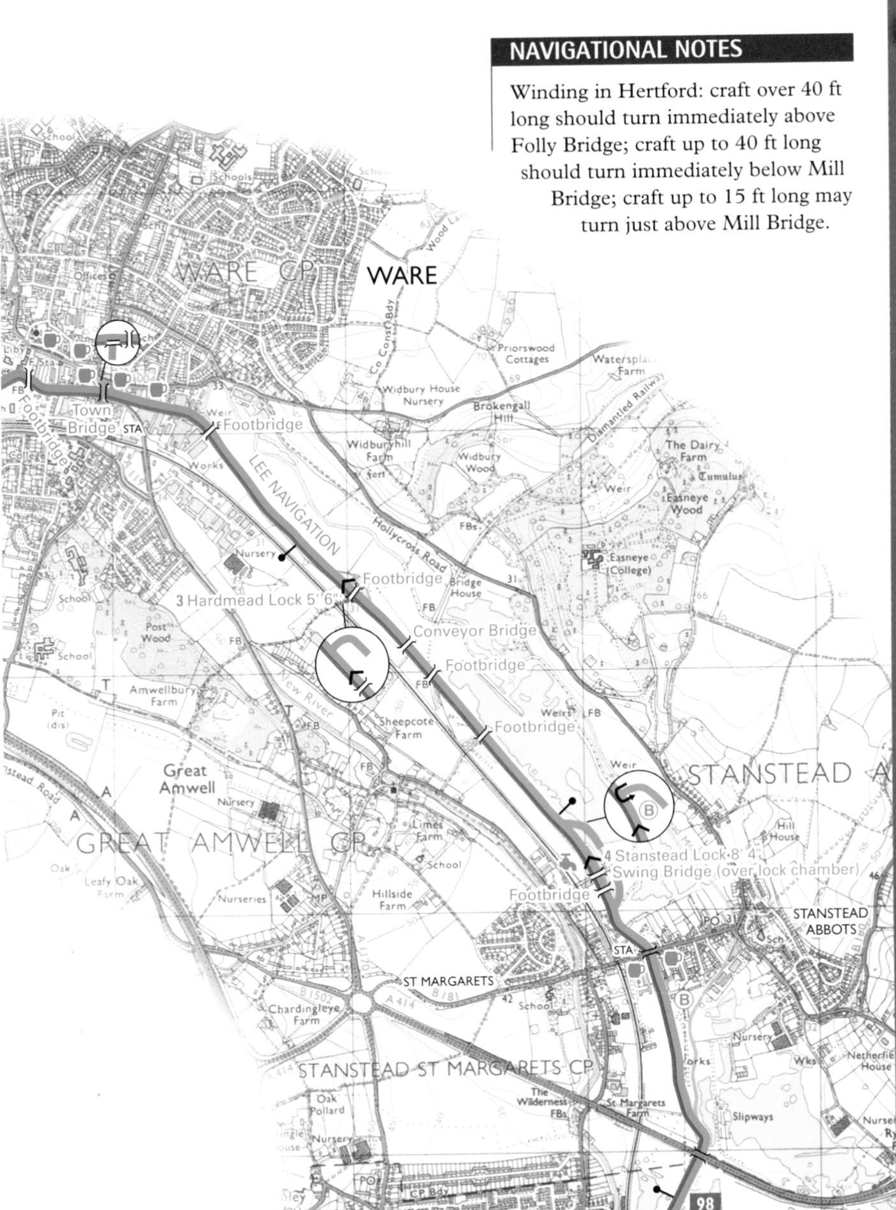

Ware

Herts. PO, tel, stores, garage, station. A busy town, still attractive around the old Town Hall. You can find evidence of a former medieval town here, and buildings with their projecting upper storeys show the importance of through-traffic during the coaching days. Its name means the Weirs.

Ware Priory Priory Street. Built from the remains of a Franciscan friary founded by Thomas Wake, Lord of the Manor, in 1338.

St Mary's Church Church Street. Its battlemented clock tower is surmounted by a spire. There is a fascinating story connected with the oak railings enclosing the children's corner, which are the original rails from the time of William Laud, who was Archbishop of Canterbury and adviser to Charles I, during the early part of the 17thC. The rails were the subject of a dispute when Charles Chauncy (who later became the second principal of Harvard College) was vicar, and were removed by Cromwell's army. They were discovered in a nearby garden in the 1920s by W H Lee, cleaned up, and re-installed.

New River

Opposite Ware Park is the intake from the Lee Navigation of the New River, which continues 24 miles south, terminating at Stoke Newington. It was a great feat of engineering designed by Sir Hugh Myddelton in the 17thC to bring a fresh water supply from Chadwell Spring to north London to replace the polluted supply obtained from the Thames. Work started on this remarkable plan in 1609 and the original 38-mile course, including several large wooden aqueducts, was completed within four years. As Chadwell Spring could not supply sufficient water by the end of the 19thC, most of the water in the New River is now drawn from the River Lee. A monument, overhung by weeping willows and a yew tree, commemorating Myddelton's great achievement, can be seen on an island at the foot of the slope below Great Amwell church, 1/4 mile west of the footbridge above Stanstead Lock.

Hertford

Herts. MD Mon. PO, tel, stores, garage, stations. A large and attractive county town with a long history. Two of its medieval parish churches still stand, and other buildings in the town bear witness to the Middle Ages. A relief road has unfortunately destroyed many interesting and attractive houses, but it has ensured the survival of the compact old town centre, which is now a delightful place to stroll around. In the 9thC the area was invaded with great regularity by the Danes; they were eventually seen off by King Alfred the Great. Dane End, 3 1/2 miles north of Hertford, marks the northern limit of their incursions into this region.

The Castle Built in 1100, the Castle belonged to the Cecil family after Prince Charles, son of James I, sold it. King John of France and David Bruce of Scotland were both imprisoned here; and Bolingbroke drew up charges against Richard II that led to Richard's dethronement in 1399 within the building. A few medieval structures remain, including a 12th-C curtain wall. The lawns and trees which extend to the river make an attractive setting. The 15th-C gatehouse was extensively altered about 1800. Those houses in Water Lane numbered 4 to 16 are thought to have been outhouses of the Castle. Several buildings in Castle Street itself are noteworthy, and also those in Fore Street, including the Shire Hall, built by James Adam (brother of Robert) in the 18thC. The Castle Gardens are open from *dawn until dusk* to the public at no charge. The Castle belongs to the Council, and houses offices, although there are a few rooms containing regalia, and these are open to the public as special events on some *summer Sundays*. Ring the TIC for details *in the summer.*

Hertford Museum Bull Plain, Hertford (01992 582686). Local archaeology, history, geology and natural history just up the road from the terminus of the navigation. *Open Tue–Sat 10.00–17.00.* No charge.

Tourist Information Centre 10 Market Place, Hertford (01992 584322). Friendly and helpful service.

A TRANSPORT EXPLOSION

The late 17thC saw the establishment of a gunpowder factory at Waltham Abbey, using the River Lee to transport the finished material, in what was considered to be relative safety, to the Royal Small Arms factory at Enfield; to London; and to Weedon, on the Grand Union. On 4 September 1874 a gunpowder barge was left unattended at Bromley when the flour mills nearby caught fire. It is said that red hot embers were landing close to this volatile cargo . . . *Less than a week later* a gunpowder barge on the Regent's Canal exploded, with devastating consequences. George Corble, a Lee Conservancy clerk, suggested this should be taken as a 'warning not to moor such craft in a thickly populated district'.

Pubs and Restaurants

The Victoria (01920 462565). A friendly riverside pub, just below Town Bridge, Ware, serving McMullen real ale, and a variety of food *lunchtimes and evenings (not Wed or Sun evenings) every day*. There are always vegetarian options. Children are welcomed, and moorings are available.

Saracen's High Street, Ware (01920 463640). A modern riverside pub serving McMullen real ale together with bar food. There is a fine terrace.

Old Punch House West Street, Ware (01920 467675). A comfortable pub set in the centre of the town serving Courage and Greene King real ales and bar meals *lunchtimes and evenings*, with vegetarian options. Regular pool and darts competitions. There is a garden.

Old Barge The Folly, Hertford (01992 581871). A waterside pub run by a real ale enthusiast and offering an extensive menu, at reasonable prices, served in the bar or in the restaurant *lunchtimes and evenings (not Sun, Mon or Fri evenings)*, with vegetarian food available. Burton, Marston's and Morland's real ales. Waterside patio for the *summer months*. Children welcome, and there is entertainment with a quiz night and music *once a month*.

White Hart Salisbury Square, Hertford (01992 583605). A pub with a cosy atmosphere dispensing McMullen real ale. Bar meals are available *lunchtimes and evenings every day*. There are vegetarian options. Children are welcome. Occasional entertainment. The family owned McMullen brewery, established in the town in 1827, is not far away.

Woolpack Near Mill Bridge, Hertford (01992 583766). This small town pub serves McMullen real ale and bar meals at *lunchtimes*, with Sunday roasts. Vegetarian options are always available. Children are welcome, and there is a garden.

Salisbury Arms Hotel Fore Street, Hertford (01992 583091). Restaurant and bar meals are served *lunchtimes and evenings* with vegetarian options, together with McMullen real ale. There is a special area for children.

George IV Great Amwell (01920 870039). About 10 minutes walk west from the picnic site between Stanstead and Hardmead Locks. A popular pub situated above a pool on the New River, where you can see the memorial to the New River Engineers amongst the shady willows. Restaurant and bar meals are served *lunchtimes and evenings every day*, with vegetarian choices. Children are welcome in the dining room. Adnams, Greene King and Tetley's real ale is available, and there is pleasant outside seating.

The Castle, Hertford (see page 104)

Sawbridgeworth

Leaving Eastwick to the north, the navigation passes the attractive Little Parndon Mill, then Burnt Mill; perhaps the name explains its absence. South of the railway lies Harlow New Town; it does not intrude on the navigation, which passes it by amidst pleasant parkland and quiet meadows – the station is, however, close to Burnt Mill Lock. Winding on north eastwards up the valley, the navigation reaches Harlow Mill, a large pub with a vast garden. Walkers should note that the towpath changes side at this point – do not be deceived by the path continuing along the west bank. Passing under the A11, the river continues to wind to Sawbridgeworth, passing the isolated Feakes Lock – indeed Sheering Mill Lock is a good point from which to enter this attractive town. A little further north, beyond attractively converted malthouses and granaries, is Sawbridgeworth Lock and Mill. Leaving the town, the river passes a low railway bridge and wanders round to Tednambury Lock. Just to the north of this an arm leads off to Little Hallingbury Mill, in an attractive setting at the bottom of a hill.

● **Harlow**
Essex. MD Tue, Fri, Sat. PO, tel, stores, garage, station, cinema. Harlow Old Town, which contains several 18th-C houses, a Norman chapel at Harlowbury and the site of a Romano-Celtic temple, has been swallowed up by Harlow New Town, set up in 1947 as a balanced area for London's over-spilling population. Frederick Gibberd master-minded the plan, and the New Town is now well known as an important breakthrough in town planning.
Harlow Town Pets' Corner Harlow Town Park (01279 422790). Here you can see animals roaming free in the park. There is also an aquarium, a vivarium (artificial habitat) and aviaries. *Open daily 11.00-17.00.* No charge.

● **Sawbridgeworth**
Herts. PO, tel, stores, garage, station. An attractive town with houses from the 16th to the 19thC, including many white clapboarded ones. The large 14th- and 15th-C church is rich in monuments and brasses, and has a collection of 18th-C gravestones of great elegance.
Sawbridgeworth Marsh Essex Wildlife Trust, South Green Road, Fingrinhoe, Colchester (01206 729678).

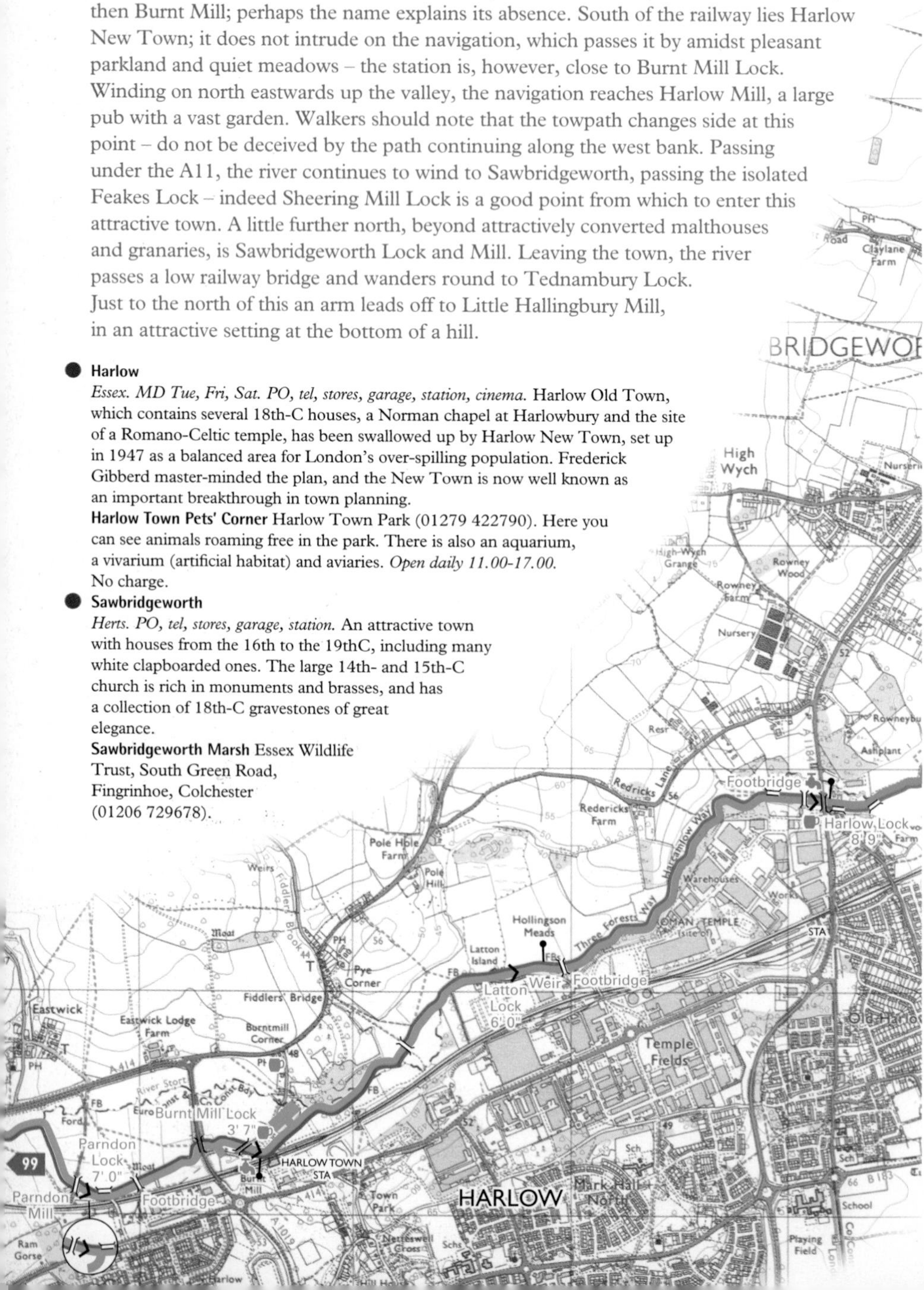

99

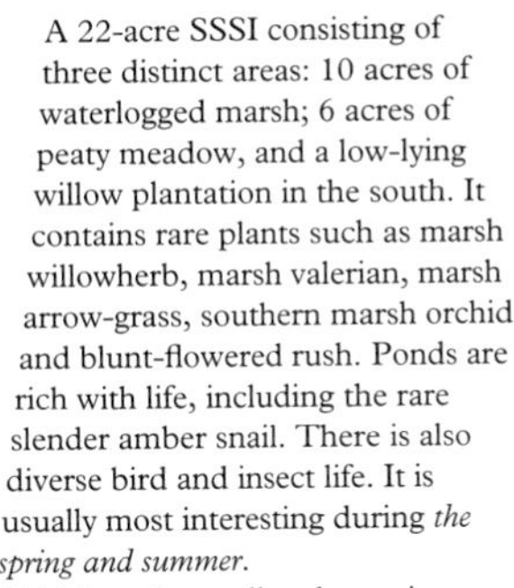

A 22-acre SSSI consisting of three distinct areas: 10 acres of waterlogged marsh; 6 acres of peaty meadow, and a low-lying willow plantation in the south. It contains rare plants such as marsh willowherb, marsh valerian, marsh arrow-grass, southern marsh orchid and blunt-flowered rush. Ponds are rich with life, including the rare slender amber snail. There is also diverse bird and insect life. It is usually most interesting during *the spring and summer.*

Pishiobury A castellated mansion rebuilt in 1782 by James Wyatt from an earlier Tudor house, it still retains some Tudor and Jacobean work inside. The park and lake were designed by Capability Brown and can be explored from an access point on the towpath.

Boatyards

Ⓑ **Lea & Stort Cruisers** Hallingbury Marina (01279 723568). D E Pump-out (by appointment only), gas, overnight & long-term mooring, dry dock, boat & engine repairs, telephone, toilets, showers, BW keys, windlasses.

Ⓑ **Moorhen Marina** Above Burnt Mill Lock Card-operated pump-out (from BW at Enfield), pub and restaurant.

Pubs and Restaurants

Dusty Miller (01279 424180). About a 1/4 mile north of Burnt Mill Lock. Excellent McMullen's real ale and bar meals *lunchtimes and evenings every day,* with vegetarian choices and a children's menu. There is a garden with a play area, and occasional entertainment.

Harlow Mill (01279 442545). By Harlow Lock. A pretty pub in the old mill, with a vast and attractive riverside garden. An excellent choice of real ales is always available, and meals are served *lunchtimes and evenings every day,* with lots of vegetarian choices. Children are welcomed. Occasional quiz nights, and special evenings for Hallowe'en and the like.

King William IV Vantorts Road, Fairgreen, Sawbridgeworth (01279 722322). A short walk west of Sheering Mill Lock. An old, quiet but popular pub opening onto a courtyard. Courage real ale is served, and home-cooked bar meals and snacks are available *lunchtimes (not Sun),* with a vegetarian choice. Children are welcome *for meals.* There is outside seating for the summer and a log fire for the winter.

Market House Hotel Knight Street, Sawbridgeworth (01279 722807). Set on the crossroads, at the heart of the village, this 400-year-old hotel provides both bar meals and an à la carte menu in the restaurant *lunchtimes and evenings.* Vegetarians are catered for. Courage and a guest real ale are served, and children are welcomed.

The Moorhen (01279 423066). By the Marina. Greene King real ale and a restaurant. Children's indoor and outdoor play areas.

Bishop's Stortford

Just above Spellbrook Lock lies Walbury Camp, said to date from the Iron Age – it is shielded by woods and there is little to be seen from the river. There follows a short stretch of open country before reaching Twyford House, Mill and Lock, which form an attractive group in the water meadows that flank the river; then a final sweep past trees and fields brings the outskirts of Bishop's Stortford into view. Two pubs are passed as the navigation finally makes its way into the town, passing a few surviving timber yards and some handsome restored maltings, to finish at the Causeway. There is a fine crane just below the bridge, and splendid gardens above it, beneath the castle.

Pubs and Restaurants

Old Bull's Head London Road, Bishop's Stortford (01279 652666). A riverside pub serving Wadworth's real ales. The choice of over 100 home-cooked bar meals (including ten vegetarian meals) is available *lunchtimes and evenings every day.* Children are welcome and there is a garden. Regular quiz nights.

Tanner's Arms Station Road, Bishop's Stortford (01279 651837). Cosy and beamy riverside pub, with a garden, serving a varied menu (incredibly neatly written) *lunchtimes,* with vegetarian options. McMullen's real ale is served. Children are welcome, and they will enjoy seeing the tropical fish. Regular entertainment with karaoke and discos.

The Falcon Station Road, Bishop's Stortford (01279 654995). A town local. Children are welcome and there is a garden. Discos are held *at weekends.*

George Hotel Bishop's Stortford (01279 654042). In the centre of the town and serving Tetley's real ale. Bar meals are available *lunchtimes and evenings Mon–Fri* with a vegetarian choice. Children are welcome.

Three Horseshoes Spellbrook Lane East (01279 722849). About 1/4 mile north of Spellbrook Lock. An interesting squat timber-framed building, thatched and dating from 1449. Tetley, Greenalls and guest real ales are served, and restaurant meals are available *Sun–Thu 12.00–21.30 and Fri & Sat 12.00–22.00,* with vegetarian options. Children are welcome and there is a large garden with a play area.

Little Hallingbury
Essex. PO, tel. The church has a Norman doorway made with Roman bricks; the south porch is of timber. Note also the pretty timber-framed house behind the pond.

Rushy Mead Nature Reserve Maintained by the Essex Wildlife Trust, Rushy Mead is mentioned on an old tithe map and was the site of a sewage pumping station, which ceased operating during the 1950s. Water is always present close to the surface here, giving prolific growths of reed and sedge, which, naturally, attract reed and sedge warblers, together with snipe, water rail and other birds. Dragonflies breed in the pools, and grass snakes and harvest mice may be found. *Open 09.00–17.00 (or dusk if earlier).*

Bishop's Stortford
Herts. MD Thu, Sat. PO, tel, stores, garage, station. A thriving market town that has retained much of its old-world atmosphere – indeed many of the inns are quite ancient. St Michael's Church has a Norman font, which survived from an earlier church built on the same site.

Waytemore Castle Bridge Street. Only the foundations of the rectangular keep remain. What used to be the bailey is now a riverside pleasure garden.

Rhodes Memorial Museum South Road, Bishop's Stortford (01279 651746). Contains a collection illustrating Cecil Rhodes' life, particularly in relation to his activities in Rhodesia. The old vicarage where Rhodes was born contains descriptive maps, pictures and documents devoted to him. *Open Tue–Sat 10.00–16.00. Closed Sun, Mon and B. Hols.* Modest entry fee. Groups may visit by *prior arrangement* provided there are no more than 35 people. There is also free entry to view the 28ft embroidered mural depicting local history which is displayed in the entrance to the museum. This was sponsored by an ex-mayor, designed by a local resident, and completed by local people in 1991.

Local History Museum Cemetery Lodge, Apton Road (01279 722557). *Open May-Sep on Fri, and on the first Sun of each month 14.00–17.00.* Free.

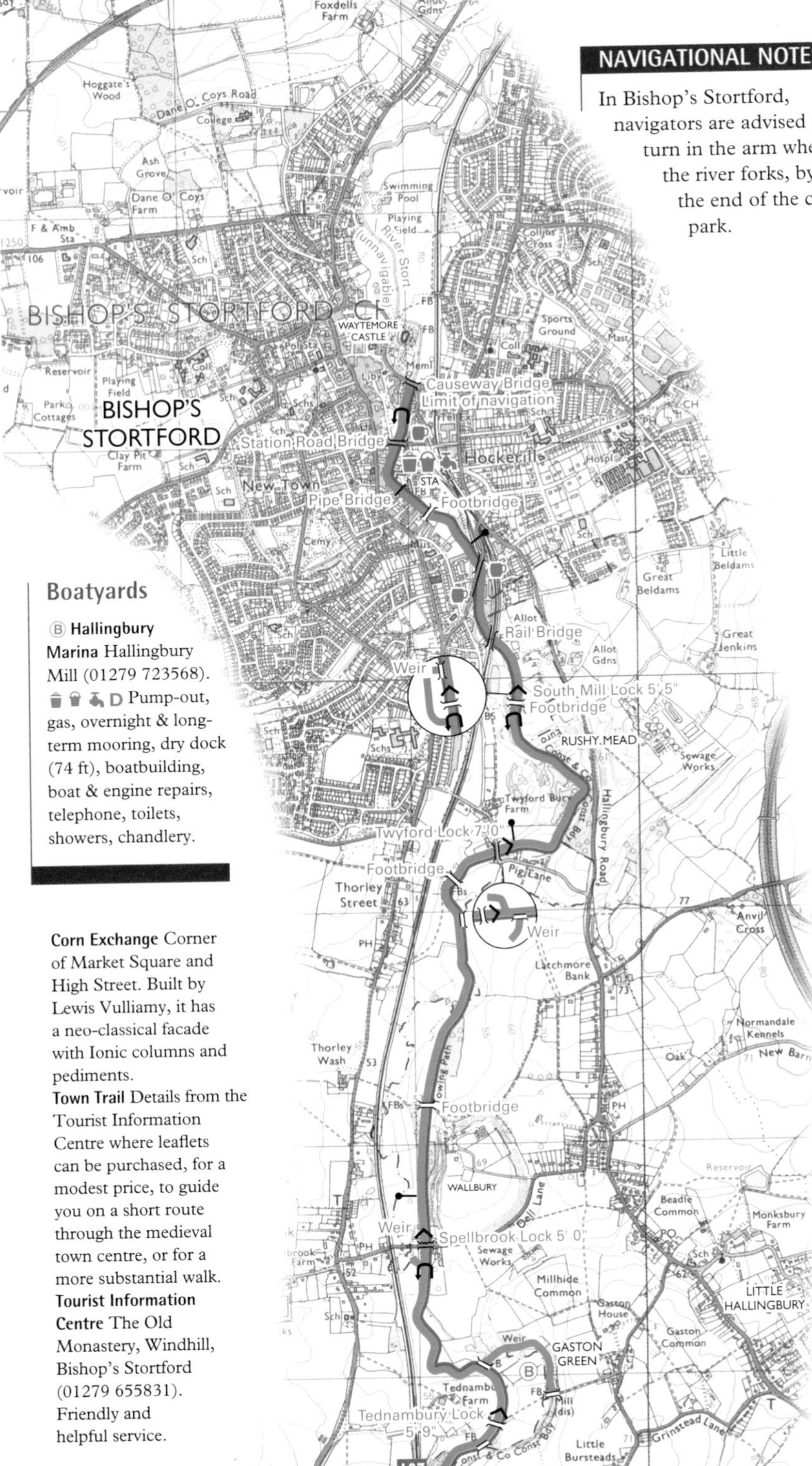

NAVIGATIONAL NOTES

In Bishop's Stortford, navigators are advised to turn in the arm where the river forks, by the end of the car park.

Boatyards

Ⓑ **Hallingbury Marina** Hallingbury Mill (01279 723568). D Pump-out, gas, overnight & long-term mooring, dry dock (74 ft), boatbuilding, boat & engine repairs, telephone, toilets, showers, chandlery.

Corn Exchange Corner of Market Square and High Street. Built by Lewis Vulliamy, it has a neo-classical facade with Ionic columns and pediments.
Town Trail Details from the Tourist Information Centre where leaflets can be purchased, for a modest price, to guide you on a short route through the medieval town centre, or for a more substantial walk.
Tourist Information Centre The Old Monastery, Windhill, Bishop's Stortford (01279 655831). Friendly and helpful service.

OXFORD CANAL

MAXIMUM DIMENSIONS

Oxford to Napton
Length: 72'
Beam: 6' 10"
Headroom: 6' 6"

Braunston to Hawkesbury
Length: 70'
Beam: 7'
Headroom: 6'

MANAGER

01788 890666

MILEAGE

OXFORD (River Thames) to
Duke's Cut: 3 miles
Thrupp: 7 1/2 miles
Lower Heyford: 14 3/4 miles
Aynho Wharf: 20 1/4 miles
Banbury: 27 miles
Cropredy: 31 1/2 miles
Fenny Compton Wharf: 37 3/4 miles
Napton Bottom Lock: 48 miles
NAPTON JUNCTION (Grand Union Canal): 49 1/4 miles
BRAUNSTON TURN (Grand Union Canal): 54 1/4 miles
Hillmorton Bottom Lock: 61 3/4 miles
Rugby Wharf Arm: 64 1/2 miles
Stretton Stop: 69 3/4 miles
HAWKESBURY JUNCTION (Coventry Canal): 77 miles

Locks: 43

This was one of the earliest and for many years one of the most important canals in southern England. It was authorised in 1769, when the Coventry Canal was in the offing, and was intended to fetch coal southwards from the Warwickshire coalfield to Banbury and Oxford, at the same time giving access to the River Thames. James Brindley was appointed engineer; he built a winding contour canal 91 miles long, which soon began to look thoroughly out-dated and inefficient for the carriage of goods. Brindley died in 1772, and was replaced by Samuel Simcock; he completed the line from Longford, where a junction was made with the Coventry Canal, to Banbury in 1778. After a long pause, the canal was finally brought into Oxford in 1790, and thereafter through-traffic flowed constantly along this important new trade route.

In 1805, however, the Grand Junction Canal opened (excepting the tunnel at Blisworth) from London to Braunston, and the Warwick & Napton and Warwick & Birmingham canals completed the new short route from London to Birmingham. This had the natural – and intended – effect of drawing traffic off the Oxford Canal, especially south of Napton Junction; but the Oxford company protected itself effectively against this powerful opposition by charging outrageously high tolls for their 5 1/2-mile stretch between Braunston and Napton, which had become part of the new London-Birmingham through route. Thus the Oxford maintained its revenue and high dividends for many years to come.

By the late 1820s, however, the Oxford Canal had become conspicuously out of date with its extravagant winding course; and under the threat of various schemes for big new canals which, if built, would render the Oxford Canal almost redundant, the company decided to modernise the northern part of their navigation. Tremendous engineering works were carried out, completely changing the face of the canal north of Braunston. Aqueducts, massive embankments and deep cuttings were built, carrying the canal in great sweeps through the countryside and cutting almost 14 miles off the original 36 miles between Braunston Junction and the Coventry Canal. Much of the old main line suddenly became a series of loops and branches leading nowhere, crossed by elegant new towpath bridges inscribed Horseley Ironworks 1828. Now most of these old loops are abandoned and weeded up, although their twisting course can still be easily traced.

This expensive programme was well worth while. Although toll rates, and thus revenue, began to fall because of keen competition from the railways, dividends were kept at a high level for years; indeed a respectable profit was still shown right through to the 20th century. Now, there is no trade on the canal – but this beautiful waterway has become one of the most popular canals in Britain for pleasure cruising, fishing and walking. However, water shortages on the long top pound have always presented problems during dry summer months and can lead to restricted lock opening times on the Claydon and Napton flights.

Isis Lock, Oxford (see page 112)

Oxford

The Oxford Canal can be reached from the Thames in two places; one, via Duke's Cut, is convenient but bypasses Oxford altogether; the other, via a backwater under the north end of Oxford Station to the canal at Isis Lock, is more enjoyable. A railway swing bridge here was once a notorious obstruction, but this is now left open. Beyond this bridge, boats continue for 50yds along the backwater and should then join the canal by turning sharp left into Isis Lock. The canal continues southwards for 1/4 mile past Worcester College to its terminus near Nuffield College, where there are visitor moorings. The original terminal basin, sold to Lord Nuffield in 1936 and eventaully infilled, has become a car park. There are now serious proposals to restore it, and bring back life to an otherwise dreary part of this fine city. Isis Lock, with its pretty iron turnover bridge, is wooded and secluded, despite its nearness to the centre of Oxford. The canal proceeds northwards, flanked by houses to the east, whose gardens run down to the water. This is an attractive stretch of urban canal. After passing several wharves the houses give way to industry, while Port Meadow lies to the west. The first Oxford Canal lift bridge appears followed by an electric lift bridge, opened by push button controls during working hours, and left open at other times. Beyond the railway bridge is Wolvercote, where the canal starts the long climb up to the Midlands. After a series of main road bridges, carrying the A40 and the A34, Duke's Cut branches off to the west to join a backwater of the River Thames, and the canal moves into open country, leaving Oxford behind.

NAVIGATIONAL NOTES

Those wishing to cruise on the River Thames will require a licence from: The Environment Agency, Thames Region, King's Meadow House, King's Meadow Road, Reading, Berks RG1 8DQ (0118 953 5650). Short period registration is available from Thames locks adjacent to the canal.

Pubs and Restaurants

There are many fine pubs, restaurants and wine bars in Oxford.

Antiquity Hall (01865 249153). A pleasant riverside pub at the very end of the canal, serving Marston's, Morland's, Tetley's and a guest real ale, and meals *lunchtimes, with snacks the rest of the day*. Outside you may relax on a patio area. *Wed* is quiz night.

Gardener's Arms Plantation Road, Oxford (01865 559814). A small friendly pub, with a garden, which attracts locals from the pretty cottages nearby. They serve Morrells real ale, and meals *lunchtimes (except Sat) and evenings (except Sun)*. Children are welcome.

Turf Tavern Bath Place, off Holywell Street (01865 243235). Surprisingly secluded from the bustle of the city, this pub is one of the most distinctive in Oxford. Made famous through Hardy's *Jude the Obscure*, the 13th-C tavern has become popular with both students and tourists. Large choice of real ales. Bar meals available *all day*. Outside seating. Children welcome.

The Anchor 01865 510282). By bridge 240. A sociable brick-built pub serving Wadworth's real ale, and food, with vegetarian options *lunchtimes and evenings every day (not Sun evenings)*. Children are welcome, and there is a garden.

✕ **The Plough** Wolvercote Green, Upper Wolvercote (01865 556969). Morrells real ale is served, and food is available *lunchtimes and evenings (except Sun lunchtimes or Mon evenings)*. Vegetarian options are always available. The restaurant, previously the local morgue, now serves an exciting à la carte menu. A library is kept in the pub, so you can browse while you wait for your food. No dogs. Garden.

Trout Inn Godstow Road, Wolvercote (01865 554485). On the River Thames near Godstow Lock, 10 minutes walk south east from canal bridge 235. Dating from the 12thC, this pub is in a beautiful setting overlooking the river. Bass and Worthington real ale are served, and meals are available *lunchtimes and evenings*, with vegetarian options. Children are welcome.

The towpath
This is passable for walkers, but impossible in many places for all but the most agile cross-country cyclists.

● **City of Oxford**
Oxon. All shops and services. The town was founded in the 10thC and has been a university city since the 13thC. Today it is a lively cosmopolitan centre of learning, tourism and industry.
Tourist Information Centre The Old School, Gloucester Green, Oxford (01865 726871). Here you will find a good selection of city guides and maps, and helpful, informative staff. It is, of course, the 39 colleges which give Oxford its unique character – they can all be visited, but opening times vary, so consult with the Tourist Information Centre before you go. Those noted here are particularly representative of their periods.
Merton College dates from 1264 and is one of the earliest collegiate foundations that is almost unrestored. Typical of the Perpendicular and Decorative periods. The Grove buildings are by Butterfield.
New College Founded by William of Wykeham, Bishop of Winchester, in 1379. The Perpendicular chapel was greatly restored by Sir George Gilbert Scott in the 19thC.
Keble College Built by Butterfield in 1870 entirely in the Victorian Gothic style.
Sheldonian Theatre Broad Street. Built by Sir Christopher Wren in the 17thC under the auspices of Gilbert Sheldon, Archbishop of Canterbury, who disapproved of the annual performances of plays in St Mary's Church. University degrees are awarded here. It has an attractive ceiling by Robert Streeter.
Ashmolean Museum Beaumont Street. Outstanding collection of Near Eastern and European archaeology, the Farrer collection of 17th- and 18th-C silver, a display of early coins and some drawings of Michelangelo and Raphael.
Christ Church Picture Gallery Christ Church. Built by Powell and Moya in 1967, it contains drawings by Michelangelo, Veronese and Tintoretto, and 14th-18thC paintings, mainly Italian.
Museum of Modern Art Pembroke Street. Gives unusual art exhibitions – anything from environment to architecture, graphics and photography.
University Museum Parks Road. A high Victorian Gothic building by Deane and Woodward. Natural history, including the head and claw of a dodo. *Open weekdays.*
Christ Church Meadows Approach from St Aldate's. A path leads down to the Thames, where the rowing eights are to be seen.
University Botanic Gardens High Street. The oldest botanic garden in Britain, founded by Henry Danvers, Earl of Danby. In the 17thC the garden was intended for the culture of medicinal plants, but today it fosters extensive collections of rare plants for research and teaching. The gateway is by Inigo Jones.

● **Wolvercote**
Oxon. PO, tel, stores, garage. Oxford spreads north along the Woodstock and Banbury roads, making Wolvercote inseparable from the city. There is little of interest, although it is useful as a supply centre.

Boatyards

Ⓑ **College Cruisers** Combe Road Wharf, Oxford (01865 554343). D Pump-out, gas, narrow boat hire, day hire craft, crane, boat & engine repairs, chandlery.

A SPATE OF PROBLEMS

The Oxford Canal and the River Cherwell share a course between Shipton Weir Lock and Baker's Lock, and care should be taken on this section if the river is in spate. William Blake, in his *Strange Adventures of a Houseboat*, published in 1889, recorded how his boat, the *Nameless Barge*, almost came to grief here:

'As this is a candid history, the writer will confess that he was very nearly being the death of all those members of the party who happened to be afloat. Steering at the time, and observing that the heaviest rush of the river was along the western shore, he naturally thought he could cheat the current by edging out towards mid-stream, and proceeded to do so with all imaginary caution. But the moment the heavy weight of water got a grip of the bow, the boat was twisted round, so that the full force of the stream bore down upon her broadside on; while the strain of the tow rope, acting at this awkward angle, proceeded to tilt us over in a very alarming fashion. It was an affair of only a moment or two, for by jamming the tiller over she was presently righted'.

Thrupp

Continuing northwards the canal runs through lightly wooded fields and meadows to Kidlington, which is hidden from the canal by a low cutting. Keeping Kidlington in the distance, it then joins the Cherwell valley at the pretty canalside village of Thrupp. From here the canal closely follows the Cherwell and adopts the meandering characteristics of a contour canal. Much of the waterway is tree-lined, while its shallow banks and close relationship with the villages make it seem very river like. At Shipton Weir Lock, whose 1ft rise is made up by its great width, the Cherwell and the canal merge and share a common course for the next mile. The Cherwell swings away west under an elegant iron bridge before Baker's Lock, but soon returns to run parallel to the canal. Wooded hills now determine the course of the waterway, which passes plenty of villages and places of interest. Only Thrupp yard and the moored maintenance boats, the bridges and the occasional locks give away the fact that this was a commercial waterway. It is indeed a truly delightful stretch of rural canal.

NAVIGATIONAL NOTES

Bridge 228 is very low. Take care.

- **Kidlington**
  Oxon. PO, tel, stores, garage. The canal skirts round Kidlington, an extended suburb of Oxford. Parts of an older village survive to the north around the tall-spired church, including Sir William Morton's 17th-C gabled almshouses. Nearby is the Oxford Air Training School, one of only 20 such places in the world training airline pilots. The town is most easily reached from bridge 228.
- **Thrupp**
  Oxon. PO box, tel. A wonderfully romantic canal village, with a terrace of stone houses running along beside the towpath, a pub at one end and a British Waterways yard at the other. The quality of the village makes it an unusual survival of early canal prosperity.
- **Hampton Gay**
  Oxon. A deserted village. The church stands by itself, overlooking the River Cherwell, and can only be approached on foot, its seclusion and peace rather disturbed by the railway that almost runs through the churchyard. To the east, half-hidden by trees, are the romantic ruins of the manor: gaunt broken stone walls and windows open to the winds. The whole is well worth exploration, but is difficult to approach owing to the presence of the River Cherwell. Leave the canal at bridge 220 and walk east.
- **Shipton-on-Cherwell**
  Oxon. PO box, tel. A village in a magnificent situation: the wooded church overlooks the bridge and the canal, which curls round the foot of the church yard. Behind, the grey stone manor and farm look out over rolling fields to the west. Shipton Bridge, a 1/4 mile to the east of the village, was the scene of a railway disaster on Christmas Eve 1874. Nine carriages fell from the bridge on to the frozen canal below and 34 people were killed. In the 1860s the thigh-bones of an immense dinosaur, cetiosaurus oxoniensis, were found in the nearby Enslow quarry. They are now in the University Museum, Oxford.

Boatyards

Ⓑ **BW Thrupp Yard** (01865 841570). This yard is not regularly manned. Moorings, toilets.

Ⓑ **Kingsground Narrowboats** Enslow Mill Wharf, Enslow, Kidlington (01869 233444). By bridge 216A. D Pump-out, gas, long-term mooring, boat & engine repairs, boat building, telephone, toilets, showers, small shop.

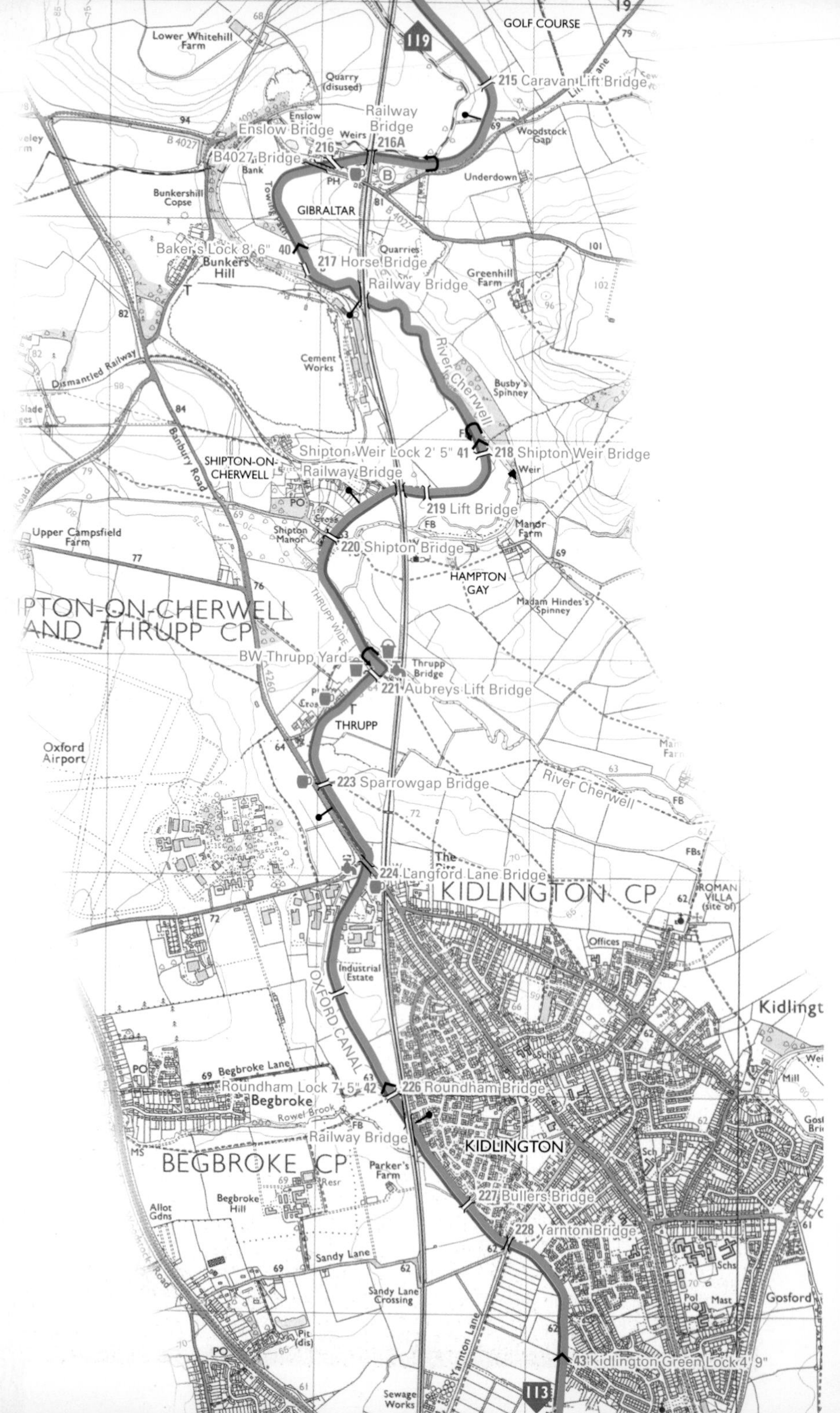

19
119
GOLF COURSE
Lower Whitehill Farm
Quarry (disused)
215 Caravan Lift Bridge
Railway Bridge
Enslow
Enslow Bridge
Weirs
216
216A
B4027 Bridge
Woodstock Gap
Underdown
Bank
PH
Bunkershill Copse
GIBRALTAR
Towing Path
B 4027
Baker's Lock 8' 6" 40
217 Horse Bridge
Quarries
Bunkers Hill
Railway Bridge
Greenhill Farm
Cement Works
River Cherwell
Busby's Spinney
Dismantled Railway
Banbury Road
Shipton Weir Lock 2' 5" 41
218 Shipton Weir Bridge
SHIPTON-ON-CHERWELL
Railway Bridge
Weir
PO
219 Lift Bridge
Cross
Manor Farm
Upper Campsfield Farm
Shipton Manor
220 Shipton Bridge
HAMPTON GAY
THRUPP WIDE
Madam Hindes's Spinney
SHIPTON-ON-CHERWELL AND THRUPP CP
BW Thrupp Yard
Thrupp Bridge
221 Aubreys Lift Bridge
THRUPP
Oxford Airport
223 Sparrowgap Bridge
River Cherwell
224 Langford Lane Bridge
KIDLINGTON CP
ROMAN VILLA (site of)
Offices
Industrial Estate
OXFORD CANAL
Kidlingt
Begbroke Lane
Roundham Lock 7' 5" 42
226 Roundham Bridge
Begbroke
Rowel Brook
Mill
Railway Bridge
KIDLINGTON
BEGBROKE CP
Parker's Farm
227 Bullers Bridge
Begbroke Hill
Allot Gdns
228 Yarnton Bridge
Sandy Lane
Schs
Sandy Lane Crossing
Mast
Gosford
Pit (dis)
Yarnton Lane
43 Kidlington Green Lock 4' 9"
Sewage Works
113

NAVIGATIONAL NOTES

Between Shipton Weir Lock and Baker's Lock the canal and river share a common course – this stretch can be hazardous when the river is in flood.

Pubs and Restaurants

Wise Alderman Banbury Road, Kidlington (01865 372281). Canalside at bridge 224. A comfortable village pub, with a canalside garden, dispensing Hook Norton, Wadworth and Tetley's real ales. Food *lunchtimes and evenings*, with vegetarian options. At certain times, during the close season for fishing, you may see carp going through their breeding rituals, splashing around amongst tree roots, at the water's edge at the bottom of the pub garden. It is an amazing sight. Mooring.

Jolly Boatman Banbury Road, Thrupp (01865 373775). A smart family run pub, by bridge 223, which was originally two cottages, now serving food *lunchtimes and evenings* in both the bar and the restaurant, along with Morrells real ale. Children are welcome and the pub has a canalside patio. Disabled access.

Boat Inn Thrupp (01865 374279). Canalside near bridge 221. An attractive stone-built and flower-bedecked pub which is popular with boaters, serving Morrells real ale and bar meals *lunchtimes and evenings,* with vegetarian options. The pub has a large garden, and children are welcome. An episode of the TV series *Inspector Morse* was filmed here.

Rock of Gibraltar Enslow (01869 331223). Canalside at bridge 216. Henry Baker, once landlord of this pub and a contractor during the building of the canal, has a nearby lock named after him. The pub has a fine stone interior, with a stone fireplace, and a vast and attractive garden, with children's playthings and a junior assault course. Good food is available *lunchtimes and evenings (not Sun or Mon evenings in winter)* from the servery in this well-kept establishment, and there are vegetarian choices. Courage real ale can be enjoyed, as well as a good selection of wines.

Brinklow (see page 136)

Lower Heyford

The canal continues to follow the Cherwell, winding its way through wooded undulating scenery. The waterway does not intrude at all, in fact it is so well landscaped as to be often invisible from the hills on either side. At first the woods are thick, the overhanging trees forming a tunnel through which the canal passes, bounded by old stone walls. Pigeon Lock marks the centre of the woods, which gradually diminish to reveal rolling farmland to the east and the water meadows of the Cherwell to the west. The canal passes over the route of Akeman Street, and then the trees and the isolation return to conceal the canal from the grounds of Rousham House. As it reaches Lower Heyford the landscape opens out, exposing pretty farmland. The locks continue the rise towards Claydon. Kirtlington and Tackley are set up on ridges away from the canal, but Lower Heyford actually reaches its banks. Here the wharf is now a hire boat base. The railway follows the canal very closely, and Heyford station is very convenient.

● **Kirtlington**
Oxon. 1 mile east of Pigeon Lock. *PO, tel, stores.* A stone village laid out around a green.

● **Tackley**
Oxon. PO, tel, stores, garage. About 1 mile north west of Pigeons Lock, across the Cherwell – access from the canal is by the footpath and a bridge leading from Pigeon Lock. It is a pleasant walk. A residential stone village, spreading down towards the canal to include Nethercott, where there is a small station – Tackley Halt. The church, set on a hill to the south, contains fine monuments.

Northbrook Bridge The stone canal bridge adjoins a much earlier packhorse bridge which crosses the Cherwell to the east.

Rousham House Steeple Aston (01869 347110). A lively picture of fighting during the Civil War is conjured up by the shooting holes made in the doors, which are preserved from the time when a Royalist garrison used the house. It dates from 1635 and was enlarged and its gardens landscaped in 1730 by William Kent. *Open Apr–Sep, Wed & Sun 14.00–16.30 (last entry). Gardens open daily 10.00–16.30 (last entry).* Charge. No children under 15, and no dogs.

● **Lower Heyford**
Oxon. PO box, tel, station. Built among woods along the south bank of the Cherwell, and hence the canal. The church, with fine stained glass, overlooks the canal from a slight hill that conceals many of the cottages in a village where motor cars still seem intruders. To the north is a fine and ancient water mill, screened by a line of willow trees.

Pubs and Restaurants

Dashwood Arms South Green, Kirtlington (01869 350225). An attractive pub overlooking the village green, serving Wadworth's and a guest real ale. Food is available *lunchtimes and evenings during the summer,* including vegetarian options, and there is a garden. Children welcome.

✕ **Oxford Arms** Troy Lane, Kirtlington (01869 350208). Food is available in both the bar and restaurant *lunchtimes and evenings every day,* including vegetarian options. Real ales change regularly, but may include Archers and Greene King. Children are welcomed if eating, and there is a garden.

Gardiners Arms Tackley (01869 331266). Morrell's plus a guest real ale are served in this pleasant pub, along with food *lunchtimes and evenings every day.* Vegetarian options are always available, children are welcomed, and there is a garden.

Bell Market Square, Lower Heyford (01869 347176). An attractive 17th-C inn just off the towpath. Moorings can be found by Heyford Mill lift bridge (205). ABC, Benskins, Burton and Tetley's real ales are served and meals are available *Tue–Sat lunchtimes and evenings, and lunchtime only on Sun. No food on Mon.* There are vegetarian options. Children are welcome and there is a garden.

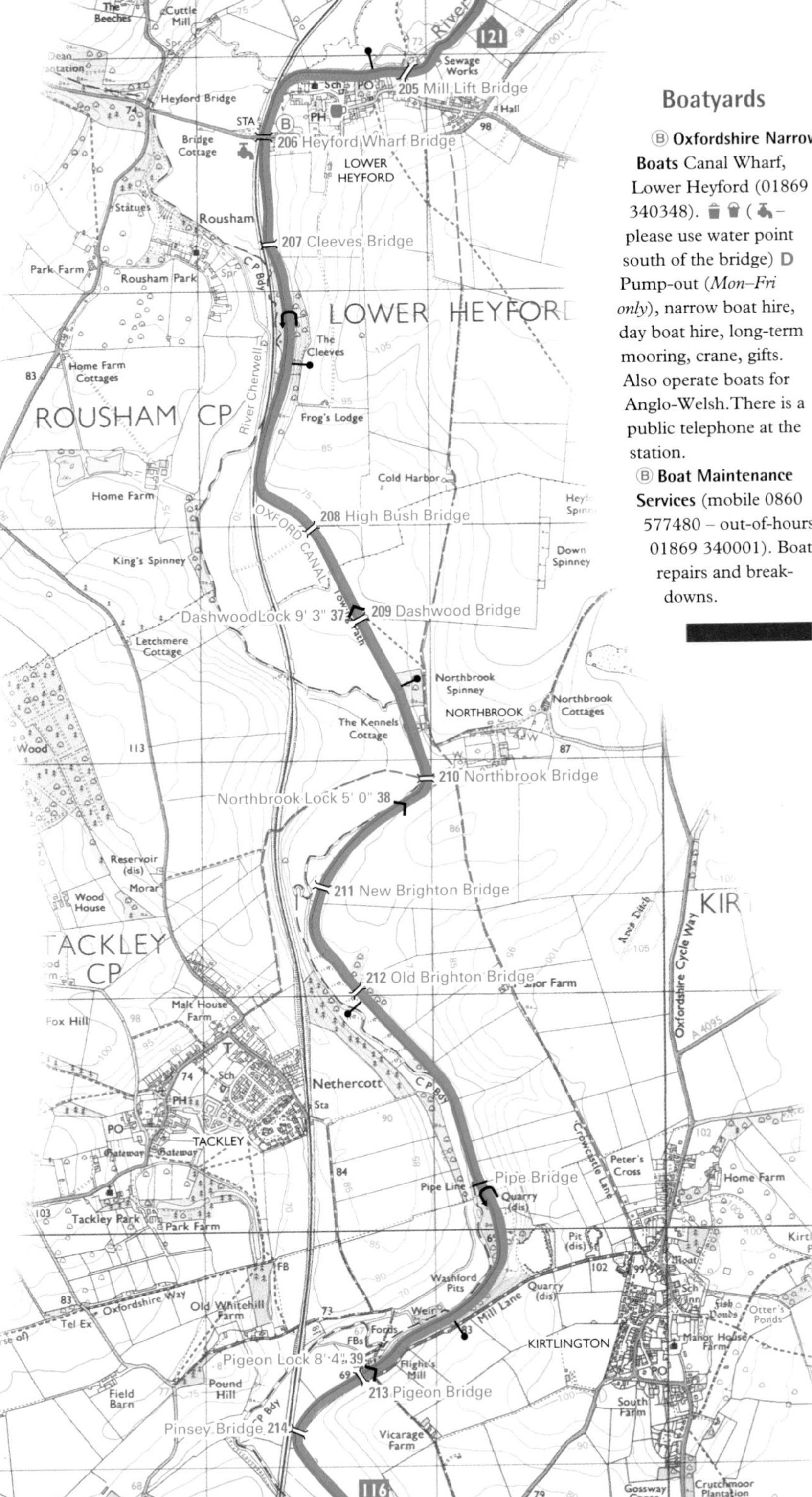

Boatyards

Ⓑ **Oxfordshire Narrow Boats** Canal Wharf, Lower Heyford (01869 340348). (– please use water point south of the bridge) D Pump-out (*Mon–Fri only*), narrow boat hire, day boat hire, long-term mooring, crane, gifts. Also operate boats for Anglo-Welsh. There is a public telephone at the station.

Ⓑ **Boat Maintenance Services** (mobile 0860 577480 – out-of-hours 01869 340001). Boat repairs and breakdowns.

Somerton

Continuing north along the Cherwell valley, the canal wanders through water meadows, the high towpath hedge often obscuring the fine views across the valley. As it curves towards Somerton the canal enters a short cutting and then moves out into open pastureland. Somerton climbs away from the wharf up the hillside to the east, altogether a very attractive situation. Just beyond the bridge four strange sculptured posts are passed, but there are few other intrusions and the canal remains isolated in the middle of the landscape – the locks are generally remote, and set amongst trees, a pattern only broken at Heyford Common Lock. However, the open country continues after Somerton Deep Lock, where the bridge retains its old number, harking back to the great modernisation of the 1820s, when the northern section of the canal was shortened, and the bridges were re-numbered. The canal then pursues a straighter course towards Banbury. After Somerton two railways run side by side to the east of the canal, before joining at Aynho.

● **Upper Heyford**
Oxon. PO box, tel. A main street of thatched stone cottages falls steeply to the canal, with views across the valley to Steeple Aston. The church overlooks the canal, as does a fine barn.

● **Somerton**
Oxon. PO box, tel. A straggling grey stone village winding up the hill to the east of the canal. On the highest point is the church with its decorated tower: there are good 16th-C tombs inside. In all the villages along the Cherwell valley, the churches are placed on mounds or higher ground, overlooking the valley.

Boatyards

Ⓑ **Aynho Wharf** Banbury (01869 338483).
D Pump-out, gas, overnight & long-term mooring, boat & engine sales and repairs, boatbuilding, boat painting and signwriting, telephone nearby, toilets, small shop.

RALLY AROUND THE OXFORD

Save the Oxford Canal? Who needs to *save* the Oxford Canal? It is as much an integral part of the network as the Grand Union and the Leeds & Liverpool, and the system would seem bleak without it. But 'twas not always so . . .

In 1955 the *British Waterways Board of Survey Report* was not at all favourable towards the retention of the *narrow* canals, and the Oxford was directly under threat. Then, as now, there were thankfully many enthusiasts prepared to direct their skills and energy towards the retainment of the waterways, and so it was that Joan Marston and the Midlands Branch of the IWA organised a rally at Banbury on 1 August 1955.

Over 50 boats arrived to support the occasion, and estimates of visitors vary between 5000 and 10,000. The weather was splendid, and the attractions (in addition to the canal) included waterways films, an exhibition, canoe races, a mobile grocery store, a Saturday night reception and a supper dance on Monday. And a beer tent, of course.

The *Banbury Guardian* reported 'Never has the town had such a water borne spree'. Those of us who enjoy the Oxford Canal today should be very thankful.

BOAT TRIPS
From Aynho Wharf, Banbury (01869 338483). Public trips and private charter.

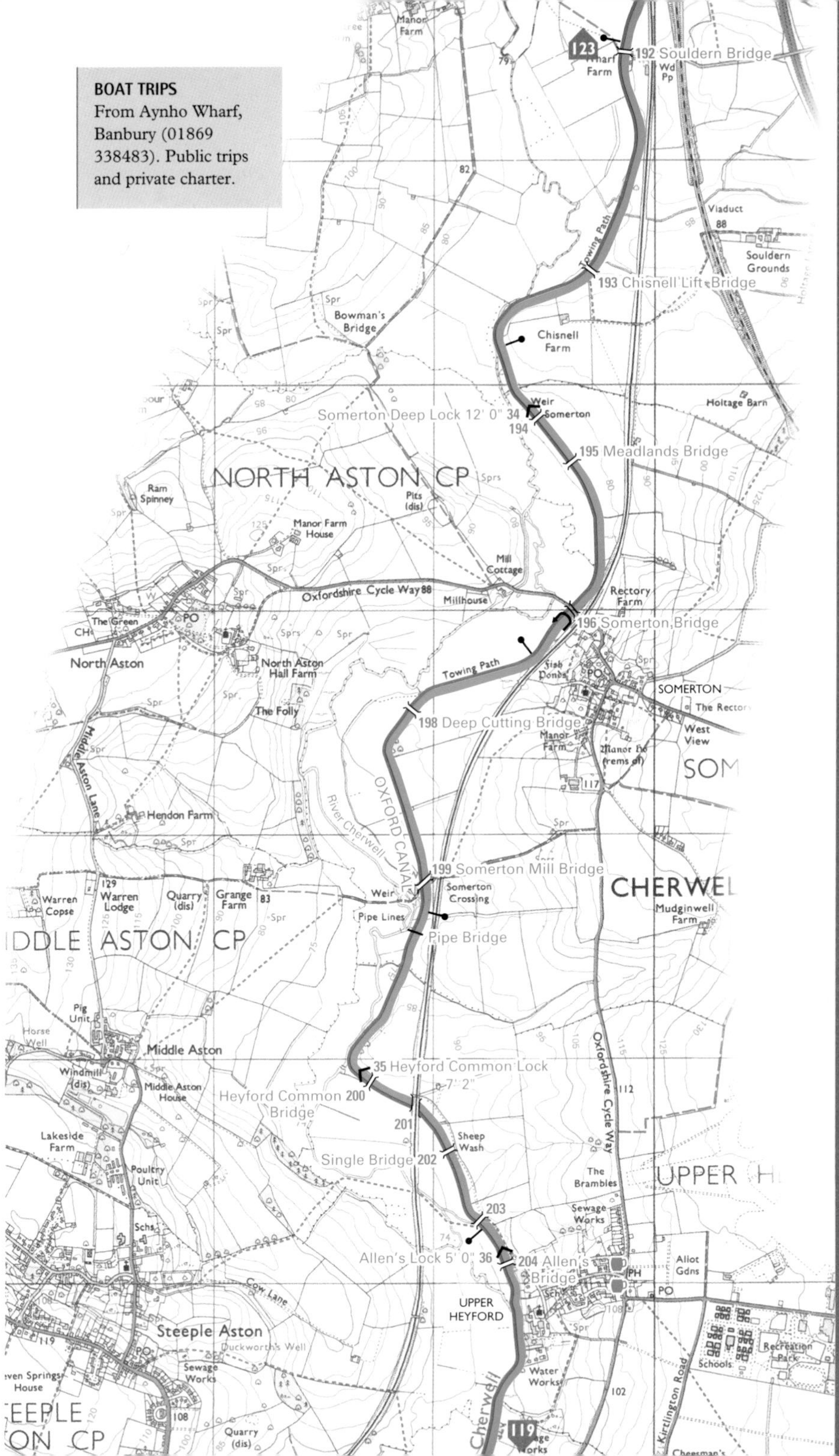

King's Sutton

The canal continues through wooded open country with a background of hills to the east. The Cherwell crosses the canal at Aynho Weir Lock before continuing parallel to it and forming a large loop lined by trees as it approaches King's Sutton, with its pretty lock and cottage. Then the tall spire of the church comes into view. Locks continue the rise to Banbury: the very narrow Nell Bridge, is one of the oldest, having survived the various road-widening schemes. The railway follows the canal to the east. This pleasant rural stretch of the canal along the Cherwell valley is well punctuated by the characteristic wooden lift bridges: luckily most of these are nowadays left open (raised). Railway and motorway now bracket the canal intruding into its rural peace. In parts the sinking of the motorway into deep cuttings has helped to lessen its impact upon the countryside, but the steady drone of the traffic is still discernible.

Pubs and Restaurants

Great Western Arms Station Road, Aynho Wharf (bridge 190) (01869 338288). The interior of this good-humoured pub is devoted to memorabilia of the GWR. They serve Hook Norton real ale and bar meals *Easter–Oct (not Sun and Mon in winter), lunchtimes and evenings.* The pub also has a family room and a garden.

X **Duke of Cumberland's Head** Clifton (01869 338534). This attractive thatched 16th-C pub has the largest hen salmon caught with a fly in the UK. Hook Norton, Adnams, Hampshire (King Alfreds) and a guest real ale can be enjoyed, along with good food *lunchtimes and evenings every day*, with vegetarian options. Children are welcome if dining, and there is a garden.

Three Tuns King's Sutton. A cosy and friendly local, with a garden.

Butcher's Arms King's Sutton (01295 730750). A family pub serving Hook Norton real ale. Children welcome, garden.

X **Red Lion Hotel** The Green, Adderbury (01295 810269). Overlooking the village green this fine old coaching inn has been beautifully restored. Features discovered during the restoration work indicate that this ancient Royalist hostelry dates from before the civil war. Hook Norton, Martson's and Theakstons real ale are served, and food is available in both the bar and restaurant *lunchtimes and evenings.* Vegetarians are catered for. There is a garden, and children are welcome.

X **Bell Inn** High Street, Adderbury (01295 810338). It is worth the walk down the village street to find this little pub dating back to 1779. Hook Norton and a guest real ale are available, and bar and restaurant meals are served *lunchtimes and evenings every day.* Children are welcome, and there is a pretty patio garden.

- **Clifton**
  Oxon. PO box, tel. A small village, overlooking the canal.
- **Aynho**
  Northants. PO, tel. It is worth walking a mile east of Aynho Wharf to visit this village. A self-contained village square sheltered from the road, unchanged and complete in rich stone. New houses have been carefully blended with the old, and peach trees have been trained along the walls of many of the cottages. On the other side of the road is the formal classical façade of:
  Aynho Park (01869 810636). A 17th-C mansion rebuilt by Sir John Soane in the late 18thC, the house is large but restrained, and does not look out of place in a village street. Fine paintings, furniture and Venetian glass. The church beside the house was classicised at the same time: the strange façade added to the nave wall makes it a charming folly. *Open May–Sep, Wed & Thu afternoons.* Charge.
- **King's Sutton**
  Northants. PO, tel, stores, garage, station. An attractive village of narrow streets that wander in every direction. The centre is round a green, at the top of a hill, where rows of thatched cottages, two pubs and the church stand in quiet harmony. The church is superb: beautifully proportioned with a tall, slender spire. The Saxon font, found buried in the churchyard in 1923, has been linked with the baptism in 662 AD of St Rumbold who was born at nearby Walton Fields. The River Cherwell makes access to this village difficult from the canal; the only practicable access is by walking south east for 1½ miles from bridge 177.
- **Adderbury**
  Oxon. PO, tel, stores, garage. West of bridge 177. The large expanse of village green surrounded by

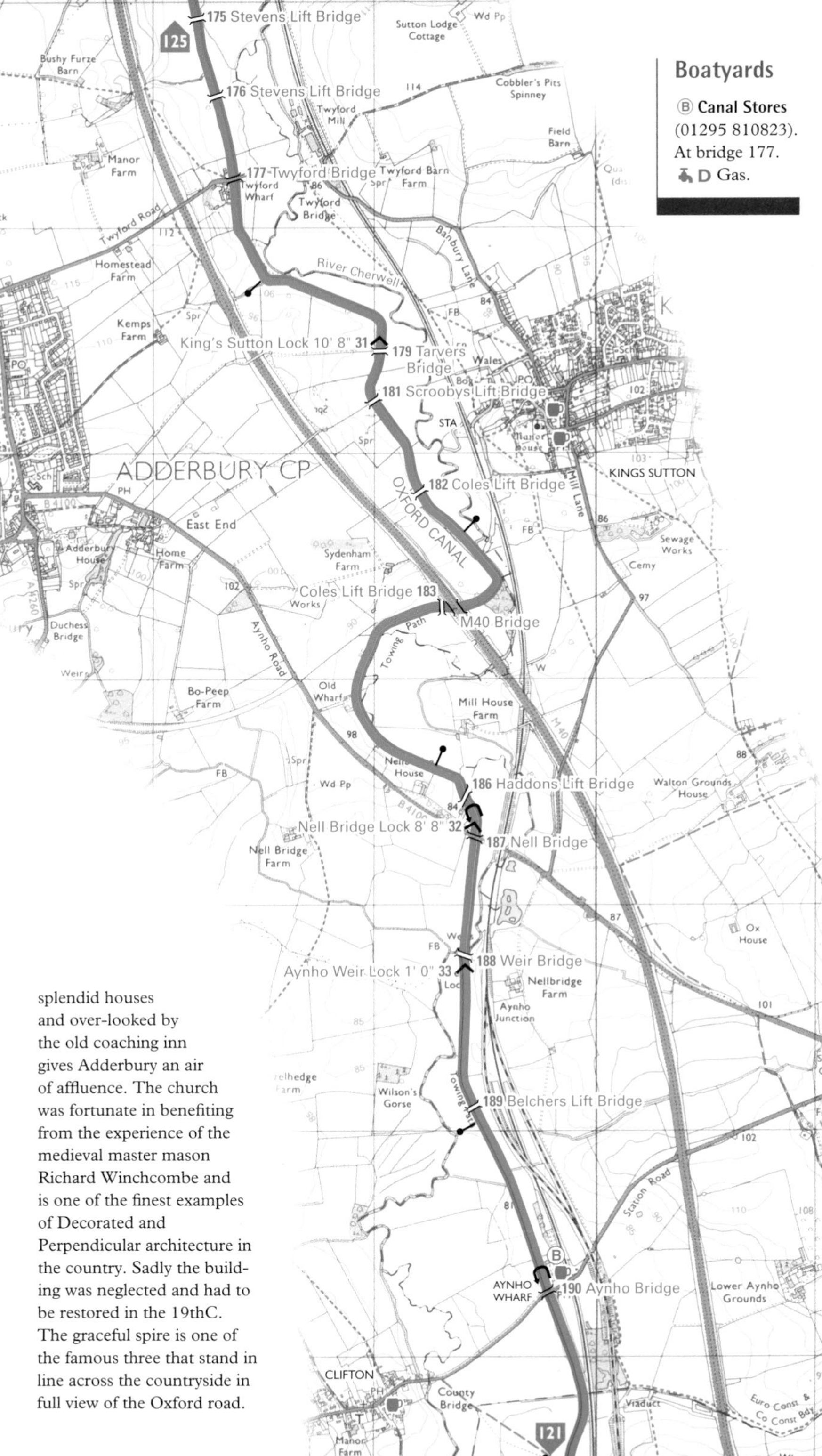

Boatyards

Ⓑ **Canal Stores** (01295 810823). At bridge 177. **D** Gas.

splendid houses and over-looked by the old coaching inn gives Adderbury an air of affluence. The church was fortunate in benefiting from the experience of the medieval master mason Richard Winchcombe and is one of the finest examples of Decorated and Perpendicular architecture in the country. Sadly the building was neglected and had to be restored in the 19thC. The graceful spire is one of the famous three that stand in line across the countryside in full view of the Oxford road.

Banbury

Continuing north west along the Cherwell valley the canal enters Banbury beside housing estates and an industrial area. It passes through the centre in a flurry of bridges, and soon skirts Spiceball Country Park, a pleasant area of parkland. There are good moorings, and shops nearby. Industry remains generally confined to the east – it is not until Hardwick Lock and the M40 bridge are passed that surroundings more typical of the Oxford Canal return, as the canal swings to the north and hills reappear to the west. Locks continue the steady rise throughout this stretch, and from here on all the locks feature double bottom gates, which make for lighter work. The railway follows the canal but crosses to the west after Banbury.

● **Banbury**
Oxon. MD Thu, Sat. PO, tel, stores, garage, cinema, station. Originally a wool town, the castle was pulled down by Cromwell's forces in 1646 and now no trace remains. The ancient cross of nursery rhyme fame in the town centre was demolished in 1602, and the present cross is a 19th-C replica. The church was built in 1793 by S P Cockrell. The original bake house, which produced the spiced Banbury cakes, survived until 1968.
The Mill Arts Centre (01295 252050). By Banbury Lock. Plays, theatre, dance and music. A café is *open 10.00–15.00*, and a bar is open during *normal licensing hours*. Tickets can often be purchased on the night.
Tourist Information Centre & Museum Castle Quay, Banbury (01295 259855). The museum, which overlooks the Banbury Cross and is next door to Tooleys Boatyard (see below), gives a graphic representation of local history. It is housed in this new development, which also includes:
Tooley's Boatyard This historic boatyard, the last remaining element of the old Banbury canal terminus surviving since 1780 has, it seems, been saved. It was here that Tom Rolt's boat *Cressy* was prepared for his honeymoon cruise with new wife in 1939. This cruise was the basis of his now classic book *Narrow Boat*, which in turn led to the formation of the Inland Waterways Association in 1946 aboard *Cressy*, moored at the top of the Tardebigge Flight on the Worcester & Birmingham (see Book 2, Worcester & Birmingham, page 150). Tooley's Boatyard still has a working forge and an operational dry dock, together with all the tools needed to build a wooden narrow boat. The yard is being restored, and will open, as part of the museum, in 2001.

● **Little Bourton**
Oxon. 1/2 mile west of bridge 158. *PO box, tel, stores, garage.* A quiet residential village to the west of the beautifully kept Little Bourton Lock and cottage. Stores at the garage are *open each day till late.*

Boatyards

Ⓑ **Sovereign Narrowboats** Sovereign Wharf, Compton Road, Banbury (01295 275657). (charge) D Pump-out, gas, overnight and long-term mooring.

Pubs and Restaurants

Ye Olde Reindeer Inn Parsons Street, Banbury (01295 264031). Dating from 1570, this pub offers Hook Norton real ale and meals *Mon–Sat lunchtimes*, with vegetarian options. Have a look at the Globe Room. Children are welcome, and there is an outside seating area.

Ye Olde Auctioneer Parsons Street, Banbury (01295 251820). A cosy town pub. Food is served *Mon-Thu all day, Fri & Sat 11.00-18.00 & 21.00-23.45, Sun lunchtimes.* Seats outside in summer.

Woolpack Horsefair, Banbury (01295 262915). Courage real ale is served. Children welcome, small garden.

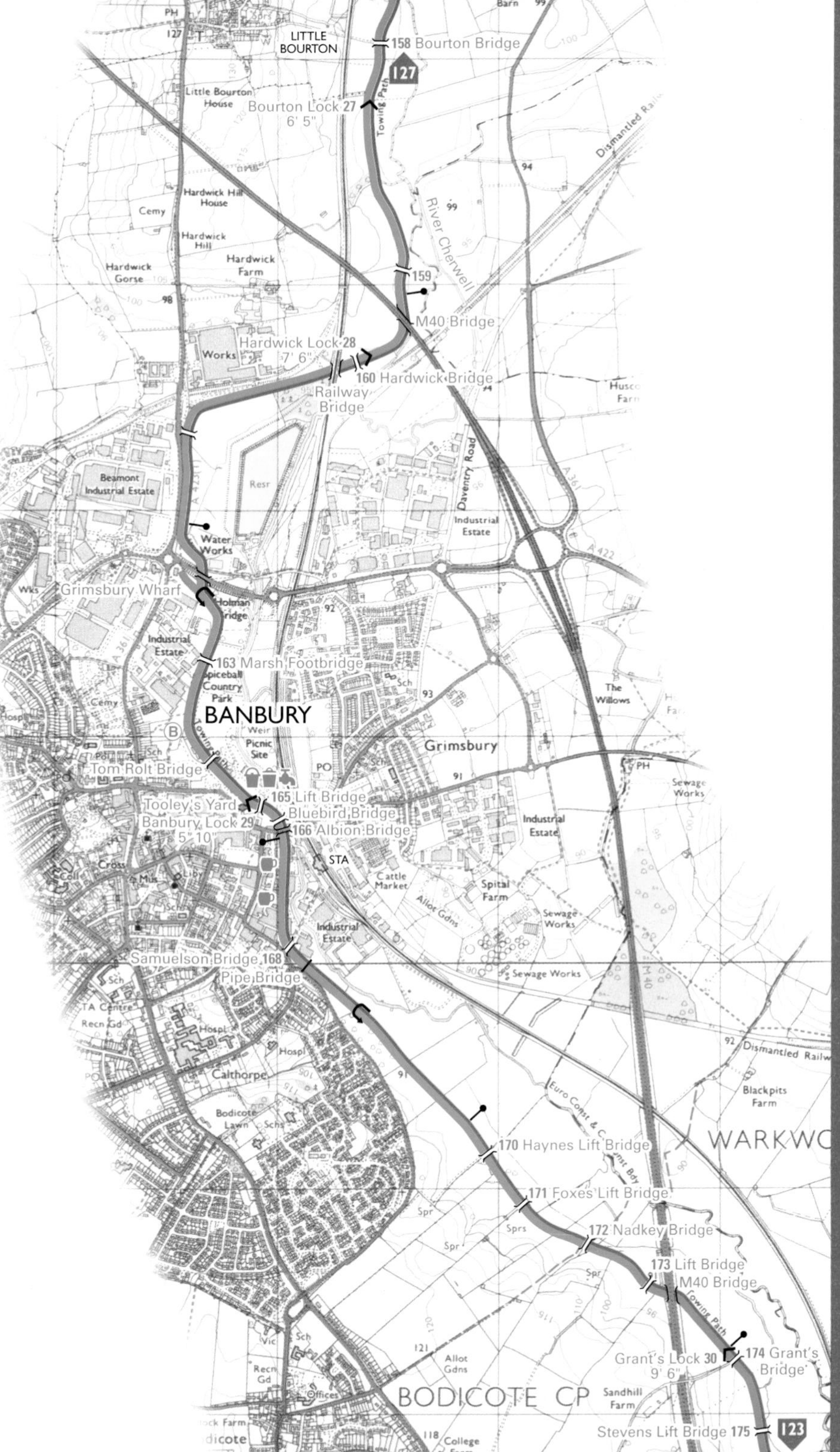
LITTLE BOURTON
158 Bourton Bridge
127
Little Bourton House
Bourton Lock 27
6' 5"
Towing Path
Dismantled Railway
River Cherwell
Hardwick Hill House
Cemy
Hardwick Hill
Hardwick Farm
Hardwick Gorse
159
M40 Bridge
Works
Hardwick Lock 28
7' 6"
160 Hardwick Bridge
Railway Bridge
Resr
Beamont Industrial Estate
Daventry Road
Industrial Estate
Water Works
A 361
A 422
Grimsbury Wharf
Wks
Holman Bridge
Industrial Estate
163 Marsh Footbridge
Spiceball Country Park
Cemy
BANBURY
Weir
Picnic Site
The Willows
Grimsbury
Tom Rolt Bridge
PO
165 Lift Bridge
Tooley's Yard
Bluebird Bridge
Banbury Lock 29
5' 10"
166 Albion Bridge
STA
Sewage Works
Industrial Estate
Cross
Mus
Liby
Cattle Market
Spital Farm
Allot Gdns
Sewage Works
Industrial Estate
Samuelson Bridge 168
Pipe Bridge
Sewage Works
M 40
TA Centre
Recn Gd
Hospl
Hospl
Calthorpe
Dismantled Railway
Blackpits Farm
Bodicote Lawn
Euro Const & Cty Bdy
170 Haynes Lift Bridge
WARKWO
171 Foxes Lift Bridge
172 Nadkey Bridge
173 Lift Bridge
M40 Bridge
Towing Path
Grant's Lock 30
9' 6"
174 Grant's Bridge
Allot Gdns
BODICOTE CP
Sandhill Farm
Offices
Stevens Lift Bridge 175
123
College Farm

Cropredy

Continuing north along the Cherwell valley the canal enters Cropredy, whose stone cottages and wharf have been visible for some time. The village flanks the canal on the west bank, and the useful stores are right beside Cropredy Wharf Bridge. After the village the high towpath hedge conceals the open fields beyond, although there are views across the valley to the west. There is a useful shop at Broadmoor Lock selling fenders, mooring pins and so on. Near Varney's and Elkington's Locks the old ridge and furrow field patterns are very pronounced. Soon Claydon comes into sight – here five locks take the canal to the summit level. Light woods border the canal, which is both shallow and very narrow in places. Near the second lock the remains of the handsome old red-brick stabling for boat horses can be seen.

● **Cropredy**
Oxon. PO, tel, stores. A quiet village with wandering streets of old brick houses. There is no real centre, but the whole village is very close to the canal. The stately sandstone church contains fine woodwork; the slow swing of the clock pendulum in the belfry seems to echo the sleepy nature of the village, which only bursts into life during the annual Folk Festival, now Europe's largest. It is held on the *second weekend in August.* It all began in 1979, when Fairport Convention held their farewell concert here. The Old Coal Wharf by the bridge is available for teas and light meals.
Battle of Cropredy 29 June 1644. Cromwell's forces under Waller attacked Cropredy Bridge in an attempt to open a way to Oxford. Despite greatly inferior numbers, the Royalist cavalry managed to scatter Waller's army and capture his artillery, thus protecting Oxford. A plaque on the river bridge recalls the battle.

● **Claydon**
Oxon. PO, tel. Set in a rolling open landscape to the west of the canal. Claydon is an old-fashioned brown-stone village; in spite of some new development it preserves a quiet unpretentious charm. The curiously irregular Church of St James the Great provides a focal point – parts of it date from before the 12thC and the tower, which has a saddle back roof, contains a clock. There is no face, but the hour is chimed. Clattercote Priory, just to the south, still remains, although the village pub is no more.
The Bygones Museum Butlin Farm, Claydon (01295 690258). Andrew Fox's fascinating museum of local relics continues to grow and never fails to entrance visitors. Children love to handle the objects, and his recreation of a 19th-C cottage kitchen is remarkably atmospheric. Outside there are tractors, a traction engine, a steam roller and various stationary steam engines, which are in steam on the *first Sun of each month, and Summer B. Hols.* There is a well-stocked gift shop and a licensed restaurant. *Open 10.00–17.00 (closed Mon except B. Hols).* Charge.

Pubs and Restaurants

Brasenose Arms Station Road, Cropredy (01295 750244). A welcoming 16th-C thatched stone pub with Canadian hosts and a resident ghost. A choice of three or four real ales are available, and food is served *lunchtimes and evenings (not Mon lunchtimes).* Large garden, and children are welcome.

Red Lion Red Lion Street, Cropredy (01295 750224). A beautiful 15th-C thatched terraced pub opposite the church, covered with wisteria, where you can enjoy real ales in a bar which has stone walls and flagged floors. There is a fine well to the rear. Good meals at reasonable prices are served *lunchtimes and evenings every day in season (not Mon–Wed evening at quieter times, but booking is advisable during the summer).* Vegetarian options are always available, children are welcome, and there is a garden. There is no juke box.

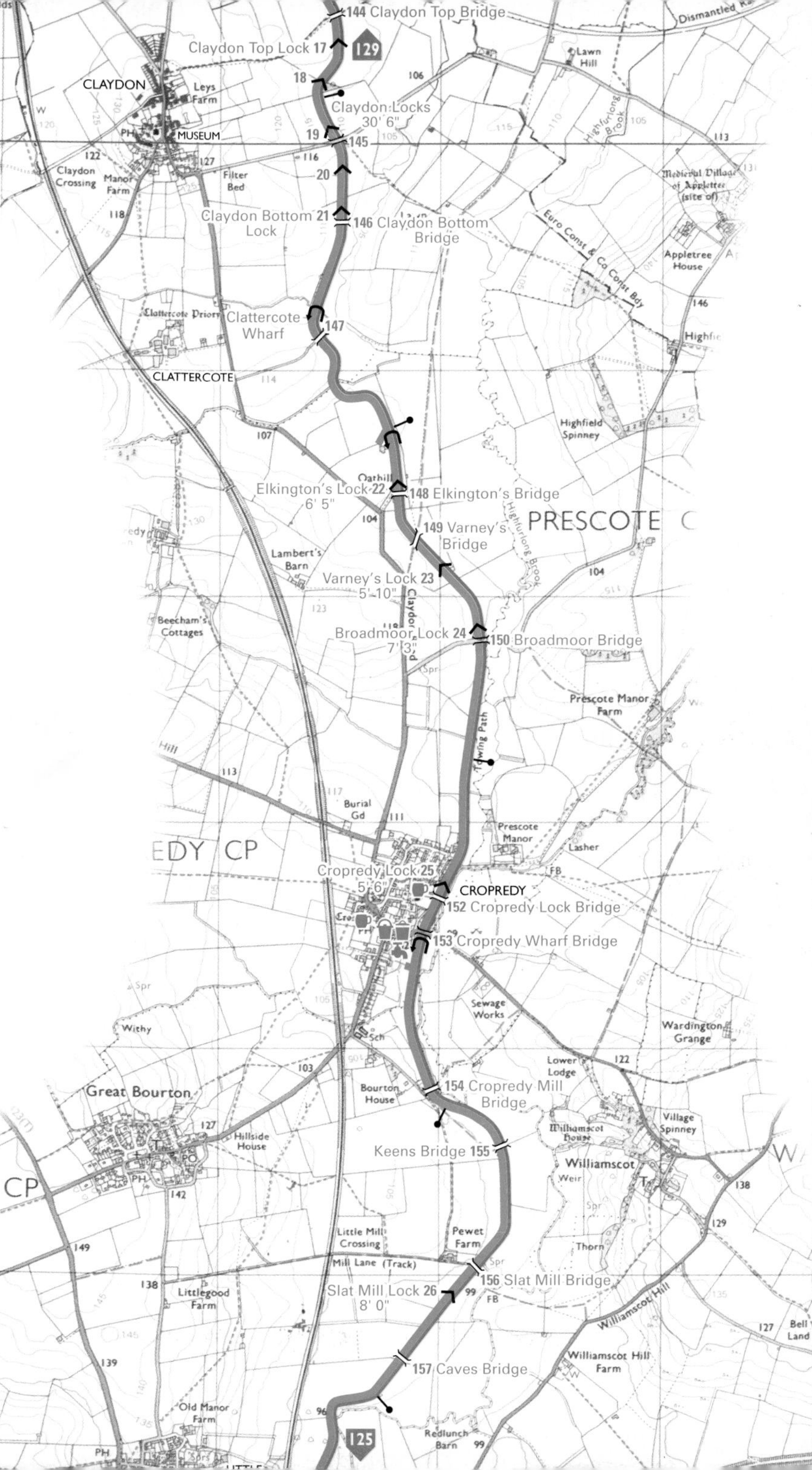
144 Claydon Top Bridge
Claydon Top Lock 17
129
18
Claydon Locks
30' 6"
19
145
20
Claydon Bottom 21
Lock
146 Claydon Bottom
Bridge
CLAYDON
Leys
Farm
MUSEUM
PH
Claydon
Crossing
Manor
Farm
Filter
Bed
Clattercote Priory
Clattercote
Wharf
147
CLATTERCOTE
Lawn
Hill
Dismantled Rly
Highfurlong
Brook
Medieval Village
of Appletree
(site of)
Euro Const & Co Const Bdy
Appletree
House
Highfield
Spinney
Oathill
Elkington's Lock 22
6' 5"
148 Elkington's Bridge
149 Varney's
Bridge
PRESCOTE
Lambert's
Barn
Varney's Lock 23
5' 10"
Claydon Road
Beecham's
Cottages
Broadmoor Lock 24
7' 3"
150 Broadmoor Bridge
Prescote Manor
Farm
Towing Path
Burial
Gd
EDY CP
Prescote
Manor
Lasher
FB
Cropredy Lock 25
5' 6"
CROPREDY
152 Cropredy Lock Bridge
153 Cropredy Wharf Bridge
Sewage
Works
Withy
Sch
Wardington
Grange
Lower
Lodge
Great Bourton
Bourton
House
154 Cropredy Mill
Bridge
Hillside
House
Williamscot
House
Village
Spinney
Keens Bridge 155
Williamscot
Weir
PO
PH
CP
Thorn
Little Mill
Crossing
Pewet
Farm
Mill Lane (Track)
156 Slat Mill Bridge
Slat Mill Lock 26
8' 0"
Littlegood
Farm
Williamscot Hill
Bell
Land
157 Caves Bridge
Williamscot Hill
Farm
Old Manor
Farm
125
Redlunch
Barn

Fenny Compton

After Claydon Locks the canal twists and turns. Hills and trees close in, preparing for the cutting that marks the course of the old tunnel. The feeder from Boddington reservoir, 2½ miles to the east, enters the canal through the towpath bridge 142. The railway, which moved to the west after Cropredy, reappears beside the canal. The canal continues along the Fenny Compton Tunnel, a steep, thickly wooded cutting which ends as it swings in a wide loop eastwards towards Fenny Compton Wharf. The hills retreat for a while, although their influence is still present in the extravagantly indirect course taken by the canal. The long winding route involves a large number of brick arch accommodation bridges and many are now not-numbered – it is easy to become disorientated here. The canal first runs west before doubling back on itself and running east to Stoneton Manor, where a steep ridge causes it to resume a north westerly direction towards Napton. Fenny Compton and Wormleighton are both about a mile from the canal; Priors Hardwick is nearer, across the fields, but has no supplies. The railway disappears to the west after Fenny Compton Wharf.

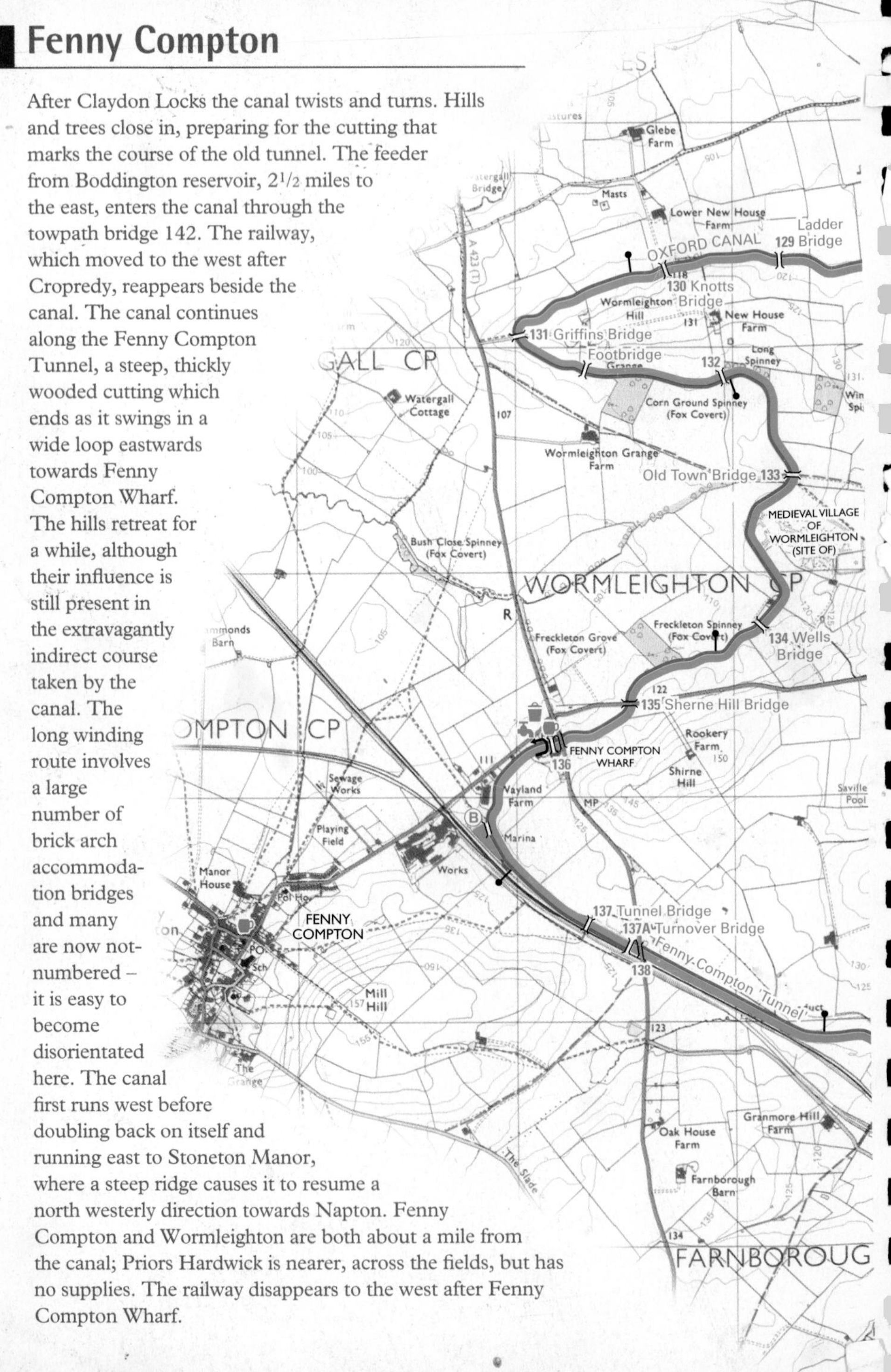

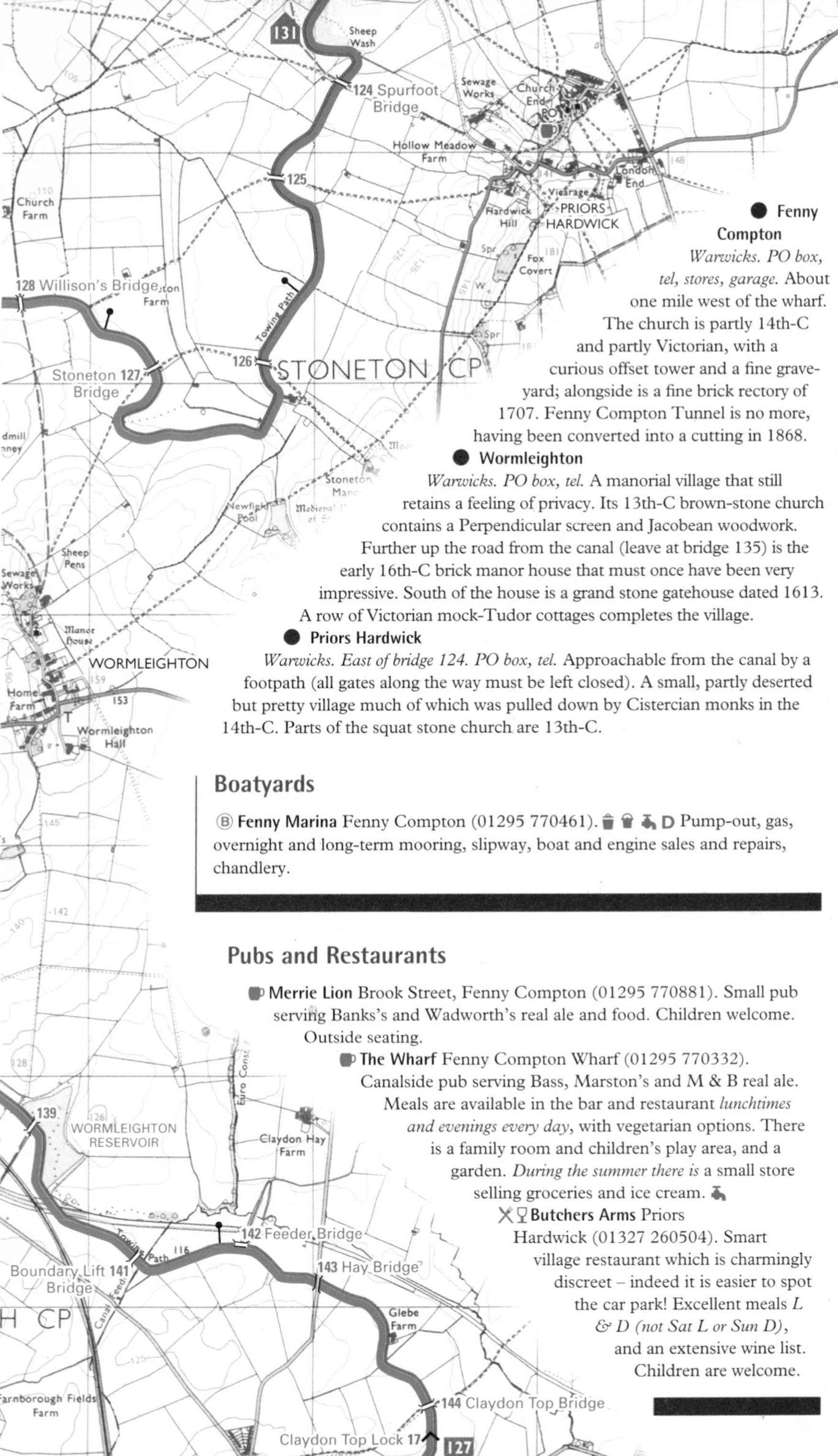

● **Fenny Compton**

Warwicks. PO box, tel, stores, garage. About one mile west of the wharf. The church is partly 14th-C and partly Victorian, with a curious offset tower and a fine graveyard; alongside is a fine brick rectory of 1707. Fenny Compton Tunnel is no more, having been converted into a cutting in 1868.

● **Wormleighton**

Warwicks. PO box, tel. A manorial village that still retains a feeling of privacy. Its 13th-C brown-stone church contains a Perpendicular screen and Jacobean woodwork. Further up the road from the canal (leave at bridge 135) is the early 16th-C brick manor house that must once have been very impressive. South of the house is a grand stone gatehouse dated 1613. A row of Victorian mock-Tudor cottages completes the village.

● **Priors Hardwick**

Warwicks. East of bridge 124. PO box, tel. Approachable from the canal by a footpath (all gates along the way must be left closed). A small, partly deserted but pretty village much of which was pulled down by Cistercian monks in the 14th-C. Parts of the squat stone church are 13th-C.

Boatyards

Ⓑ **Fenny Marina** Fenny Compton (01295 770461). D Pump-out, gas, overnight and long-term mooring, slipway, boat and engine sales and repairs, chandlery.

Pubs and Restaurants

Merrie Lion Brook Street, Fenny Compton (01295 770881). Small pub serving Banks's and Wadworth's real ale and food. Children welcome. Outside seating.

The Wharf Fenny Compton Wharf (01295 770332). Canalside pub serving Bass, Marston's and M & B real ale. Meals are available in the bar and restaurant *lunchtimes and evenings every day*, with vegetarian options. There is a family room and children's play area, and a garden. *During the summer there is* a small store selling groceries and ice cream.

Butchers Arms Priors Hardwick (01327 260504). Smart village restaurant which is charmingly discreet – indeed it is easier to spot the car park! Excellent meals *L & D (not Sat L or Sun D)*, and an extensive wine list. Children are welcome.

Napton

The canal continues northwards through rolling open farmland, with the view to the west concealed by the towpath hedge. At Marston Doles the country opens out and the windmill on top of Napton Hill comes into view. Here the summit level ends and the canal starts the fall towards the junction. The arm to the east, now used for private moorings, once lead to the site of a former pump house – it has now been shortened to the site of the first bridge. A useful shop will be found by the Folly pub (bridge 113) – the canal then swings to the west of Napton Hill, passing Brickyard Bridge, and then turns east to meet the Grand Union at the junction. Marston Doles, at the top of the flight, is a typical canal settlement, but Napton, larger and prosperous, is set to the east on the side of the hill. There are moorings available at Napton Bottom Lock.

Marston Doles
Warwicks. PO box, tel. A tiny settlement which owes its existence to the canal – towing horses used to be stabled here. To the north, at the end of a foreshortened arm, are the remains of the pumping house that used to pump water up to the summit from the bottom of the Napton flight.

Napton-on-the-Hill
Warwicks. PO, tel, stores, garage. Rising to over 400ft, Napton Hill dominates the immediate landscape. The village is scattered all over the hill, climbing steeply up the sides. The shops and pubs are at the bottom, however, and so only those wishing to enjoy the view or visit the 13th-C church need climb to the top. Legend has it that the church was to be built on the village green but the devil persisted in carrying the building stones to the present site where the church was eventually built. Seven counties can be seen from this high vantage point. Near the church is the restored windmill alone on the hilltop. The canal wanders round the base of the hill, bypassing the village except for the wharf alongside Brickyard Bridge. Best access is from either bridge 113 or 110.

Pubs and Restaurants

Folly Inn Folly Lane, Napton (01926 815185). Next to bridge 113. A welcoming family pub dispensing Banks's and Camerons real ales. Re-opened after a 40-year closure, the rooms are pleasantly decorated with charming bygones, and there is a larger collection out the back. An unusual menu offers various different pies, including vegetarian, available *lunchtimes and evenings every day*. There is a large garden, and children are welcome. Bike hire nearby.

X **Napton Bridge Inn** (01926 812466). Canalside at bridge 111 on the Oxford Canal. Excellent food is served *lunchtimes and evenings every day*, with restaurant meals *L & D*. You can choose from steaks to fish to spicy pasta. Vegetarians are well looked after, and children are welcomed. Flowers, Tetley's and a guest real ale are available. There is a pleasant garden with a children's play area, and often entertainment during *the summer months*.

X **Ye Olde Kings Head** Napton-on-the-Hill (01926 812202). Just 200yds south of bridge 109. Marston's, Morland's plus seven constantly changing real ales and a wide range of bar and restaurant meals *lunchtimes and evenings every day (all day at weekends, when there is a Sunday carvery)*. Children are welcome, there is a children's menu, and a large garden.

X **Crown Inn** High Street, Napton (01926 812484). 1/2 mile east of bridge 113, with *PO and stores* nearby. A friendly village pub with a garden area to the rear. Boddingtons and Flowers real ales are served, and there are bar meals *lunchtimes and evenings every day*, and restaurant meals *Thu–Sat evenings*. Vegetarian options are always available. A large horse chestnut tree planted to commemorate the coronation of George V provides a shady drinking area on the green, and there is a windmill around the back. Children are welcomed, and there is a pool room.

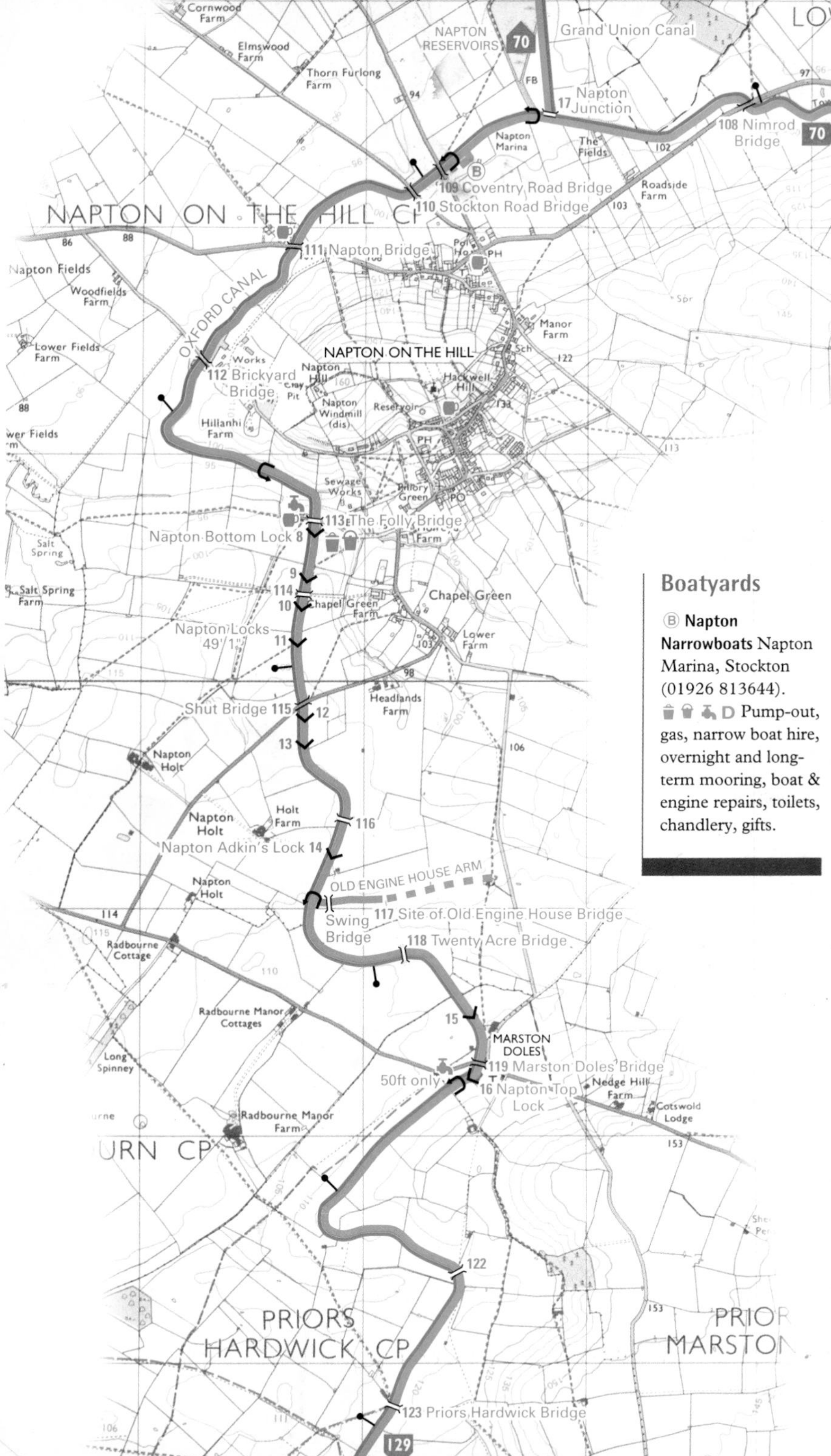

Boatyards

Ⓑ **Napton Narrowboats** Napton Marina, Stockton (01926 813644).
D Pump-out, gas, narrow boat hire, overnight and long-term mooring, boat & engine repairs, toilets, chandlery, gifts.

Willoughby

North of Braunston the Oxford Canal soon leaves behind the excitement and interest of the village to run through wide open country, backed by bare hills to the east. It is an ancient landscape, and by bridge 87 medieval ridge and furrow field patterns are in evidence. These were created as villagers cleared forested land, and each ploughed strips throwing soil towards the centre. Gradually a collection of strips, all running parallel to each other, made up a furlong or cultura. This was then enclosed by a low bank and an access track (usually difficult to identify today) was created. Fields, consisting of dozens of furlongs, were then sometimes fenced. Skirting round Barby Hill, the canal swings north east towards Hillmorton and Rugby. The M45 makes a noisy crossing after Barby Hill.

Boatyards

All the following are on the *Grand Union Canal* at Braunston.

The Boat Shop (01788 891310). Started on board a boat moored at Braunston Turn, this is now a shop by Braunston Top Lock selling basic chandlery, coal, groceries, fruit and vegetables canal ware, brass ware and much more. *Open Jun–Sep 08.00–20.00, Oct–May 08.00–18.00.*

Ⓑ **Braunston Boats** Bottom Lock, Braunston (01788 891079). **D** Pump-out, gas, narrow boat hire, long-term mooring by arrangement only.

Ⓑ **Union Canal Carriers** Canalside at Braunston pump house, Dark Lane (01788 890784). **D** Pump-out, gas, narrow boat hire, overnight mooring by arrangement, books and maps, boat building, boat and engine sales and repairs. *24hr* breakdown service (telephone 01788 812156 *outside working hours*).

Ⓑ **Braunston Marina** The Wharf, Braunston (01788 891373). Through the fine bridge dated 1834 and into an historic canal wharf. **D E** Gas, pump-out, overnight and long-term mooring, dry and wet dock, chandlery, boat building sales and repairs, engineering – all services. Toilets and showers, public telephone, chandlery, gift shop selling books and maps. Laundrette.

Ⓑ **Midland Chandlers** Canalside, Braunston Turn (01788 891401). A wide range of chandlery.

Pubs and Restaurants

Rose Inn Main Street, Willoughby (01788 890567). An attractively maintained thatched village pub, offering Courage real ale. Bar, restaurant and carvery meals *lunchtimes and evenings (not Mon & Wed lunchtimes or Sun evenings)*, with vegetarian choices. Outside seating with children's play area. Regular entertainment with theme nights.

The Mill House London Road, Braunston (01788 890450). Once the Rose & Castle, now a comfortable and friendly modern pub/restaurant. Bass and Worthington real ale, and food *Mon–Sat 12.00–21.30 (Sun until 21.00)*. Children's room and fine canalside garden. Overnight mooring for patrons.

Wheatsheaf The Green, Braunston (01788 890748). A locals' pub with a warm atmosphere, and traditional bar games. Everards, Flowers and guest real ales. Food *lunchtimes and evenings,* along with some interesting wines. Children welcome until early evening.

Old Plough Inn High Street, Braunston (01788 890000). Popular village pub of great character, with an open fire. Built around 1672, it has had only thirteen landlords since then. Wadworth's real ale, with good food *lunchtimes and evenings every day*, including vegetarian dishes. Children are welcome, and there is a garden.

BOAT TRIPS

Rachael Operating from Braunston Marina, this licensed restaurant boat can accommodate 20 people. It makes regular *3 hour evening trips during the summer* on the Oxford Canal, and can also be chartered for *lunchtime* cruises. Telephone 07071 880784 for details.

The Rambler Operating from the Mill House (see below). Seating 12 people, this boat provides *lunchtime* cruises, *afternoon* cream tea cruises, and *evening* trips to the Napton Bridge Inn *Fri-Sat*, plus *hourly trips each Sun, throughout the summer.* It is also available for private charter. Details from Braunston Cruises, 14 Countryside, Braunston (01788 890373). Booking is essential.

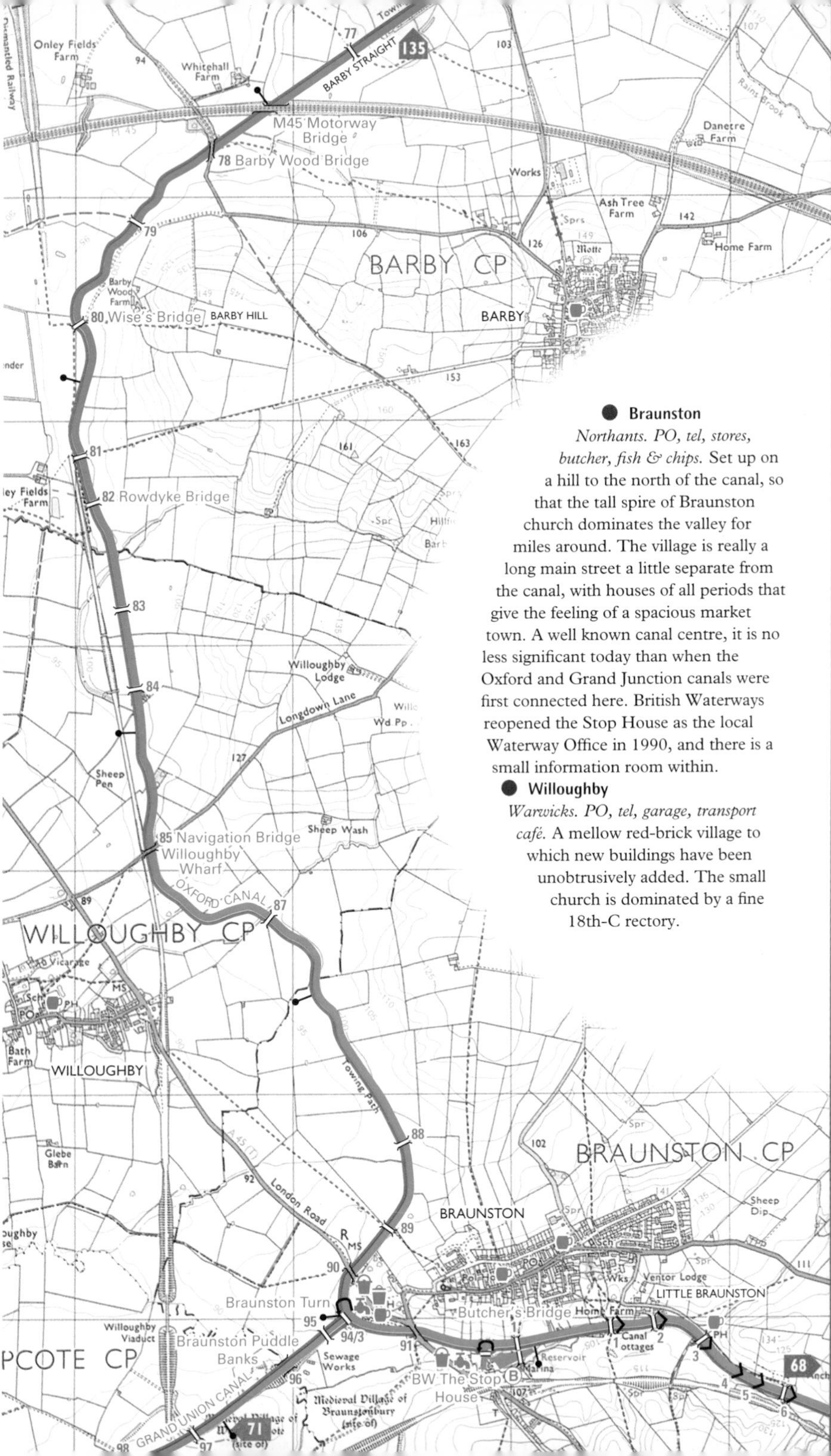

Braunston

Northants. PO, tel, stores, butcher, fish & chips. Set up on a hill to the north of the canal, so that the tall spire of Braunston church dominates the valley for miles around. The village is really a long main street a little separate from the canal, with houses of all periods that give the feeling of a spacious market town. A well known canal centre, it is no less significant today than when the Oxford and Grand Junction canals were first connected here. British Waterways reopened the Stop House as the local Waterway Office in 1990, and there is a small information room within.

Willoughby

Warwicks. PO, tel, garage, transport café. A mellow red-brick village to which new buildings have been unobtrusively added. The small church is dominated by a fine 18th-C rectory.

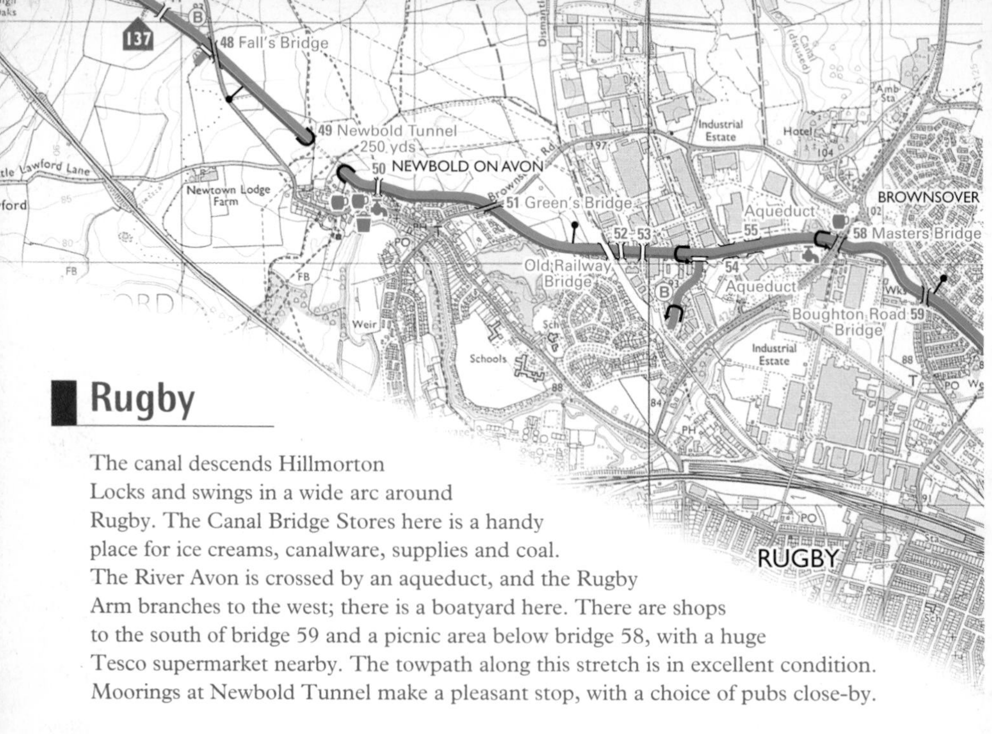

Rugby

The canal descends Hillmorton Locks and swings in a wide arc around Rugby. The Canal Bridge Stores here is a handy place for ice creams, canalware, supplies and coal. The River Avon is crossed by an aqueduct, and the Rugby Arm branches to the west; there is a boatyard here. There are shops to the south of bridge 59 and a picnic area below bridge 58, with a huge Tesco supermarket nearby. The towpath along this stretch is in excellent condition. Moorings at Newbold Tunnel make a pleasant stop, with a choice of pubs close-by.

Boatyards

Ⓑ **Club Line Cruisers** Hillmorton Wharf, Crick Road, Rugby (01788 577300). Long-term mooring, dry dock with hydraulic lift.

Ⓑ **Hillmorton Boat Services** The Locks, Hillmorton (01788 578661). Wet dock and dry dock, boat sales, boat and engine repairs, boat repainting, engineering services, sign writing, boat covers. *24 hour* boat emergency breakdown call-out.

Ⓑ **Clifton Cruisers** Clifton Wharf, Vicarage Hill, Clifton on Dunsmore (01788 543570). D Pump-out, gas, narrow boat hire, overnight mooring, boat and engine repairs, boatbuilding, toilets, showers, gifts.

Ⓑ **Willow Wren Hire Cruisers** Rugby Wharf, off Consul Road, Leicester Road, Rugby (01788 562183). D Pump-out, gas, narrow boat hire, overnight and long-term mooring, toilets and showers, gifts.

Ⓑ **T. F. Yates** Falls Bridge Works, Cathiron Lane, Newbold-on-Avon (01788 569140). East of bridge 44. D Pump-out, gas, crane, engine sales, boat and engine repairs, full engineering services, real chandlery.

● **Hillmorton**

Warwicks. PO, tel, stores, garage, take-aways, but all a fair distance from the canal.

● **Rugby**

Warwicks. MD Mon, Fri, Sat. PO, tel, stores, garage, station, theatre, cinema, leisure centre. There is a pedestrianised shopping centre, a leisure centre and an open market with a town crier. Look out for the tiny shop in Chapel Street, which has stood for over 500 years and is reputedly the oldest building in the town.

James Gilbert Rugby Football Museum 5 St Matthews Street, Rugby (01788 542426). Founded by the nephew of William Gilbert, who made boots and shoes for Rugby School in his original shop in the High Street. *Open Mon–Fri 10.00–17.00, Sat 10.00–14.00. Closed Sun.* Free.

Rugby School Museum 10 Little Church Street, Rugby (01788 574117). Opposite the Temple Speech Room, opened in 1909 by King Edward VII and named after a headmaster of the school who later became Archbishop of Canterbury. Guided tours. *Open daily 10.30–16.30.* Charge.

Tourist Information Centre Rugby Library, St Matthew's Street, Rugby (01788 535348).

● **Newbold on Avon**

Warwicks. PO, tel, stores, garage, fish & chips. At the wharf near the tunnel mouth are two fine pubs right next door to each other.

Pubs and Restaurants

Old Royal Oak Crick Road, Hillmorton Wharf (01788 561401). Canalside at bridge 73. Marston's and Ansells real ale and bar meals *all day,* with a vegetarian menu. Children's room and play area. Mooring for patrons.

Clifton Inn Clifton Road, Rugby (01788 542338). South of bridge 66. Ansells, Marston's, Morland's and Tetleys real ales, bar and restaurant meals *lunchtimes and evenings every day,* with a vegetarian menu. Live music *Fri & Sat,* with a quiz on *Sun.*

Bell & Barge Brownsover Road, Rugby (01788 569466). Bridge 58. A Harvester serving Bass and M&B real ale and food *lunchtimes and evenings every day,* with vegetarian options. Garden. Children welcome.

Boat Main Street, Newbold Wharf (01788 576995). By Bridge 50. Bass and Greenalls real ale. Menu, including vegetarian food, *lunchtimes and evenings every day.* Pleasant garden and moorings. A fine variety of entertainment with traditional bar games, and Morris Dancers *in the summer.*

Barley Mow Main Street, Newbold-on-Avon (01788 544174). Canalside pub serving Bass real ale. Bar and restaurant meals and snacks available *lunchtimes and evenings every day.* Vegetarian menu. Children welcome, and there is a canalside garden with a bouncy castle. Regular entertainment, and *weekend* piano sing-alongs.

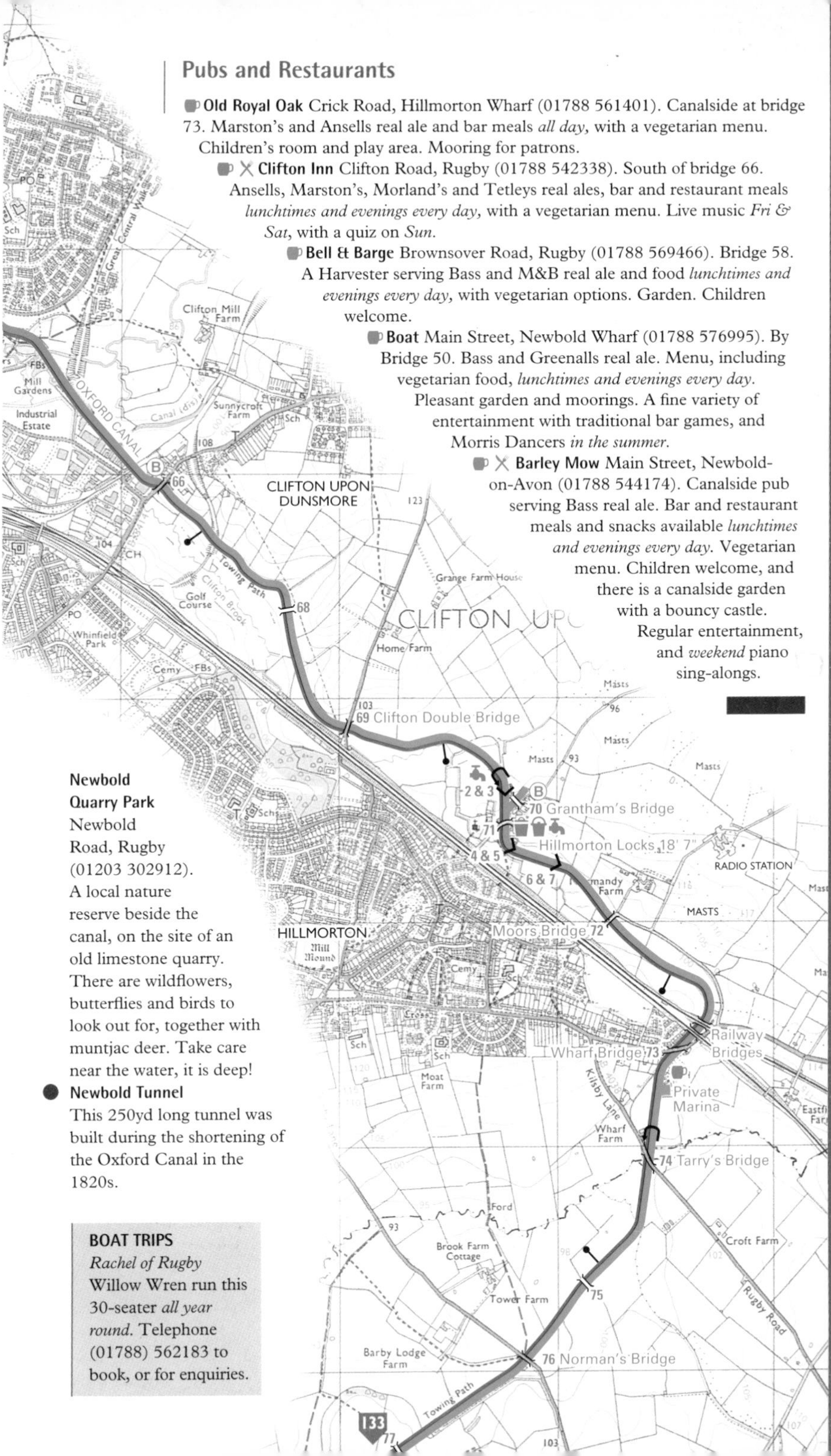

Newbold Quarry Park Newbold Road, Rugby (01203 302912). A local nature reserve beside the canal, on the site of an old limestone quarry. There are wildflowers, butterflies and birds to look out for, together with muntjac deer. Take care near the water, it is deep!

Newbold Tunnel This 250yd long tunnel was built during the shortening of the Oxford Canal in the 1820s.

BOAT TRIPS
Rachel of Rugby
Willow Wren run this 30-seater *all year round.* Telephone (01788) 562183 to book, or for enquiries.

133

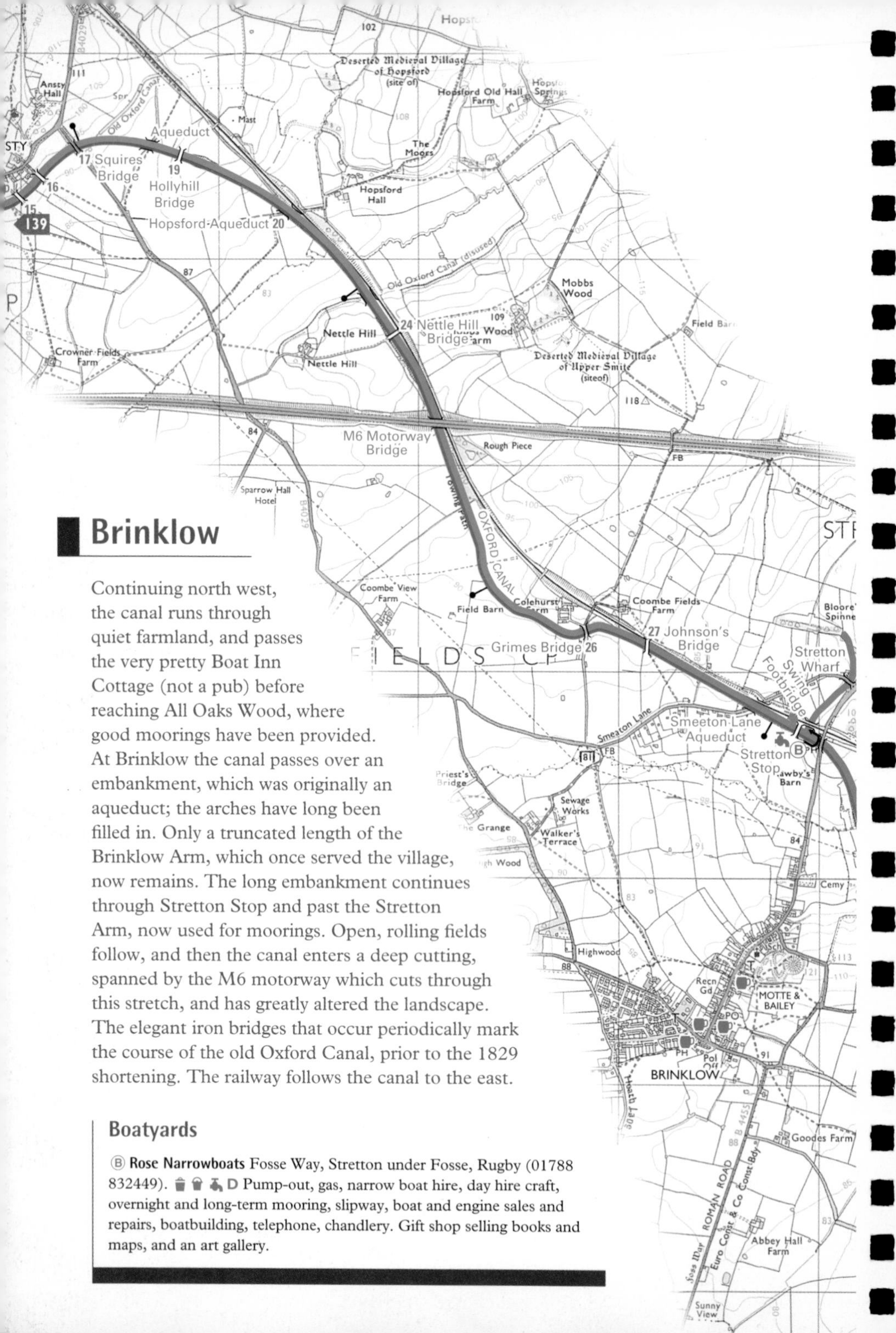

Brinklow

Continuing north west, the canal runs through quiet farmland, and passes the very pretty Boat Inn Cottage (not a pub) before reaching All Oaks Wood, where good moorings have been provided. At Brinklow the canal passes over an embankment, which was originally an aqueduct; the arches have long been filled in. Only a truncated length of the Brinklow Arm, which once served the village, now remains. The long embankment continues through Stretton Stop and past the Stretton Arm, now used for moorings. Open, rolling fields follow, and then the canal enters a deep cutting, spanned by the M6 motorway which cuts through this stretch, and has greatly altered the landscape. The elegant iron bridges that occur periodically mark the course of the old Oxford Canal, prior to the 1829 shortening. The railway follows the canal to the east.

Boatyards

Ⓑ **Rose Narrowboats** Fosse Way, Stretton under Fosse, Rugby (01788 832449). D Pump-out, gas, narrow boat hire, day hire craft, overnight and long-term mooring, slipway, boat and engine sales and repairs, boatbuilding, telephone, chandlery. Gift shop selling books and maps, and an art gallery.

● **Harborough Magna**
Warwicks. PO box, tel, stores. Quiet red-brick village one mile to the north of the canal from bridges 43 or 48. The 13th-14thC church has a Victorian west tower and many Victorian additions, including an interesting stained-glass window depicting Christ rising, with two angels, against a dark blue background.

● **Brinklow**
Warwicks. PO, tel, stores, garage, fish & chips. A spacious pre-industrial village built along a wide main street. The church of St John Baptist is of late Perpendicular style, and has some interesting 15th-C stained glass depicting birds, including a peacock. Its sloping floor climbs 12 feet from west to east. Alongside is the substantial mound of a motte and bailey castle, built to defend the Fosse Way.

Pubs and Restaurants

White Lion Broad Street, Brinklow (01788 832579). A welcoming local pub with a plush lounge and an old-fashioned bar, serving Banks's real ale and bar snacks *lunchtimes Mon–Fri.* Garden and children's room. Traditional bar games, theme and quiz nights. B & B.

Bulls Head Broad Street, Brinklow (01788 832355). A smartly furnished family pub. Food. Garden.

Raven Broad Street, Brinklow (01788 832655). A friendly family pub at the top of the village, with Banks's and Marston's real ale available. Extensive range of bar meals *lunchtimes and evenings every day,* with a vegetarian menu and traditional *Sunday lunch.* Garden.

✕ **Dun Cow** Coventry Road, Brinklow (01788 832358). A locals' pub serving Boddingtons and M & B real ale with food available in the restaurant or bar, including vegetarian choices, *lunchtimes and evenings every day.* Children welcome in the lounge. Garden.

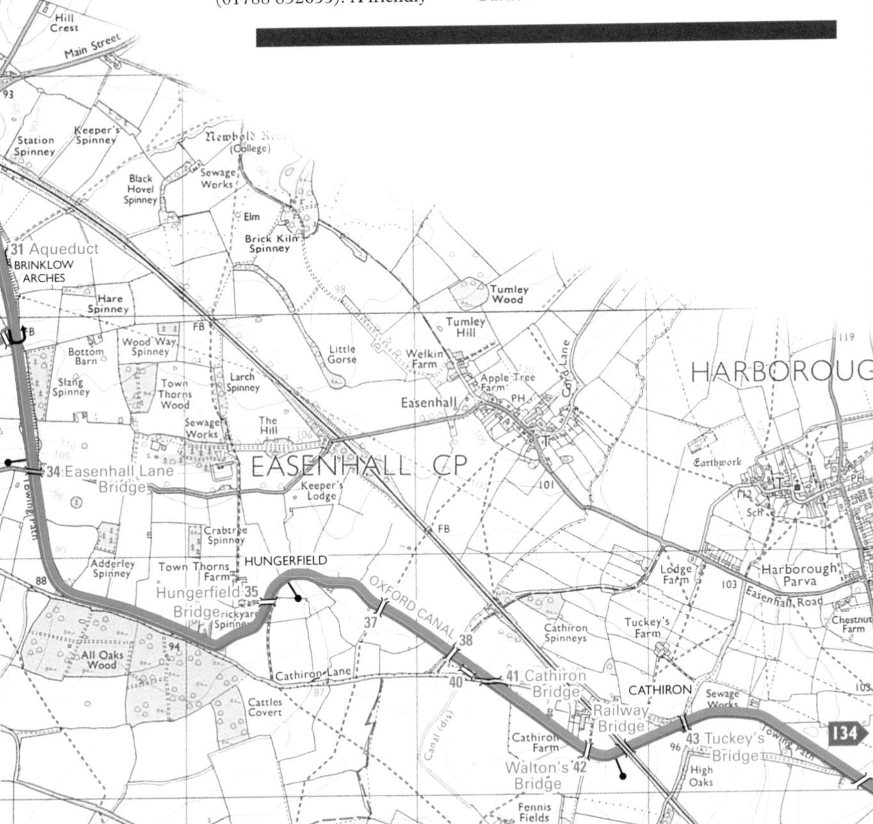

Hawkesbury Junction

The open landscape continues beyond Ansty, although the motorway is never far away. Soon the first signs of Coventry appear, with views of pylons and housing estates. The new Wyken Colliery Arm leaves to the west: it was built to replace the old one eaten up by the motorway which comes alongside the canal at this point: it is now used by the Coventry Cruising Club. Sharp bends then lead to the stop lock before Hawkesbury Junction, the end of the Oxford Canal where it joins the Coventry Canal. This last stretch of the Oxford Canal is characterised by the 1820s shortenings; straight cuttings and embankments date from this period, while the cast iron bridges mark the old route.

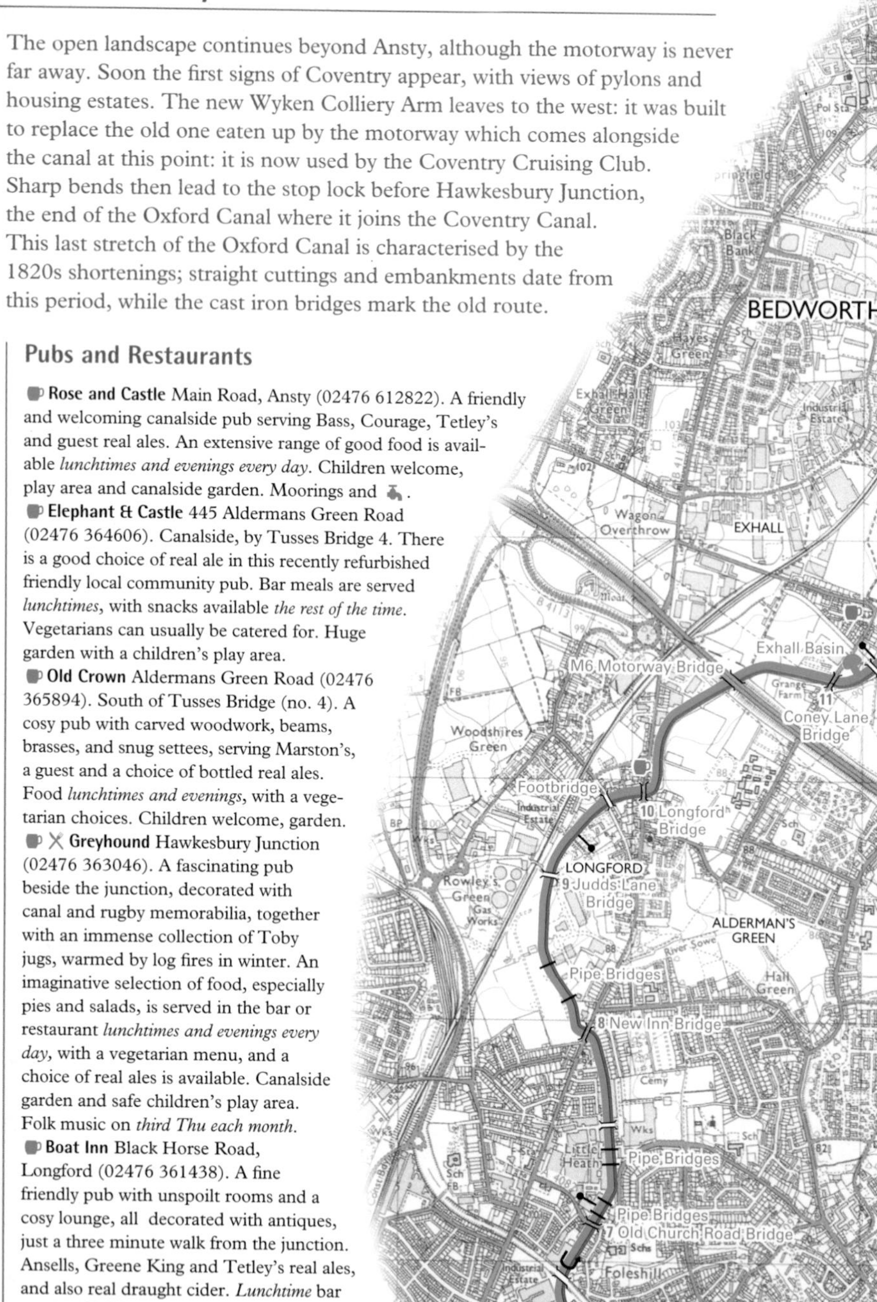

Pubs and Restaurants

Rose and Castle Main Road, Ansty (02476 612822). A friendly and welcoming canalside pub serving Bass, Courage, Tetley's and guest real ales. An extensive range of good food is available *lunchtimes and evenings every day*. Children welcome, play area and canalside garden. Moorings and .

Elephant & Castle 445 Aldermans Green Road (02476 364606). Canalside, by Tusses Bridge 4. There is a good choice of real ale in this recently refurbished friendly local community pub. Bar meals are served *lunchtimes*, with snacks available *the rest of the time*. Vegetarians can usually be catered for. Huge garden with a children's play area.

Old Crown Aldermans Green Road (02476 365894). South of Tusses Bridge (no. 4). A cosy pub with carved woodwork, beams, brasses, and snug settees, serving Marston's, a guest and a choice of bottled real ales. Food *lunchtimes and evenings*, with a vegetarian choices. Children welcome, garden.

Greyhound Hawkesbury Junction (02476 363046). A fascinating pub beside the junction, decorated with canal and rugby memorabilia, together with an immense collection of Toby jugs, warmed by log fires in winter. An imaginative selection of food, especially pies and salads, is served in the bar or restaurant *lunchtimes and evenings every day,* with a vegetarian menu, and a choice of real ales is available. Canalside garden and safe children's play area. Folk music on *third Thu each month.*

Boat Inn Black Horse Road, Longford (02476 361438). A fine friendly pub with unspoilt rooms and a cosy lounge, all decorated with antiques, just a three minute walk from the junction. Ansells, Greene King and Tetley's real ales, and also real draught cider. *Lunchtime* bar snacks. Children welcome. Garden for the summer and a real fire for the winter.

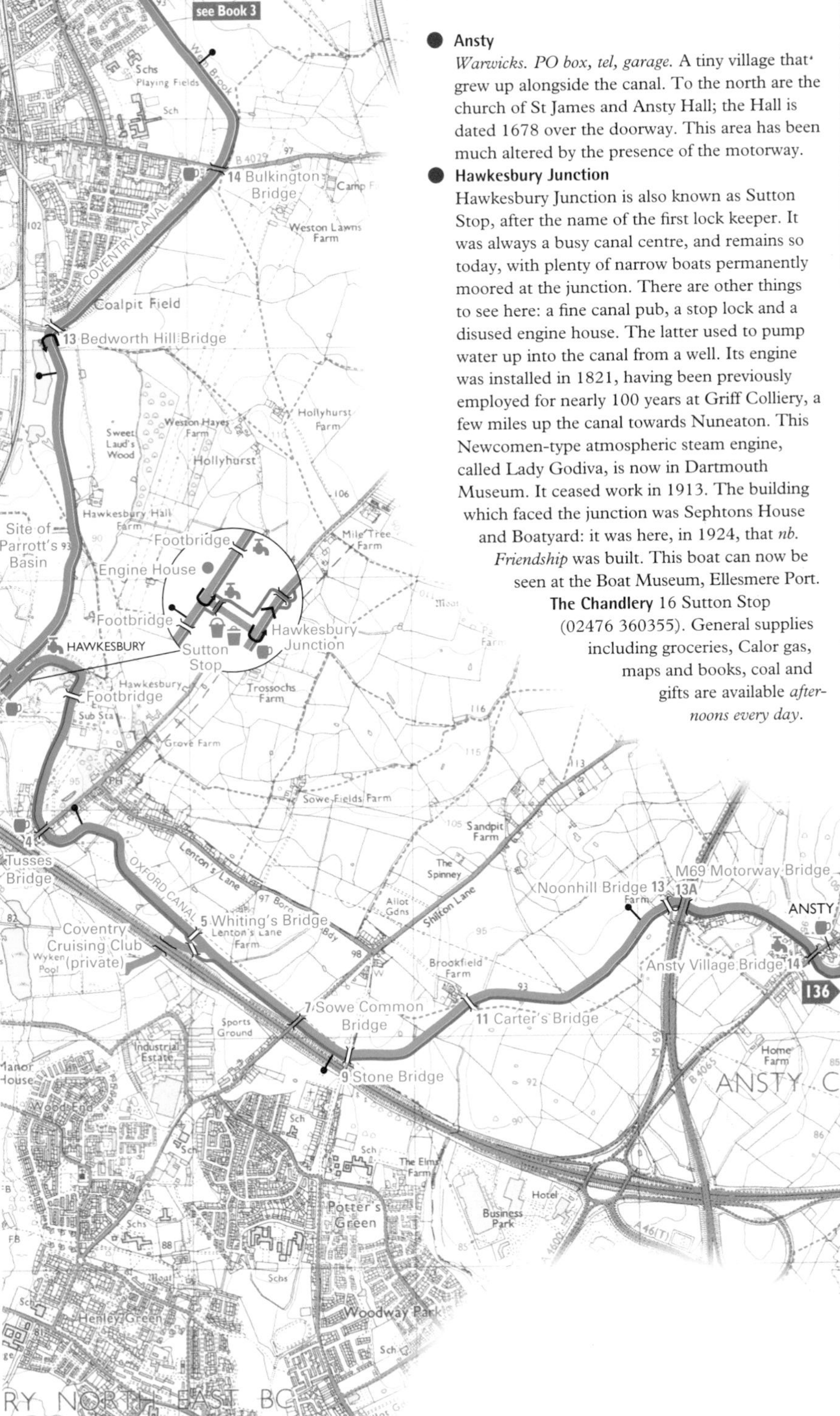

● **Ansty**

Warwicks. PO box, tel, garage. A tiny village that grew up alongside the canal. To the north are the church of St James and Ansty Hall; the Hall is dated 1678 over the doorway. This area has been much altered by the presence of the motorway.

● **Hawkesbury Junction**

Hawkesbury Junction is also known as Sutton Stop, after the name of the first lock keeper. It was always a busy canal centre, and remains so today, with plenty of narrow boats permanently moored at the junction. There are other things to see here: a fine canal pub, a stop lock and a disused engine house. The latter used to pump water up into the canal from a well. Its engine was installed in 1821, having been previously employed for nearly 100 years at Griff Colliery, a few miles up the canal towards Nuneaton. This Newcomen-type atmospheric steam engine, called Lady Godiva, is now in Dartmouth Museum. It ceased work in 1913. The building which faced the junction was Sephtons House and Boatyard: it was here, in 1924, that *nb. Friendship* was built. This boat can now be seen at the Boat Museum, Ellesmere Port.

The Chandlery 16 Sutton Stop (02476 360355). General supplies including groceries, Calor gas, maps and books, coal and gifts are available *afternoons every day.*

Napton-on-the-Hill *(see page 130)*

RIVER THAMES: LONDON

Under the Control of:
Port of London Authority
Devon House
58–60 St Katharine's Way
London E1 9LB
0207 265 2656

The Port of London Authority (PLA) issue a selection of useful free information for pleasure boaters obtainable from the office above and referred to in the Navigational Notes on the following pages.
All river users are governed by the Port of London River Bye-laws a copy of which can be obtained from (charge):

The Chief Harbour Master
London River House
Royal Pier Road
Gravesend
Kent DA12 2BG

All river movements on the section of the river covered by this guide are under the control of **Woolwich Radio** who can be contacted by telephone on 0208 855 0315 and VHF channel 14.
All vessels over 20 metres must carry VHF radio and boat owners are reminded that they should hold an appropriate licence to operate such equipment.

As a river the Thames enjoys a special place in the hearts and minds of the British population metamorphosed as a great patriarchal figure reaching back into the beginnings of time. Geographically it links the rural idyll of the Cotswolds, in the very centre of the country, with the nation's bustling capital city, flowing past the very seat of government. In terms of trade it led to London's international importance as a port, whilst nationally it functioned as a spinal carrying route, well connected to a robust inland waterways network. Virtually everything that was needed to fuel the city's 18th- and 19th-C expansion arrived by water. Goods for export, manufactured further afield, reached the massive docks complex on a boat, be it narrow or wide beam. The horse and cart played but a very subservient role in establishing London as the largest port in the world in the early 19thC.
However, the Thames is neither the longest river in the country nor does it carry the most water along its 215 mile course. The first accolade is held by the Severn at some 220 miles whilst the flow of the Trent, at its junction with the Ouse to form the Humber, is somewhat greater at 3000 cubic feet of water per second. These cold clinical facts notwithstanding, it is the sheer poetry of the river that captures the imagination, making river travel superior as a means to gain initial insight into the capital's complex makeup. For many inland boaters the chance to navigate London's arterial highway can be the culmination of maybe years spent navigating the narrow channels of more humble waterways. The thrill of seeing the sights from one's own boat, on the passage between canal and canal (or non-tidal river and canal), by far outweighs the apprehension brought on by such an expanse of turgid and sometimes choppy water. The flat-bottomed narrow boat, whilst predominant on inland navigations, is far from the ideal vessel for tidal estuaries, having the sea-going characteristics of a bathtub. Boaters wishing, for whatever reason, to sample this majestic river should beware of being swept up in the euphoria of the occasion. There are still a good number of commercial craft on the tideway carrying both passengers and all manner of bulk traffic. In what is relatively (to the inland boater) open water, choppy can soon become rough: these conditions can be severely aggravated by the wash from passing commercial craft. Your boat must comply with all the requirements laid down by the PLA (0207 265 2656) whilst the crew require experience and boat handling ability commensurate with the conditions. One excellent introduction to navigating this section of the Thames is to join a flotilla cruise and benefit from shared experience. These are conducted by St Pancras Cruising Club (0207 278 2805) who also produce cruising notes.

West London

Immediately below Brentford Dock Marina is the entrance to the Grand Union Canal, a direct link with Birmingham and places north. On the north bank opposite Kew is Strand-on-the-Green, a cluster of desirable houses and fashionable pubs facing the towpath. The Oxford and Cambridge Boat Race finish is below Chiswick Bridge, the line being marked on both banks by wooden piles and the University Stone. The river is flanked by elegant houses at Hammersmith and Chiswick, but further downstream becomes grimy and industrial. There is, however, as always on the lower Thames, plenty of interest. Below the splendid Hammersmith Bridge, on the south bank, lies one of the most bizarre buildings on the whole riverside – the Harrods Depository – a cupolated building in the same terracotta as the main store. There is a small wharf in front where a light railway used to run directly into the building.

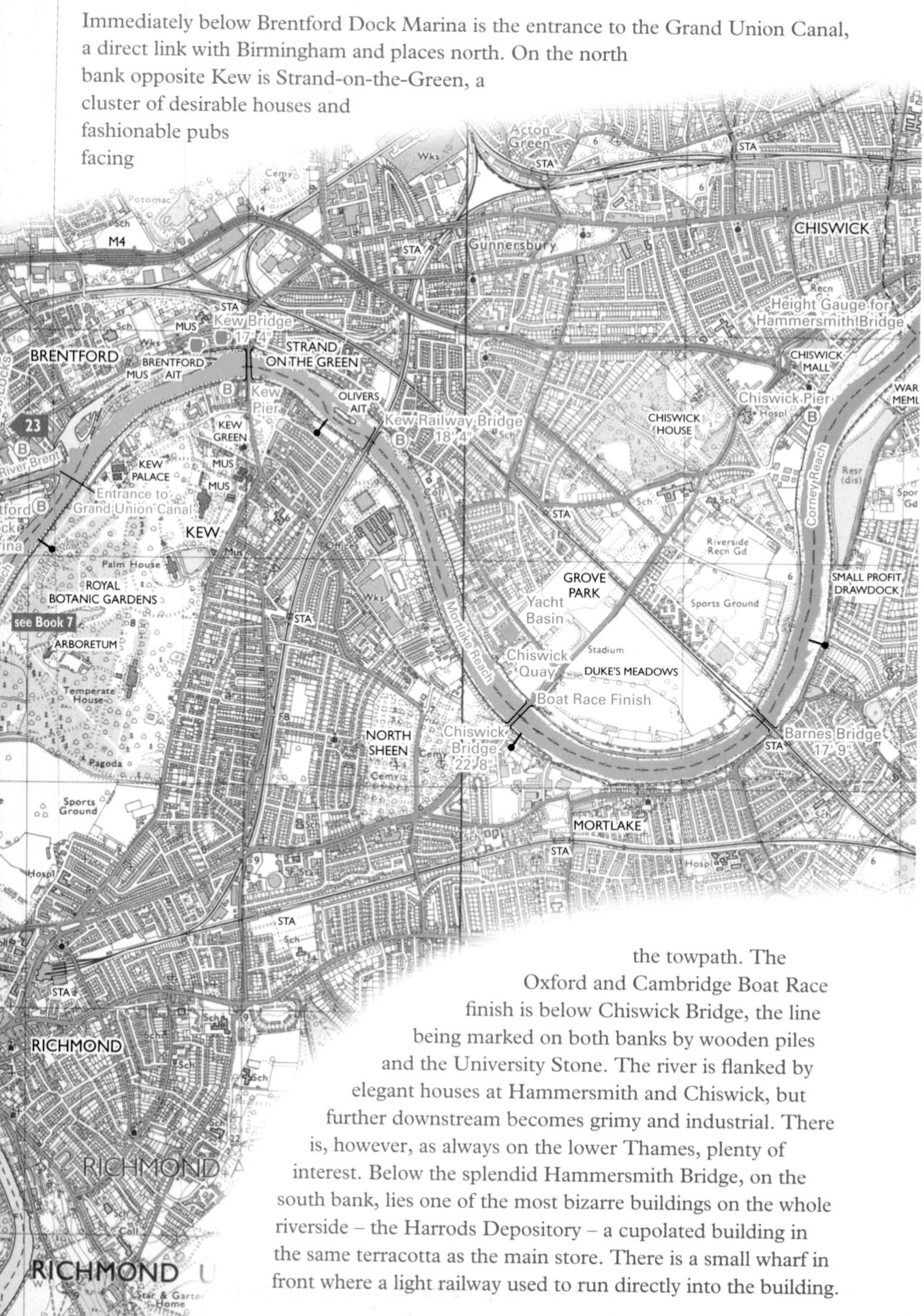

MOORING

For the inland boater the tidal River Thames should be regarded as a transit route between canals, or between the non-tidal river and the Grand Union exits. There are few opportunities for pleasure craft to moor between Brentford and Limehouse. During the summer the piers are generally too busy with trip boats to accommodate casual visitors. If you do wish to stop, you are advised to contact one of the boatyards or marinas listed in the PLA Leisure Guide (see Navigational Notes on page 144) to see if they have room for you. The PLA may have certain moorings available and they do offer limited boater facilities (usually pump-out and water) at some of their piers.

Barn Elms Reservoir is now host to a variety of watersports and is ideal for fishing and birdwatching. On the north bank is Bishop's Park, home to Fulham Palace. Putney Bridge marks the start of the Oxford and Cambridge Boat Race and gives way to a stretch of industry.

Pubs and Restaurants

For Pubs and Restaurants accessible to the boater entering the canal at either Brentford or Limehouse see pages 25 and 13.

NAVIGATIONAL NOTES

1 From **Brentford** to **Limehouse** navigation on the Thames is far more complex than on the upper reaches. The river here is a commercial waterway first and foremost, and pleasure craft must take great care. The River Thames below Teddington is controlled by the Port of London Authority (PLA) which produces a useful set of free notes, *Yachtsman's Guide for the Tidal Thames.* A separate leaflet (*PLA Facilities on the Tidal Thames*) details facilities available to boaters. For general navigational enquiries about the river contact the Assistant Harbour Master, Devon House, 58–60 St Katharine's Way, London E1 9LB (0207 265 2656). While hire companies do not allow their craft to be taken onto the tideway, owners of pleasure boats may wish to make the passage along the Thames below Teddington Locks and between the canals at Brentford and Limehouse. With proper planning this should present no particular difficulties.

2 **Brentford** to **Limehouse Basin** – leave Brentford 1/2 hour before high water to gain the benefit of the ebb tide. Limehouse Basin is fitted with sector gates and is *open Apr–Oct 08.00–18.00 & Nov–Mar 08.00–16.30. (Pre-booked passage within the core hours 05.00–22.00 is available by giving at least 24hrs notice*). Telephone Limehouse Basin (0207 308 9930) and inform them of your intentions. Limehouse listen and operate on VHF channel 80.

3 **Limehouse Basin** to **Brentford** – pass through the entrance lock at Limehouse 2 1/2 hours before high water, to gain the benefit of the flood tide. Thames Lock, Brentford is manned *for a period before, and following high water (2hrs each side if this falls within normal working hours*) and you should contact the lock keeper to pre-book passage *outside the normal working hours* (which are the same as Limehouse) on 0208 560 1120. The same core hours also apply. Brentford gauging lock is boater operated using a BW sanitary station key. Brentford listen and operate on VHF channel 74.

4 **Brentford** to **Teddington** – pass through Thames Lock, Brentford 2 hours before high water to gain the benefit of the flood tide. Teddington lock keeper can be contacted on 0208 940 8723 and Richmond lock keeper can be contacted on 0208 940 0634.

5 **VHF Radio** – all vessels of 20 metres or more in length must carry a VHF radio capable of communicating with the harbourmaster at port control – channel 14. An exception is made for narrow boats over 65ft in transit between the Grand Union Canal at Brentford and the non-tidal Thames at Teddington Locks. If no radio is available such vessels must telephone the PLA duty officer (0208 855 0315) immediately before and on completion of transit.

6 **Warning lights** – see PLA publication: *Yachtsman's Guide for the Tidal Thames.*

7 **Draught** – the depth at the centre span of Westminster Bridge is approximately 2ft 8in at chart datum (about 4ft 0in at mean low water springs). In practice there is usually a greater depth than this. The depth at all the other bridges is greater than Westminster.

8 **Headroom** – on the tidal river the clearance at bridges is given as the maximum at mean high water springs – this is less than the headroom at chart datum (lowest astronomical tide). In practice this means that there will usually be more headroom than that indicated.

9 **Canals –** those who wish to navigate on the adjoining British Waterways canals will require a licence, available from: Craft Licensing Office, Willow Grange, Church Road, Watford WD1 3QA (01923 226422). Full details of the inland waterways encountered at Brentford and Limehouse can be found on pages 9 and 22.

Notes for walkers
This is an absolutely splendid section for walking. The path keeps to the south side throughout and Kew Gardens and Kew Palace are definitely worth a visit. Across the river is Strand-on-the-Green, with its fine houses and pubs. Barnes Railway Bridge has a foot crossing, and walkers can choose which bank they take to reach Hammersmith – the scenic route is on the south bank, the pubs on the north. After the fascinating walk around Barnes to Putney, the Thames towpath terminates, giving way to road as far as Putney Bridge. The course of the river can best be followed through London by keeping to the north side. *Nicholsons London Streetfinder* is a helpful guide when detours are necessary.

● **Royal Botanic Gardens** Kew Road, Richmond (0208 940 1171). Superb botanical gardens of 300 acres founded in 1759 by Princess Augusta. Delightful natural gardens and woods bounded by the river on one side, and stocked with thousands of flowers and trees. The lake, aquatic garden and pagoda were designed by Sir William Chambers in 1760 and the magnificent curved glass Palm House and the Temperate House, 1844–8, are by Decimus Burton. Beneath the Palm House is a Marine Display which has examples of flowering marine plants and coral reef. The Princess of Wales Conservatory houses orchids, cacti, and water lilies the size of mattresses. Kew's scientific aspect was developed by its two directors Sir William and Sir Joseph Hooker and the many famous botanists who worked here. Cafeteria and gift shop in the Orangery. *One hour* tours available from the Victoria Gate Visitor Centre. Gardens *open daily 09.30–18.30 (weekends & B. Hols 19.30)*. Glasshouses, gallery and museum *close 17.30.* Charge.

Kew Bridge Opened by Edward VII in 1903 and officially called the King Edward VII Bridge. A fine stone structure designed by Sir John Wolfe Barry and Cuthbert Brereton, it replaced the earlier granite bridge of 1789.

Kew Railway Bridge When it was opened in 1869 this five-span lattice girder bridge, designed by W R Galbraith, was part of the London and South Western Railway extension.

● **KEW**

Surrey. Old Kew centres around the Green, the 18th-C houses built for members of the Court of George III, and the entrance to the Royal Botanic Gardens. The church of St Anne dates from 1714 but was greatly altered in the 19thC.

Grand Union Canal

Musical Museum St George's Church, 368 High Street, Brentford (0208 560 8108). A fascinating collection of around 200 automatic, old and odd musical instruments. Many of the instruments are played during the *one hour* conducted tour. *Telephone for details of opening times.* Charge. No small children.

Kew Bridge Steam Museum Green Dragon Lane, Brentford (0208 568 4757). Huge Victorian building housing six gigantic beam engines, restored to working order by volunteers. In steam at *weekends.* Also a collection of old traction engines and a working forge. Tea room *(weekends only). Open daily, inc B. Hols 11.00–17.00.* Charge (under 5s free).

● **CHISWICK**

W4. Chiswick stretches between Kew Bridge and Hammersmith Terrace and provides some of the most picturesque scenery on the London stretch of the Thames. Georgian houses extend along Strand-on-the-Green and again at Chiswick Mall. Between these points, running down to the riverside, originally stood three 18thC mansions: of the three, only Chiswick House remains. The site of Grove House has been built over, and Duke's Meadows, part of the grounds of Chiswick House, is now a recreation ground. Chiswick Cemetery backs on to St Nicholas Church where Lord Burlington and William Kent are buried.

Chiswick Bridge Built in 1933, designed by Sir Herbert Baker and opened to the public by the Prince of Wales, this bridge has the longest concrete arch of any bridge on the Thames. The centre span measures 150ft.

Chiswick House Burlington Lane W4. (0208 994 3299). Lovely Palladian villa built in the grand manner by 3rd Earl of Burlington 1725–30, modelled on Palladio's Villa Capra at Vicenza.

● **MORTLAKE**

SW14. In the 17thC Mortlake was famous for its tapestry workshop, established by James I and staffed by Flemish weavers. Some of the Mortlake Tapestries can still be seen in the Victoria & Albert Museum. The riverside here is picturesque along Thames Bank where there is a fine collection of 18th-C houses. Mortlake also marks the end of the Oxford and Cambridge Boat Race at Chiswick Bridge (although the first race took place at Henley in 1829).

Barnes Railway Bridge This light and elegant iron bridge by Locke was opened in 1849 to connect with the Richmond line. Similar in design to Richmond Railway Bridge.

Oxford v Cambridge Boat Race On a *Saturday afternoon in March or April* this famous annual event is held over a 4-mile course from Putney to Mortlake. Get to the riverside early for a good view.

● NORTH BANK

Hammersmith Terrace *W6.* A terrace of 17 identical houses on the river bank, built c.1750. The late Sir Alan Herbert, historian of the Thames, lived in the Terrace.

Upper Mall *W6.* Separated from Lower Mall by Furnivall Gardens, Upper Mall boasts some fine 18th-C buildings including the Dove Inn, originally a coffee house. William Morris lived in Kelmscott House between 1878–96.

Lower Mall *W6.* Bustling in the summer months with rowers from the number of boathouses and rowing clubs which have been established here for over a century, Lower Mall is home to the Rutland and Blue Anchor pubs, and a number of pretty 18th-C cottages.

Hammersmith Bridge The first suspension bridge in London. The original, built 1824 by William T Clarke, was replaced in 1883 by the present splendid construction by Sir Joseph Bazalgette.

Fulham In the 18th and 19thC Fulham was the 'great fruit and kitchen garden north of the Thames', a place of market and nursery gardens, attracting the more prosperous Londoners in search of purer air. Today little is left of the fertile village and the area has become quite built-up. Fulham has, however, remained an attractive area, nowadays better known for its abundance of restaurants and bars. Also home to two of London's most famous football clubs, Fulham and Chelsea. Bishop's Park and Hurlingham House can be seen from the river.

Fulham Palace The palace lies behind the long avenues of Bishop's Park, with grounds stretching to the river. The site was first acquired by Bishop Waldhere in 704 and continued as a residence of the Bishops of London until 1973. A fascinating mixture of architectural styles, from the Tudor courtyard with its mellow red brick to the restrained elegance of the Georgian east front.

Putney Bridge The wooden toll bridge of 1729 was replaced by the present bridge designed by Sir Joseph Bazalgette in 1884. Putney Bridge marks the start of the Oxford and Cambridge Boat Race .

Fulham Railway Bridge This trellis girder iron bridge was part of the Metropolitan extension to the District Railway. Designed by William Jacomb, it was opened in 1889 and connects with a footbridge running parallel to it. Part of the London Transport underground system.

Hurlingham House Ranelagh Gardens *SW6.* This is the only large 18th-C residence still surviving in Fulham. The house has a fine river front with Corinthian columns and is now the centre of the Hurlingham Club. Members play tennis, golf and croquet in the grounds.

● SOUTH BANK

Barnes Terrace *SW13.* The delightful village of Barnes lies behind the attractive ironwork façade of Barnes Terrace. The terrace was, and still is, a fashionable place to live, with former residents including Sheridan and Gustav Holst.

Castelnau Barnes is rich in Victorian houses and some of the most interesting are to be seen in Castelnau. Remarkably standardised, they are largely semi-detached and typical of early Victorian villa architecture with their arched windows.

Barn Elms Formerly the manor house of Barnes, the estate was later leased to Sir Francis Walsingham, Secretary of State to Elizabeth I. Today, all that remains of the former layout is part of the ornamental pond and the ice house. The Reservoir at Barn Elms now plays host to a variety of watersports, plus fishing and bird-watching.

Putney The Embankment is picturesque. The London Rowing Club and Westminster School have their boat houses here and the eights and sculls can be seen practising most afternoons.

BOAT TRIPS

One of the best ways to understand the layout of a large, water-bound city is to take a boat trip and London is no exception to this rule. There are a large number to choose from, although most originate from Westminster Pier. Broadly speaking the options available encompass a selection of down-river trips as far as the Thames Barrier (and the Visitor Centre) and a range of up-river trips, which can reach as far as Hampton Court. The latter takes a full day. There are also evening dinner and dance cruises. Visit the pier (without your boat) to compare the plethora of options and make a choice.

Central London

The short stretch of intrusive industry, sprawling along the south bank, is soon relieved at Battersea by the splendid St Mary's Church opposite Lots Road Power Station and Chelsea Harbour. Albert Bridge, restored in 1991, is a remarkable sight when illuminated at night by over 4000 bulbs. From here on the River Thames curves through the heart of the capital, and has been London's lifeline for 2000 years. Indeed it was instrumental in the Roman settlement which created London as an international port. Once used as the local bypass, being cheaper and safer than travel by road, it has carried Viking longships, Roman galleys, Elizabethan barges and Victorian steamers. One of the best ways to see London is still from the Thames. The buildings and sights lining its twisting, turning path are as varied as London itself. It is fascinating by day and magical by night.

● NORTH BANK

Wandsworth Bridge In 1938 the 19th-C bridge was replaced with the existing structure by E P Wheeler, now painted a distinctive bright blue.

Chelsea Harbour A modern development dominated by the Belvedere tower block. The golden ball on its roof slides up and down with the level of the river. The development contains offices, restaurants, a luxury hotel, smart shops, apartments and the marina. Chelsea Wharf, just along the bank, has been transformed from old warehouses into modern business units.

Battersea Railway Bridge The West London Extension Railway, of which this bridge was a part, was opened in 1863 to connect the south of England directly with the north. The line was the only one which did not end at a London terminus and was therefore a target for bombing in the Second World War.

Lots Road Power Station This huge and dominating structure was built in 1904 to provide electricity for the new underground railway.

Battersea Bridge The original Battersea Bridge, 1772, a picturesque wooden structure by Henry Holland, has been portrayed in paintings by Whistler and Turner. The replacement iron structure, opened in 1890, was designed by Sir Joseph Bazalgette.

All Saints Church Chelsea Embankment. Rebuilt in 1964 after severe bomb damage during the war. Contains two 13th-C chapels, one restored by Sir Thomas More in 1528, a Jacobean altar table and one of the best series of monuments in a London parish church. Henry VIII married Jane Seymour here before their state wedding in 1536.

Cheyne Walk *SW3*. Cheyne Walk, with its houseboats and its row of delightful riverside Queen Anne houses, has been home to Lloyd George, Hilaire Belloc, George Eliot, Isambard Kingdom Brunel, Turner and Whistler.

Carlyle's House 24 Cheyne Row *SW3*. Once the haunt of writers such as Dickens and Tennyson, and the home of Thomas and Jane Carlyle 1834–81.

Albert Bridge A delightful suspension bridge connecting Chelsea and Battersea, built by Ordish 1871–3. The bridge was strengthened in 1973 by a huge solid support under the main span. Illuminated by over 4000 bulbs, the bridge is particularly beautiful at night.

Chelsea Embankment *SW3*. Chelsea Embankment, stretching between Albert Bridge and Chelsea Bridge, was built in 1871. The embankment is bordered on the north bank by the grounds of the Chelsea Royal Hospital where the Chelsea Flower Show is held annually in *May*. Norman Shaw's famous Old Swan House stands at No. 17 Chelsea Embankment.

Tate Gallery Millbank *SW1*. Founded in 1897 by Sir Henry Tate, the sugar magnate, and designed by Sidney H J Smith. Houses representative collections of British painting from the 16thC to the present day. Fine examples of Blake, Turner, Hogarth, the pre-Raphaelites, Ben Nicolson, Spencer and Francis Bacon; sculpture by Moore and Hepworth. Also a rich collection of foreign paintings and sculpture from 1880 to the present day, including paintings by Picasso, Chagall, Mondrian, Pollock, Lichtenstein, Rothko, Degas, Marini and Giacometti. Policy of annual rotation. The Clore Gallery houses the Turner bequest.

Millbank Tower Millbank *SW1*. The traditional balance of the river bank has been overturned by this 387ft–high office building by Ronald Ward and Partners, 1963.

Victoria Tower Gardens Abingdon Street *SW1*. A sculpture of Rodin's Burghers of Calais, 1895, stands close to the river and near the entrance to the gardens is a monument to Mrs Emmeline Pankhurst and Dame Christabel Pankhurst, champions of the women's suffragette movement in the early 1900s. Emmeline Pankhurst is reputedly the last person to have been incarcerated in the cell at the bottom of Big Ben (1902).

Houses of Parliament Parliament Square *SW1*.

Originally the Palace of Westminster, and a principal royal palace until 1512. Became known as parliament or 'place to speak' in 1550. Westminster Hall, one of the few remaining parts of the original royal palace, has an impressive hammerbeam roof. The present Victorian-Gothic building was designed 1847 by Sir Charles Barry and Augustus Pugin specifically to house Parliament and has 1100 rooms, 100 staircases and over 2 miles of passages. The Houses of Parliament and Big Ben – the bell clock housed in the adjoining St Stephen's Tower – make up London's most famous landmark.

Westminster Abbey Broad Sanctuary *SW1.* Original church by Edward the Confessor 1065. Rebuilding commenced in 1245 by Henry III who was largely influenced by the new French cathedrals. Completed by Henry Yevele and others 1376–1506 (towers incomplete and finished by Hawksmoor 1734). Henry VII Chapel added 1503; fine perpendicular with wonderful fan vaulting. The Abbey contains the Coronation Chair, and many tombs and memorials of the Kings and Queens of England. Starting place for the pilgrimage to Canterbury Cathedral. Nave and Cloisters.

Old Scotland Yard Victoria Embankment *SW1.* An asymmetrical building by Norman Shaw, 1888, with fine iron gates by Blomfield. Scotland Yard is now housed in a modern building in Victoria.

Victoria Embankment The Embankment was created by Joseph Bazalgette in 1868, reclaiming 37 acres of mud from the Thames banks, making the river narrower and the water faster flowing, thereby ending the skating era on the once-frozen waters. The building of the embankment provided a wall against flooding, a riverside walk, a new west-east sewerage system and part of the District Line Railway. It was completed in 1870, Bazalgette was knighted, and his bust incorporated into the parapet by Hungerford Bridge.

Cleopatra's Needle Victoria Embankment *SW1.* A 60ft-high ancient Egyptian granite obelisk, presented to Britain by the Viceroy of Egypt, Mohammed Ali, in 1819 and brought to London by sea in 1878. When it was erected various articles were buried beneath it for posterity – the morning's newspapers, a razor, coins, four Bibles in different languages and photographs of '12 of the best-looking Englishwomen of the day'. The bronze sphinxes were added (facing the wrong way) in 1882.

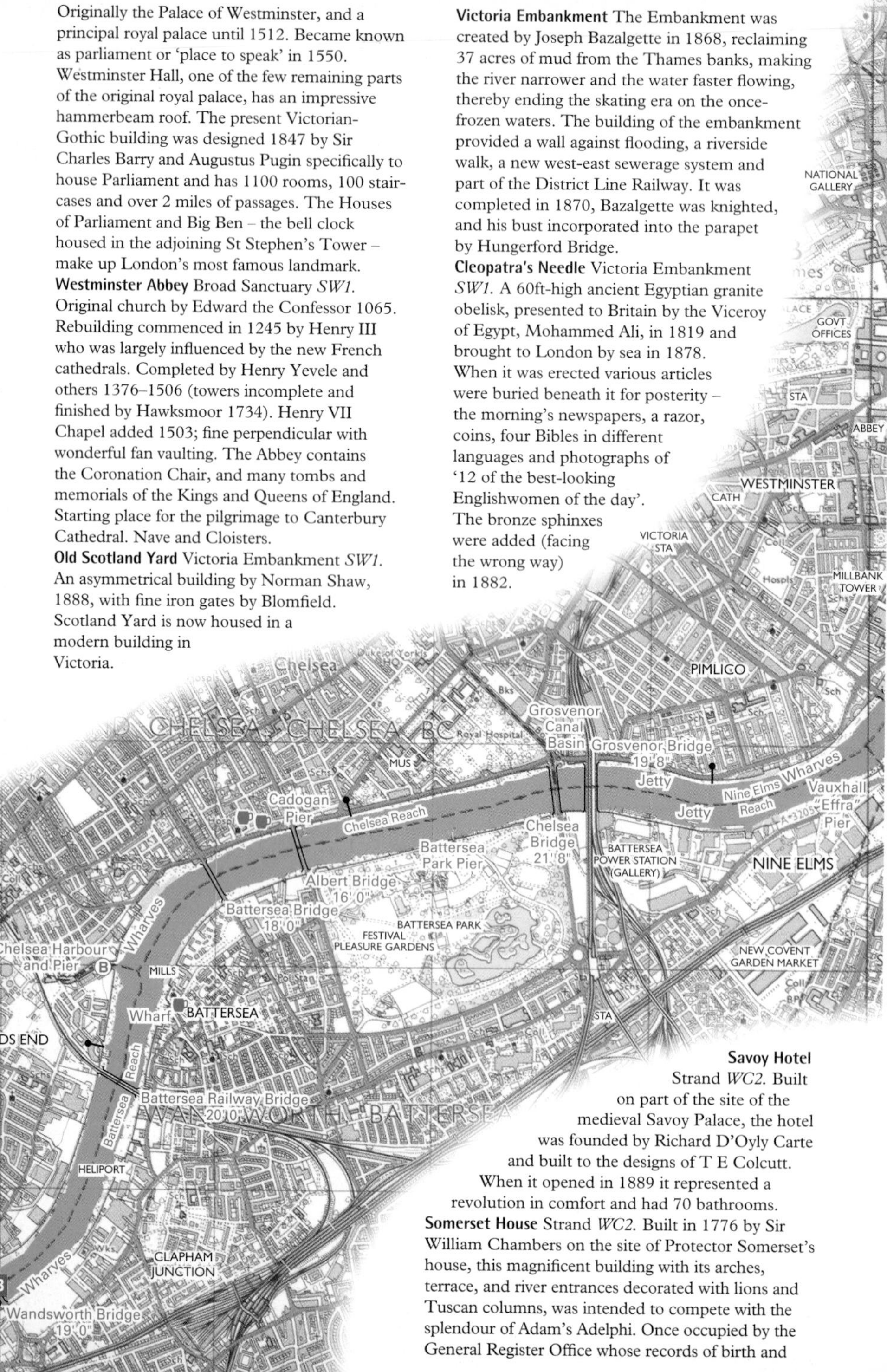

Savoy Hotel Strand *WC2.* Built on part of the site of the medieval Savoy Palace, the hotel was founded by Richard D'Oyly Carte and built to the designs of T E Colcutt. When it opened in 1889 it represented a revolution in comfort and had 70 bathrooms.

Somerset House Strand *WC2.* Built in 1776 by Sir William Chambers on the site of Protector Somerset's house, this magnificent building with its arches, terrace, and river entrances decorated with lions and Tuscan columns, was intended to compete with the splendour of Adam's Adelphi. Once occupied by the General Register Office whose records of birth and

death go back to 1836, it now houses offices of the Inland Revenue and the Courtauld Institute Galleries. In the garden stands a bronze statue of Brunel by Marochetti, 1866. Brunel was the engineer in charge of the building of the Great Western Railway and his ship, the Great Eastern, was launched on the Thames, at Millwall.

The Temple *EC4.* The name derives from the Order of Knights Templar who occupied the site from 1160–1308. In the 17thC the Temple was leased to the benchers of the Inner and Middle Temple, two Inns of Court. These inns, together with Lincoln's Inn and Gray's Inn, hold the ancient and exclusive privilege of providing advocates in the courts of England and Wales. A visit should be made on foot, as only a few of the Temple Buildings are visible from the river. On the Embankment, Sir Joseph Bazalgette's arch and stairs mark the 19th-C access to the Temple from the river.

City of London A thriving and commercial centre, stretching between Blackfriars Bridge and London Bridge, which has within its square mile such famous institutions as the Bank of England, the Stock Exchange, the Royal Courts of Justice and the Guildhall.

Mermaid Theatre Puddle Dock *EC4.* The original theatre, the first in the City since the 16thC, was opened in a converted warehouse in 1959 following energetic campaigning by Lord Bernard Miles. It was rebuilt on a new site and reopened in 1981.

● **Fishmongers' Hall**
1 London Bridge Road *EC4.* Built in the grand classical manner in 1831–4 by Henry Roberts to replace the original hall which was burnt down in the Great Fire of 1666. The Fishmongers' Company administers the annual Doggett's Coat and Badge Race for Thames Watermen. This race, the oldest annual contested sporting event and the longest rowing race in the world (1 furlong short of 5 miles), was introduced in 1715. Doggett, an Irish comedian and staunch Hanoverian, who used the services of the watermen to ferry him to and from the theatres, decided to mark the anniversary of the accession of George I to the throne by instituting an annual race for watermen. The race is from London Bridge to Cadogan Pier, Chelsea, and is usually held at the end of *July.* The victor is presented with a red coat, breeches and cap, and a silver arm badge bearing the words 'The Gift of the late Thomas Doggett'.

Monument *EC4.* A 17thC hollow fluted column by Wren, built to commemorate the Great Fire of London. It marked the northern end of the original London Bridge and stands at 202ft, a foot in height for every foot in distance from where the fire started in Pudding Lane. Gives a magnificent view over the city.

Old Billingsgate Market Lower Thames Street *EC3.* The yellow-brick Victorian building with arcaded ground floor was built by Sir Horace Jones, 1875, although the first reference to a market at Billingsgate was made in AD870. A free fish market was established by statute in 1699, but until the 18thC coal, corn and provisions were also sold. The fish-porters wore leather hats with flat tops and wide brims, formerly known as bobbing hats. Bobbing was the charge made by the porter to carry fish from the wholesaler to the retailer. These hats enabled the porter to carry about a hundredweight of fish on his head. The market moved down river to new premises on the Isle of Dogs in 1982.

The Custom House Lower Thames Street *EC4.* A custom house has stood beside Billingsgate since AD870. The present building is by Laing, 1813–17, but the river façade was rebuilt by Smirke in 1825. Badly bombed in the war, the building has been restored.

Tower of London Tower Hill *EC3.* Although greatly restored and altered over the centuries, the Tower of London is probably the most important work of military architecture in Britain and has been used as a palace, a fortress and a prison since William the Conqueror built the White Tower in 1078.

Tower Bridge This spectacular bridge was built by Sir John Wolfe Barry in 1894 and the old hydraulic lifting mechanism was originally powered by steam.

● SOUTH BANK

Wandsworth Until the 19thC Wandsworth was a village oasis on the River Wandle – a good fishing river – and was noted for a local silk and hat industry. The course of the Wandle can still be traced near the Church of All Saints. The Surrey Iron Railway, whose wagons were drawn by horses, ran alongside the river. Past residents include Defoe, Thackeray and Voltaire, but today little remains to point to the past. There are a few Georgian houses in Church Row, but the river bank has become a grimy industrial scene.

Battersea Many of the old riverside warehouses are now gone and tall tower blocks dominate.

St Mary's Church Church Road *SW11.* The church is one of the few relics of Battersea's 18th-C village. Built in 1775 by Joseph Dixon, it is strangely Dutch in character.

Battersea Park *SW11.* The park was laid out by Sir James Pennethorne as a public garden and opened by Queen Victoria in 1858. Re-designed in the 1950s for the Festival of Britain, there is a boating lake, a deer park, an Alpine showhouse, herb garden and greenhouse, a children's zoo and sculptures by Moore, Hepworth and Epstein. The London Peace Pagoda which stands close to the river was built by monks and nuns of the Japanese Buddhist order Nipponzan Myohoji and was completed in 1985.

Battersea Power Station *SW8.* One of the most potent buildings on the river bank, this vast oblong of brick with its four chimneys was designed by Sir Giles Gilbert Scott, 1932–4, and was one of the finest examples of contemporary industrial architecture. Redundant as a power station, plans for its conversion now rest on a scheme to turn the building into a museum of modern art.

Albert Embankment *SE1.* Designed as a broad footwalk by Sir Joseph Bazalgette, 1867, the Embankment stretches between Vauxhall and Westminster Bridges. The upper Embankment was once the site of the 18thC Vauxhall Gardens, whose Chinese pavilions and walks were the envy of Europe.

Lambeth Palace Lambeth Palace Road *SE1.* The London residence of the Archbishop of Canterbury since 1197. Remarkable Tudor gatehouse, fine medieval crypt. A 14th-C Hall with a splendid roof and portraits of archbishops on its walls. The Guard Room, which houses the library, was rebuilt in medieval style in 1633.

County Hall Westminster Bridge *SE1.* Designed by Ralph Knott in 1911, this was once the headquarters of the Greater London Council but is now to become a hotel and leisure complex.

London Eye Jubilee Gardens *SE1.* A gigantic ferris wheel, open during 2000 (daily 1000–1800), offering a bird's eye view over London.

Shell Centre *SE1.* Part of the area known as the South Bank, the Shell Centre was designed by Sir Howard Robertson, 1962. Of greyish white concrete with monotonous little square windows, the flat surface is totally unrelieved – it seems more in character to view it as a physical feature rather than as architecture. The central 351ft-high skyscraper rises like a huge grey mountain.

South Bank Arts Centre *SE1.* Royal Festival Hall, the Queen Elizabeth Hall, the Purcell Room, the National Theatre, the National Film Theatre, the Hayward Gallery and the Museum of the Moving Image make up the complex which originated with the Festival of Britain in 1951. The Festival Hall, completed in 1951 and built by Sir Robert Matthew and Sir Leonard Martin, seats 3400. The Queen Elizabeth Hall by Hubert Bennett, 1967, is much smaller and intended for recitals. Bennett also designed the Hayward Gallery which opened in 1968. The Purcell Room is the smallest of the three concert halls; ideal for chamber music and solo concerts. However, the buildings are dreary and the maze of tunnels and winding staircases which lead to the terrace area can be overwhelming, the blind corners in many instances blocking the view and giving a sense of isolation. Nevertheless, the range of cultural activities on offer at the South Bank Centre is diverse and can be enjoyed by everyone.

Upper Ground *SE1.* The decrepit warehouses that used to line the south bank have been demolished, and replaced by the impressive London Weekend Television building and Gabriel's Wharf – South Bank's answer to Covent Garden. To the east of Gabriel's Wharf stands the fine art deco OXO tower, built in 1928 and decorated thus because advertising was forbidden on buildings.

Bankside *SE1.* In the 16thC the Rose Theatre, the Swan and the Globe were all situated around Bankside, and until the 19thC the area was the site of playhouses and amusement gardens. Today the area has been developed and almost all is changing apart from the few remaining 17th-C and 18th-C houses and the Anchor pub, an historic tavern with strong smuggling connections. A tudor theatre has been reconstructed near the site of the original Globe Theatre as part of the International Shakespeare Globe Centre, and the Shakespeare Globe Museum illustrates the theatre of the age. From Bankside are fine views of St Paul's Cathedral and the City and it is thought that Wren lived in No. 49 Bankside during the construction of St Paul's.

Shakespeare Globe Museum 1 Bear Gardens, Bankside *SE1.* Converted 18th-C warehouse on the site of a 16th-C bear-baiting ring and the Hope Playhouse.

Bankside Power Station *SE1.* Designed in 1935 by Sir Giles Gilbert Scott, architect of the Battersea Power Station. Like its counterpart, Bankside Power Station now stands redundant, its distinctive single chimney dominating the landscape.

Southwark Cathedral Borough High Street *SE1.* Built by Augustinian Canons but destroyed by fire in 1206 and greatly restored. The tower was built c.1520 and the nave, by Blomfield, 1894–7. In the Middle Ages the cathedral was part of the Augustinian Priory of St Mary Overie. Despite its 19th-C additions, it is still one of the most impressive Gothic buildings in London. Apart from the wealth of monuments, the model in the retro-choir showing the priory and Winchester Palace in 1540 is of special interest, as is the collection of carved wooden bosses from the 15th-C roof.

Kathleen & May St Mary Overy Dock. Last surviving three-masted, topsail, trading schooner and now a floating museum.

BRIDGES

Chelsea Bridge The original bridge designed by Thomas Page, 1858, was rebuilt as a suspension bridge in 1934 by Rendel, Palmer & Tritton.

Victoria Railway Bridge When it was opened in 1859, this was the widest railway bridge in the world – 132ft wide and 900ft long – and it provided ten separate accesses to Victoria Station. It has now been widened further to meet the demands of modern transport.

Vauxhall Bridge James Walker's Regent's Bridge which opened in 1816 was the first iron bridge to span the Thames in London. The present structure, designed by Sir Alexander Binnie, was opened in 1906. The bronze figures alongside the bridge represent Agriculture, Architecture, Engineering, Learning, the Fine Arts and Astronomy.

Lambeth Bridge Originally the site of a horse ferry, the first bridge was built here in 1861, designed by P W Barlow. This was replaced in 1932 by the present steel-arch bridge designed by George Humphreys and Sir Reginald Blomfield.

Westminster Bridge Built in 1750, Westminster Bridge was the second bridge to be built across the Thames in central London. The present bridge, by Thomas Page, replaced the old stone one in 1862.

Charing Cross Railway Bridge Also known as Hungerford Bridge, it has replaced the original suspension bridge which was demolished in 1864. A separate footbridge runs alongside to Waterloo Station with excellent views of the City.

Waterloo Bridge John Rennie's early 19th-C bridge, a beautiful design of Greek columns and nine elliptical arches, was replaced in 1945 by Sir Giles Gilbert Scott's concrete bridge, faced with Portland stone.

Millennium Bridge Constructed in 1999 and, in conjunction with the new walkway on the upstream side of Hungerford Bridge, forms part of the City's Cross River Partnership initiative to provide an integrated transport and regeneration strategy for Thames side in central London.

Southwark Bridge Southwark Bridge was built in 1814 and was the largest bridge ever built of cast iron. Replaced 1912–21 by the present five-span steel bridge of Mott and Hay, with Sir Ernest George as architect. Southwark Causeway, the steps on the south side, were used by Wren when he travelled across the river to supervise work on St Paul's.

Cannon Street Railway Bridge Built in 1866 as part of the extension of the South Eastern Railway, the bridge's engineers were J Hawkshaw and J W Barry. A prominent structure on account of the 19th-C train shed jutting out to the side of the bridge.

London Bridge Until 1749 London Bridge was the only bridge to span the Thames in London. The first recorded wooden bridge was Saxon, but it is possible that a Roman structure may have existed here. In 1176 the wooden bridge was replaced by a stone structure, with houses, shops and a church built upon it, similar in appearance to the Ponte Vecchio in Florence. The heads of traitors were displayed on the spikes of the fortified gates at either end. In 1831 this bridge was demolished and a new bridge, by John Rennie, replaced it. A granite bridge with five arches, this soon became too narrow to meet the demands of modern traffic and because of structural faults could not be widened. A new bridge, constructed under the direction of the City Engineer, was opened to traffic in 1973. Built out of concrete, it has a flat-arched profile in three spans carried on slender piers. The McCulloch Corporation of Arizona paid $2,460,000 for the facing materials of Rennie's bridge, which has been reconstructed spanning Lake Havasu.

Blackfriars Bridge Blackfriars Bridge was built in 1760. It cost £230,000 and was mainly paid for by fines which had accumulated from men refusing the post of Sheriff. Replaced by the present structure in 1860. Note the pulpits, a reminder of the religious significance of its name.

Blackfriars Railway Bridge Built in 1886 for the London, Chatham and Dover Railway, this elegant iron bridge, with its high parapet and decorative coat of arms at each end, can best be seen from the road bridge.

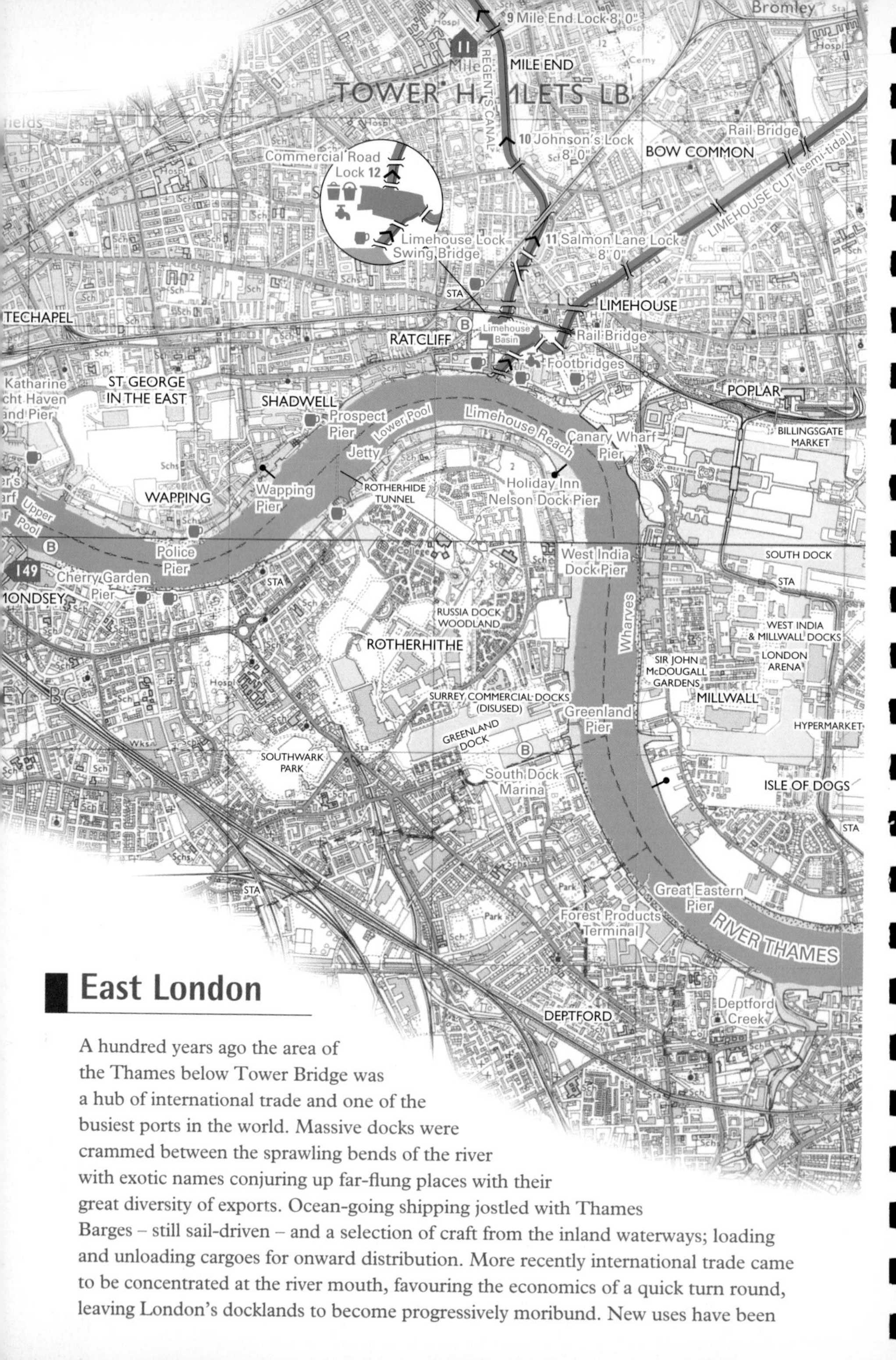

East London

A hundred years ago the area of the Thames below Tower Bridge was a hub of international trade and one of the busiest ports in the world. Massive docks were crammed between the sprawling bends of the river with exotic names conjuring up far-flung places with their great diversity of exports. Ocean-going shipping jostled with Thames Barges – still sail-driven – and a selection of craft from the inland waterways; loading and unloading cargoes for onward distribution. More recently international trade came to be concentrated at the river mouth, favouring the economics of a quick turn round, leaving London's docklands to become progressively moribund. New uses have been

devised for these huge areas of dereliction, ranging from the City Airport to the Canary Wharf development. New housing and new industry have been drafted in, often with scant regard for established communities and cultures. In converting redundant warehouses the value of these solid symbols of a previous prosperity and optimism has at least been recognised.

NAVIGATIONAL NOTES

1 From **Limehouse** to **Brentford** navigation on the Thames is far more complex than on the upper reaches. The river here is a commercial waterway first and foremost, and pleasure craft must take great care. The River Thames below Teddington is controlled by the Port of London Authority (PLA) which produces a useful set of free notes, *Yachtsman's Guide for the Tidal Thames.* A separate leaflet (*PLA Facilities on the Tidal Thames*) details facilities available to boaters. For general navigational enquiries about the river contact the Assistant Harbour Master, Devon House, 58–60 St Katharine's Way, London E1 9LB (0207 265 2656). While hire companies do not allow their craft to be taken onto the tideway, owners of pleasure boats may wish to make the passage along the Thames to Teddington Locks and between the canals at Limehouse and Brentford. With proper planning this should present no particular difficulties.

2 **Limehouse Basin** to **Brentford** – pass through the entrance lock at Limehouse 2½ hours before high water, to gain the benefit of the flood tide. Thames Lock, Brentford is manned *for a period before, and following high water (2hrs each side if this falls within normal working hours*) and you should contact the lock keeper to pre-book passage *outside the normal working hours* (*Apr–Oct 08.00–18.00 & Nov–Mar 08.00–16.30*) on 0208 560 1120; Core hours *05.00–22.00.* Brentford gauging lock is boater operated using a BW sanitary station key. Brentford listen and operate on VHF channel 74.

3 **Limehouse Basin** to **Teddington Locks** – pass through the entrance lock at Limehouse 3½ hours before high water, to gain the benefit of the flood tide. Teddington lock keeper can be contacted on 0208 940 8723 and Richmond lock keeper can be contacted on 0208 940 0634.

4 **VHF Radio** – all vessels of 20 metres or more in length must carry a VHF radio capable of communicating with the harbourmaster at port control – channel 14.

5 **The Non-tidal Thames** – those who wish to navigate on the River Thames above Teddington Lock will require a licence, available from: Navigation and Recreation Manager, Environment Agency, 1/2 Napier Court, c/o Kings Meadow House, Kings Meadow Road, Reading, Berks, RG1 8DQ (01734 535525). The non-tidal Thames is covered in Book 7, Thames, Wey, Kennet & Avon.

6 See also notes 2, 6, 7 & 8 on page 144 and reference to mooring on page 143.

THE THAMES BARGE

Around the coasts of Britain every tidal estuary, together with its river navigation, spawned its variant of the sail-driven, cargo-carrying barge. Usually the dimensions and type of rig were determined by the constraints of bridges and locks met on its passage upstream. The Thames barge, however, rarely strayed above the Port of London – the territory of the inland waterways wide and narrow boats – and consequently it evolved into a coastal craft with capacities sometimes in excess of 150 tons.
To move this tonnage smartly through the water – as smartly as a blunt bow and flat bottom can ever allow – it carried a potentially copious array of sail to supplement the spritsail main. Here the constraining factor was that the boat could be handled, in its entirety, by one man and a boy.
The activities of the Thames barge were by no means restricted to the Thames and adjoining estuaries. Cargoes were regularly carried north, to east coast ports as far afield as Newcastle upon Tyne and south west to ports along the English Channel. The flat bottom allowed easy access into shallow estuaries that often dried out completely at low tide. Its capabilities in open sea are impressive, given its fundamental design, and passages across the Atlantic have been recorded. Under sail leeboards, pivoting down from the gunwales, enable boats to sail surprisingly close to the wind and to see a racing barge tacking today, its traditional mud-brown sails sheeted in tight, is a truly awesome sight.

Pubs and Restaurants

For Pubs and Restaurants accessible to the boater entering the canal at either Brentford or Limehouse see pages 13 and 25.

St Katharine Dock St Katharine Dock was the first of the docks to be rejuvenated. Built on 23 acres in 1828, from a design by Thomas Telford, the original docks were closed down in 1968. Five years later an £80 million building scheme was begun which included the Tower Thistle Hotel and the World Trade Centre. The magnificent warehouses have been restored and now house shops, apartments, offices, restaurants, a yacht club and marina. Visiting cruisers nestle alongside resident yachts and barges.

Tobacco Dock Pennington Street *E1.* Designed by Terry Farrell in 1989, this 19th-C former warehouse has been converted into a shopping and leisure complex. Development work was carried out using original suppliers of materials wherever possible.

Butler's Wharf Transformed from narrow alleys, where Oliver Twist's Bill Sikes met his end, into a smart restaurant, shopping and office complex including the Conran restaurants – Le Pont de la Tour, the Cantina del Ponte and the Butler's Wharf Chop House.

The Design Museum Butler's Wharf, Shad Thames *SE1.* A fascinating introduction to 20th-C design, technology and consumer culture.

Cherry Garden Pier Where ships sound their signal if they want Tower Bridge to be raised. Turner sat here to paint *The Fighting Temeraire* as she returned from the Battle of Trafalgar.

Rotherhithe Tunnel Built 1904–8 by Sir Maurice Fitzmarice, the tunnel is still used as a thoroughfare between Rotherhithe and Stepney. The top of the tunnel is 48ft below the high-water mark to allow for large ships passing above.

YHA Island Yard, Salter Road *SE16.* This prominent landmark on the south bank of the river is a luxurious youth hostel catering for families, groups and individual travellers.

Limehouse Basin *E14.* This used to be called the Regent's Canal Dock, and forms part of the Grand Union Canal system, which was opened in 1820 to allow barges to trade between London and Birmingham. The Limehouse Cut also provides access to the River Lea.

Royal Naval Victualling Yard Grove Street SE8. Founded in 1513 as the Royal Dock for Henry VIII's navy, the yard became the principal naval dockyard in the kingdom, rivalling Woolwich. Sir Francis Drake was knighted here after his world voyage on the *Golden Hind,* and it was from this yard that Captain Cook's *Discovery* set sail.

Docklands Stretching from Tower Pier to Beckton is London's Docklands. The area has undergone massive change from a thriving, commercial port through closure to regeneration. The London Docklands Development Corporation (LDDC) was set up in 1981 to create a new city for the 21stC incorporating riverside apartments, shops, restaurants and offices.

Canary Wharf Tower One Canada Square, Canary Wharf *E14.* Designed by Cesar Pelli, 1988–90, this 800ft building is the tallest in the UK. Clad in stainless steel and topped with a pyramid, the 50-storey building boasts a magnificent lobby finished in Italian and Guatemalan marble. Thirty-two passenger lifts operate from the lobby and are the fastest in the country. Canary Wharf itself is full of elegant architecture, stately streets, well-planted squares and outdoor spaces.

Isle of Dogs Until the industrialisation of the early 19thC, the Isle of Dogs was mainly pastureland and marshes. Windmills stood by the river. By 1799 the Port of London had become so overcrowded that Parliament authorised the building of a new dock on the Isle of Dogs, under the auspices of the West India Company. Built by William Jessop, the two West India Docks were opened in 1802. In 1870 the South Dock was added. It was built on the site of the City Canal which had connected Limehouse Reach and Blackwall Reach between 1805 and 1829. The Millwall Docks, the most southern, were completed in 1864. The West India Docks are also the site of Billingsgate Fish Market, which was moved here from its old site near London Bridge in 1982.

Island Gardens Saunders Ness Road *E14.* This small park at the south tip of the Isle of Dogs was opened in 1895 to commemorate the spot which Wren considered had the best view of Greenwich Palace across the water.

Greenwich Tunnel The Blackwall Tunnel, opened in 1897, was designed as a road traffic tunnel. In 1902 it was decided to build a pedestrian subway to link Greenwich with the Isle of Dogs. There was opposition from the watermen and lightermen who, rightly, feared for their jobs. The southern entrance to the footway is in Cutty Sark Gardens, Greenwich, and the northern entrance is in Island Gardens, Isle of Dogs.

Greenwich *SE10.* Once a small fishing village, the historic town of Greenwich marks the eastern approach to London. Its royal and naval past is illustrated by the magnificent riverside grouping of the Queen's House, the Royal Naval College, the National Maritime Museum and the Old Royal Observatory. From the Observatory the views are magnificent, spanning Docklands and the City right through to Westminster. Museums, bookshops, antique shops, and a daily street market make for a bustling village atmosphere away from the industrialisation of the Docklands area.

A Thames sailing barge at Greenwich

The Cutty Sark King William Walk *SE10.* One of the great 19th-C tea and wool sailing clippers, stands in dry dock. The history of the *Cutty Sark* is displayed in drawings and photographs. Close by stands *Gipsy Moth IV,* the yacht in which Sir Francis Chichester made his solo circumnavigation of the world in 1966.
Greenwich Park *SE10.* The park, laid out for Charles II by the French royal landscape gardener André Le Nôtre, commands a magnificent view of the Royal Naval College and of the river. It contains 13 acres of woodland and deer park, a bird sanctuary and archaeological sites. Crooms Hill lies to the west of the park, lined with a wealth of 17th-, 18th- and 19th-C houses, the oldest being at the southern end near Blackheath. Greenwich Theatre stands at the foot of the hill.
Old Royal Observatory Greenwich Park *SE10.* The original observatory, still standing, was built by Wren for Flamsteed, first Astronomer Royal, in the 17thC. Astronomical instruments and exhibits relating to the history of astronomy are displayed in the old observatory buildings and the time ball which provided the first public time signal in 1833 still operates. Home to the Meridian Line, interactive science stations and the largest refracting telescope in the UK.
Royal Naval College Greenwich *SE10.* Mary II commissioned Wren to rebuild the palace as a hospital for aged and disabled seamen. Designed in the Baroque style, it was completed in 1705. The Painted Hall, or Dining Hall, has a swirling Baroque ceiling by Thornhill, one of the finest of its period. The neo-classical chapel dates from 1789. In 1873 the hospital became the Royal Naval College to provide for the higher education of naval officers.
Queen's House Romney Road, Greenwich *SE10.* Now part of the National Maritime Museum, this delightful white house in the Palladian style was built for Queen Anne of Denmark by Inigo Jones, 1618.
Execution Dock At the entrance to Blackwall Tunnel. This is where, until the late 19thC, the bodies of convicted pirates were hung in iron cages until three tides had washed over them.
Millennium Dome The centre piece of the country's Millennium celebrations, comprising a translucent canopy made from 328,100 square feet of fabric, held up with 43 miles of high-strength cable suspended from 12 vast 105-tonne yellow steel masts. The Dome will be open during 2000, featuring many diverse events and activities. You can arrive by river: at peak times boats will leave Waterloo every 15 minutes, travelling via Blackfriars. You can also follow the riverside walkway/cycleway from Greenwich. Telephone 0870 606 2000 for ticket details. The Greenwich Tourist Information Centre can be contacted on 0208 858 6376.
Blackwall Tunnel Built in 1897 by Sir Alexander Binnie. There are now two tunnels; the second opened in 1967. One is for northbound traffic, the other for southbound.
Thames Flood Barrier The Flood Barrier is best seen from the river. As you round the bend, the steel fins rise up from the water. Completed in 1982, it is the world's largest movable flood barrier and is designed to swing up from the river bed and create a stainless steel barrage to stem periodically dangerous high tides. Each gate weighs 3000 tonnes and is the equivalent of a five-storey building in height. The structures housing the machines which operate the gates seem to have been inspired by the sails of Sydney Opera House. Blackwall Reach, on the way to the Flood Barrier, was where, in 1606, Captain John Smith and the Virginia Settlers left on their journey to found the first permanent colony in America.

Thames 2000
The London Tube map has, arguably, become both a part of the national consciousness and a work of art. This diagrammatic representation of a huge portion of the Capital's transport network has been progressively added to over the decades to become the web of multi-coloured lines that it is today. Now another layer of activity is to be superimposed, integrating land and water-based systems in a sustainable transport initiative designed to last well into the new millennium. Since Roman times the importance of the Thames has been recognised as a highway for both commerce and passenger carrying alike, with ferries and their attendant piers developing where necessary. In the latter half of this century there has been a move away from the river to buses, tubes and taxis; the river piers largely reduced to serving pleasure traffic. Under the *Thames 2000* initiative these piers are being extended or rebuilt and new ones added under the the auspices of London River Services: a subsidiary of London Transport. Onto this revitalised infrastructure a series of central London fast ferry services have been grafted, operating alongside shuttle services to Greenwich and (in the short-term) to the Dome. Similarly as other areas of the river bank are redeveloped they too will be integrated into the river-based transport network. Still more piers on the foreshore: to be used exclusively as 'river-bus stops' and not for boaters to park at.

INDEX